FRENCH COLONIAL EMPIRE AND
THE POPULAR FRONT

Also by Tony Chafer and from the same publishers

FRANCE: From the Cold War to the New World Order (*co-editor with Brian Jenkins*)

French Colonial Empire and the Popular Front

Hope and Disillusion

Edited by

Tony Chafer
Principal Lecturer in French and African Studies
University of Portsmouth

and

Amanda Sackur
Research Associate in Francophone Area Studies
University of Portsmouth

First published in Great Britain 1999 by
MACMILLAN PRESS LTD
Houndmills, Basingstoke, Hampshire RG21 6XS and London
Companies and representatives throughout the world

A catalogue record for this book is available from the British Library.

ISBN 0–333–72973–0

First published in the United States of America 1999 by
ST. MARTIN'S PRESS, INC.,
Scholarly and Reference Division,
175 Fifth Avenue, New York, N.Y. 10010

ISBN 0–312–21826–5

Library of Congress Cataloging-in-Publication Data
French colonial empire and the Popular Front : hope and disillusion /
edited by Tony Chafer [and] Amanda Sackur.
p.   cm.
Includes bibliographical references and index.
ISBN 0–312–21826–5 (cloth)
1. Front populaire—Influence.   2. France—Colonies—History.
3. France—Politics and government—20th century.
4. Decolonization—France—Influence.   I. Chafer, Tony.
II. Sackur, Amanda.
DC396.F74   1999
909'.0971244081—dc21   98–37554
                                                              CIP

Selection, editorial matter and Introduction © Tony Chafer and Amanda Sackur 1999
Chapters 1–12 © Macmillan Press Ltd 1999

This book is printed on paper suitable for recycling and made from fully managed and sustained forest sources.

10   9   8   7   6   5   4   3   2   1
08   07   06   05   04   03   02   01   00   99

Printed and bound in Great Britain by
Antony Rowe Ltd, Chippenham, Wiltshire

Contents

Part II   Diversity of Outcomes

List of Figures

Acknowledgments

This book arises from a conference on Popular Front and Empire organised by the Francophone Area Studies Research Group, which was held at the University of Portsmouth in February 1996. The group is undertaking a long-term research project on colonialism, decolonisation and post-colonialism in France, the primary focus of which is to study the ways in which empire has shaped contemporary France and French national identity. This book is one of a series on the theme of French imperialism which is currently being published by members of the Research Group.

Particular thanks are due to Martin Evans, who put forward the idea for the conference and whose constant support and encouragement have been essential to the success of the project. The editors also wish to thank the Centre for European Studies Research at the University of Portsmouth and the Association for the Study of Modern and Contemporary France for their financial support, without which the conference and this book would not have been possible.

TONY CHAFER
AMANDA SACKUR

Abbreviations

AEF	Afrique Equatoriale Française (Federation of French Equatorial Africa)
AFIMA	Association pour la Formation Intellectuelle et Morale des Annamites
ANG	Archives Nationales de Guinée
ANS	Archives Nationales du Sénégal
ANSOM	Archives Nationales de France, Section Outre-Mer, Aix-en-Provence (comprises documents from the former Ministère des Colonies, subsequently the Ministère de la France d'Outre-Mer)
ANY	Archives Nationales de Yaoundé
AOF	Afrique Occidentale Française (Federation of French West Africa)
AOM	Archives d'Outre-Mer, Aix-en-Provence (comprises documents returned to France from overseas)
CFLN	Comité Français de la Libération Nationale
CGT	Confédération Générale du Travail
CGTT	Confédération Générale des Travailleurs Tunisiens
CGTU	Confédération Générale du Travail Unitaire
CHEAM	Centre des Hautes Etudes d'Administration Musulmane
ENA	Etoile Nord-Africaine
ENFOM	Ecole Nationale de la France d'Outre-Mer
IAI	International Institute of African Language and Cultures
IFAN	Institut Français d'Afrique Noire
ILO	International Labour Organisation
JOTC	*Journal Officiel des Territoires du Cameroun*
OAS	Organisation of African States
PCA	Parti Communiste Algérien
PCF	Parti Communiste Français
RASDN	Rapport Annuel à la Société des Nations (Annual Report to the League of Nations' Permanent Mandate Commission)
SFIO	Section Française de l'Internationale Ouvrière
SIP	Sociétés Indigènes de Prévoyance

Glossary

bachelier

A *bachelier* is someone who has passed the *baccalauréat*, the examination that marks the end of secondary schooling in France and which qualifies students to enter university.

beldi

Arabic for 'townsfolk'. Used in contradistinction to the Arabi ('countryfolk') by a middle class of craftsmen, merchants and *ulema* of moorish descent, generally residents of the Tunis *madina* (old town).

cabinet

A Minister's private office, consisting of a director (*directeur du cabinet*) and staff. Usually appointed by the Minister from among ministerial staff considered sympathetic to the Minister's political views.

capitation

In AOF, the tax was a flat rate for all native tax-payers and was payable per head, hence the name '*capitation*' (poll tax).

Cartel
des Gauches

This was an alliance between the SFIO and the Radicals which won the legislative elections of 1924. The government was run by the Radicals with the 'support without participation' of the SFIO (i.e. there were no SFIO ministers but the socialists voted with the government in the Chamber of Deputies). In theory, this alliance ought to have run the country until 1928, but the 1926 financial crisis caused certain Radicals to change camps, with the result that the moderate right, under the leadership of Raymond Poincaré, came to power.

colonie

Dependent territory of an imperial state (for

example, France). In theory French colonies were usually ruled directly, unlike protectorates (q. v.), and often settled by metropolitan settlers.

CGT Confédération Générale du Travail, one of the main French trades unions established in 1895. Representative of mainstream social democracy until after the Second World War when it became predominantly Communist.

Comintern Shorthand for the Communist or Third International, the international organisation of communist parties formed in Moscow in 1919.

déclassé This was the term used to describe those in the colonial population who had received a French education, but who subsequently were unable to find employment commensurate with their educational qualifications. The fear was that their social marginalisation would make them into a potential source of political discontent if their numbers grew.

Destour Arabic for 'constitution'. Name adopted by first Tunisian nationalist party established in 1920 under the leadership of Abd. al-Aziz Thaalbi.

direct rule The system of colonial rule by which colonies were governed directly by the colonial administration, excluding traditional local rulers or institutions.

ENFOM Ecole Nationale de la France d'Outre-Mer (formerly known as the Ecole Coloniale and often referred to informally as 'Colo'). The Grande Ecole (q. v.) which trained colonial administrators to serve in the colonies of sub-Saharan Africa, Indochina, Madagascar, the Caribbean, Indian and Pacific Oceans.

évolué	The *évolués*, in the vocabulary of the period (educated natives is the equivalent term in British colonies), were those who had received education of a European type: clerks, skilled workers or minor officials. They were therefore, in part at least, acculturated.
Grandes Ecoles	Institutions of higher education in France, parallel to the universities, the historical purpose of which was to train high-ranking engineers, civil servants, teachers and functionaries of the French state.
Hexagone	Figurative term referring to mainland France as opposed to the wider France including overseas *départements*, based roughly on the shape of the country.
Hôtel de Matignon	Prime Minister's Paris residence, used as a shorthand to refer to the Prime Minister.
indigénat	The *indigénat* was a legislative code that allowed colonial officials to punish any native with a prison sentence or a fine, as a matter of discipline and without trial.
indirect rule	The system of colonial rule by which colonies were administered indirectly by the colonial administration, using traditional local rulers (or their replacements) as intermediaries who retained some measure of competence and authority, e.g. tax-raising powers.
Abd. el-Krim	Full name Mohammed Abd. al-Karim al-Khattabi (1882–1963). Leader of Rifian revolt against Spanish and French encroachment in northern Morocco, (1921–26) during which time he established the Rifian Republic.
Loi-Cadre	Framework Law or Enabling Law, defining the framework and principles to a subsequent

set of more detailed legislation. The Loi-cadre of 1956, (also known as the loi Defferre, after the Ministre de la France d'Outre-mer, Gaston Defferre) set the framework for legislation implementing a measure of self-government in the French colonies of sub-Saharan Africa. It was superseded by the provisions for the French 'Communauté' in the constitution of 1958.

Matignon agreements Set of agreements on paid holidays, a 40-hour week and collective bargaining signed by representatives of the CGT (q. v.), the government and employers at the Hôtel de Matignon (q. v.) on 7 June 1936.

prestation This was the name given to forced labour on road construction and maintenance. It was hated by the population: every man liable had to provide in theory eight days' work a year, under the supervision of the *commandant de cercle*, but in practice injustice and abuse were widespread, thus feeding discontent.

protectorat Legal–administrative entity established to enable rule of one polity by another without the full transfer of sovereignty as in colonies. Often used to impose 'law and order' and ensure economic viability of bankrupt regimes. In theory, the existing ruler continued to rule subordinate to the 'Protecting Power'. Tunisia became a protectorate of France by virtue of the Treaty of Bardo (1881) and the al-Marsa Convention (1884).

Quai d'Orsay Paris address of French Ministry of Foreign Affairs and often used as a shorthand for the Ministry itself.

Rassemblement Populaire	Electoral coalition of progressive forces in Tunisia, formed in June 1936 as a mirror of metropolitan Popular Front.
Rue Oudinot	Paris address of Ministry of Colonies (later renamed Ministry of Overseas France) and often used as a shorthand for the Ministry itself.
Regency	Name given by French invaders to the pre-colonial Turkish administrative entity known as a beylic, ruled by a bey (governor). Under the French protectorate of Tunisia, a French administrative apparatus was superimposed on the existing beylical institutions thus warranting the continued use of the term 'Regency'.
SFIO	Section Française de l'Internationale Ouvrière. Formed in 1905 as a unitary organisation of working-class parties. Main socialist organisation in France until the split at the Congress of Tours in 1920 which led to the creation of separate and antagonistic Socialist and Communist parties.

Notes on the Contributors

Michel Brot obtained his doctorate, which was on the Guinée/ Sierra Leone borderlands, 1900–58, from the Université de Provence in 1994. He has published a book on the Popular Front period in the Alpes-Maritimes and a number of articles on African history. He teaches at the Institute for American Universities in Aix-en-Provence and is a member of the Institut d'Histoire Comparée des Civilisations at the Université de Provence.

Tony Chafer is Principal Lecturer in French and African Studies and coordinator of the Francophone Area Studies Research Group at the University of Portsmouth. He recently edited a special issue of the journal *Modern and Contemporary France* on 'France and black Africa' and is preparing a book on decolonisation in French West Africa.

Alejandro Colás is Lecturer in International Relations at the University of Sussex. His previous publications include, 'The Promises of International Civil Society', *Global Society: Interdisciplinary Journal of International Relations*, II: 3 (Sept. 1997) and 'Putting Cosmopolitanism into Practice: the Case of Socialist Internationalism', *Millennium: Journal of International Studies*, 23:3 (Winter 1994).

Catherine Coquery-Vidrovitch is Professeur d'Histoire Contemporaine de l'Afrique at the Université de Paris VII and Director of the research group 'Dynamiques comparées des sociétés en Développement'. She is the author of around 15 studies of Africa and other Third World countries. She is currently writing an 'Histoire de l'Afrique au XIXe siècle' for Armand Colin.

Gilles de Gantès is *agrégé d'histoire* and wrote his doctorate on French colonialism in Indochina. His current research is on European colonialism and the history of Indochina in the nineteenth and twentieth centuries.

John Hargreaves is Emeritus Professor of History in the University of Aberdeen. He is the author of various works on European colonialism and African history. A revised edition of his *Decolonisation in Africa* was published in 1996.

Jean Koufan is Lecturer in History at the University of Yaoundé (Cameroun).

Don LaCoss is writing a PhD dissertation on surrealism and the visual culture of the Popular Front in the Department of History at the University of Michigan. He is finishing a study of Melanesian ritual masks collected by André Breton.

Ghislaine Lydon is a Graduate Assistant in the Department of History at Michigan State University. She recently published an article in the *Cahier d'Etudes Africaines* on one of the Popular Front missions of inquiry in French West Africa.

Panivong Norindr is Associate Professor of French and Comparative Literature at the University of Wisconsin-Milwaukee. He is the author of *Phantasmagoric Indochina: French Colonial Ideology in Architecture, Film and Literature* (Duke University Press, 1996).

Amanda Sackur is Research Associate in Francophone Area Studies at the University of Portsmouth.

Martin Shipway is Lecturer in Twentieth-Century French Studies at Birkbeck College, University of London. He has written on French colonialism in Indochina, sub-Saharan Africa and Madagascar, and is the author of *The Road to War: France and Vietnam, 1944–1947* (Oxford and Providence, R.I.: Berghahn Books, 1996). He is working on a comparative study of decolonisations.

France Tostain graduated in law (Université de Caen), classical Arabic (ENALCO, Paris) and Arabic (University of Westminster). She has taught at Birkbeck College, University of London, University of North London and the University of Westminster. She is currently completing a PhD on the problems of identity and language use in a multicultural setting.

Gary Wilder teaches Modern European History at Pomona College. He is completing his PhD thesis, 'Subject-Citizens and Interwar France: Negritude, Colonial Humanism, and the Imperial Nation-State', in the History and Anthropology departments of the University of Chicago.

Introduction

Within little more than a year of the Popular Front's election victory in May 1936, the Blum cabinet was forced out of power. Within two years, the Popular Front experiment was dead and buried. It generated passionate initial enthusiasm which was rapidly replaced by recrimination and disillusionment. Despite this, and although its actual achievements were modest, the Popular Front has taken on an almost mythical quality in modern French history.[1] For the left, it stands out today as a moment of left humanism and represents a privileged moment, both of progress for the French working class and of left-wing political unity, that was not to be realised again for 40 years. Within days of coming to power, average wages had been increased by 12 per cent, legislation had been introduced to establish the principle of collective bargaining, all workers were to receive a fortnight's paid holiday and the working week was reduced from 48 to 40 hours without loss of income. For the right, on the other hand, the Popular Front symbolised the fear of political revolution entrenched since 1789. The wave of strikes that broke out shortly before Blum took power, and the economic crisis and devaluation of the franc in September 1936 that followed the introduction of the measures outlined above, simply confirmed the right's worst fears.

The significance of the Popular Front for the empire is less clear. The programme of the Popular Front simply proposed a commission of enquiry into the political, economic and cultural situation in France's overseas territories, particularly North Africa and Indochina. Black Africa did not even receive a mention. However, the various missions of enquiry in the different territories had barely had time to report, and in the case of Indochina had not even started work, by the time the Popular Front government fell. It is not surprising therefore that, in seeking to identify watersheds in the history of the French empire in the twentieth century, historians rarely mention the Popular Front. The

1

First World War, the economic crisis of 1929–34 and the
Second World War are more frequently cited as key turning-
points. The first two did provoke reassessments of colonial
policy and plans for reform. Yet the concrete measures that
actually resulted were limited. The Second World War, on
the other hand, is widely seen as marking the beginning
of what was to prove a remarkably rapid process of
decolonisation. Chastened by defeat and occupation, France
was no longer in a position to resist demands for colonial
reform. Pressure for change, both from reformers within
France and from the colonial populations themselves, became
irresistible.

The end of empire is one of the most significant historical events of the twentieth century. Yet the importance of
France's empire in shaping France today has long been
neglected, or at least substantially underestimated, by historians,[2] and this despite the fact that one of the major
themes of French history in the twentieth century has been,
and still is, the tensions generated by the need to define
the imperial relationship. By the end of the Second World
War these tensions had become acute. In order to understand France's post-war history, it is therefore vital to highlight
conflicts which resulted from increasingly urgent attempts
to redefine the role of empire. Although it had already
been raised after the First World War, the experience of
the Second World War and the need for reconstruction after
the war gave new urgency to the issue of empire as a means
of salvation for the metropole. At the same time colonial
nationalism, growing rapidly, threatened to destroy the
relationship altogether. This crisis underlay many of the
significant developments of the post-war period: colonial
wars in Indochina and Algeria, conflicts in New Caledonia,
the hasty granting of independence to many other colonies
in 1960 and moves to redefine the links with others. The
impact on domestic politics, the OAS apart, is less obvious.
Nonetheless, the issue of immigration, to mention just one,
owes much to France's colonial past and neo-colonial present.

Yet, in retrospectively identifying the end of the War (and
more particularly the Brazzaville Conference of 1944) as
the point that marked the beginning of the process of
decolonisation, historians have become increasingly aware

of the need to look back to the pre-war period in order better to understand the origins and nature of developments after the war. It is therefore necessary to reassess the significance of the Popular Front, because many of the reforms put into effect in the 1940s and attributed to the changes brought about by the Second World War were in fact proposed by the Popular Front. In this sense, 1936–38 was an important turning point in French colonial history, marking the beginning of an irreversible process of reform that was ultimately to lead to decolonisation. On the other hand, the Popular Front's reform proposals were so timid and its actual achievements so limited that some have preferred to view it as simply another example of well-intentioned colonial reform that promised much but, in the end, yielded little. One of the key aims of this book is to explore this apparent paradox, which reveals that the debate concerning the significance of the Popular Front is of far greater importance to French history than may at first appear.

In keeping with the traditional neglect of empire, the more or less unanimous focus of histories of the Popular Front to date has been on metropolitan France. In seeking to redress this imbalance, the present book starts from the position that empire has played an all-important role in the definition of modern French national identity and that an understanding of colonialism and its legacy constitutes an essential component of any genuine understanding of contemporary France. Through an exploration of the links between the metropole and empire at a defining moment in their history, this book shows that the history of the former cannot be divorced from the latter, and in so doing it puts the empire in its proper place for understanding France today. At the same time, by extending our perspective to empire, the book seeks to widen our understanding of the Popular Front experience. Thus, in revisiting the Popular Front's imperial policy some 60 years after the Popular Front's fall, historians of France can understand more about both the Popular Front and the importance of empire in shaping contemporary France.

A good example of this is the relationship between the nationalism of the metropolitan left and colonial nationalism.

An integral element of the metropolitan left's nationalism was Jacobinism and, reflecting this tradition, Socialists argued that the extension of republican values and liberties to the overseas territories would put an end to colonial abuses. If such abuses existed, this was the fault of the right which had exploited the colonial populations. Left colonialism, on the other hand, was generous, progressive and modernising, and it was therefore through closer integration into a democratic and socialist France, rather than through secession from France, that the emancipation of the indigenous populations would be achieved.[3] When confronted with colonial nationalism, this produced inevitable conflict, which became evident first of all in Indochina and North Africa, and subsequently in black Africa, in the 1940s and 1950s. However, as several of the contributions to this book show, the tensions that were to lead to conflict first became evident under the Popular Front, when colonial nationalist leaders were confronted for the first time with the realisation that the Left was also deeply imbued with a colonialist mentality.

The approaches and conceptual frameworks traditionally used to analyse the Popular Front and assess its historical significance have usually discussed it in terms of success or failure; continuity and change; and reform and resistance to change. While these approaches and conceptual frameworks are not in themselves invalid, they have tended, as we shall see, to mask the critical importance of the Popular Front both for France and for the empire. By drawing together contributions from a wide range of different perspectives, and through a re-examination of the divergent experiences of the Popular Front in different parts of the empire, this book carries forward the process of reassessment of the Popular Front as a defining moment in French imperialism.

*   *   *

An underlying theme of the book is the question of how to approach the study of the Popular Front and empire. Which perspective should we adopt: that of the metropole, or that of the colonised populations? And following on from this, what is the most appropriate conceptual framework for analysing it and for understanding its ultimate failure? Is it enough to analyse the obstacles to change to understand the contrast between the hopes of the reformers and the meagre achievements on the ground? Should it be seen as marking the beginning of a significant change in France's relationship with its empire or are the elements of continuity more important?

Yet one perspective does not preclude another. On the contrary, they must go hand in hand, since we need to bear in mind that, depending on whether our perspective is Franco-centric, colony-centric or from the point of view of the colonial populations, our assessment of the Popular Front and its significance as a turning point in France's relationship with her empire will be different. Similarly, explanations for the Popular Front's ultimate failure will also be rather different, or at least will be framed rather differently, according to the perspective and conceptual framework adopted.

A second major theme of the book is the question of colonial policy-making. What were the historical and ideological roots of the Popular Front's colonial policy? What was the role of different groups, such as political parties, trade unions, writers and intellectuals? To understand more about the policy-making process it is helpful to identify the people actually making policy and to appreciate their ideological background and political stance. This is especially important as many of the people responsible for implementing the new policy were the very same politicians and colonial administrators who had been charged with carrying out the colonial policy of previous governments and who, as Shipway shows, also remained in post until the end of the Second World War. What is more, it is clear that an international dimension is important here. As Hargreaves shows, British, French and Belgian administrators and civil servants participated in a wide network which became increasingly reformist in the 1920s and especially in the 1930s.

The third major theme to be addressed is that of the impact of Popular Front policy. This varied enormously throughout the empire. What are the factors, both metropolitan and local, that can help us to understand this diversity of outcomes? It is suggested here that the most significant outcome of colonial reforms was unintended. Failure to implement significant changes provoked such disillusion that colonial populations lost hope of reform from within. At the same time, reforms which were enacted opened up a political space for independence movements to emerge. From the perspective of the metropole, the contradictions inherent in colonial humanism revealed by the Popular Front's attempts at reform began the process which ultimately led to decolonisation.

The need for an accommodation between empire and metropole has been a constant theme of modern French history, a problem which has confronted governments of both left and right. It emerged as an issue after the First World War, to be discussed by academics, writers, colonial administrators and others with a specialist interest in empire. However, the government of the Popular Front, precisely because of its commitment to reform, was the first government to have to confront this as an acute *political* problem: even if the reforms were not new in theory, the Popular Front government was the first to adopt them formally. An analysis of the issues that confronted it, of how it handled them and of the reasons for its ultimate failure are therefore of vital importance in understanding subsequent French history. The outcome of this analysis is to suggest that the Popular Front has a wider significance than has hitherto been acknowledged.

APPROACHES

The paradigm employed until now tends to force historians into an evaluation of the Popular Front in terms of *either* change *or* continuity in policy. In practice, historians' conclusions have depended very largely on the perspective from which the Popular Front is viewed. If the perspective is that of the colonised, the effervescence of political activity, the raised hopes and the disillusion which followed take centre stage: the Popular Front will therefore be seen as marking a significant turning point for the colonial populations. If, on the other hand, the perspective is a metropolitan one, the tendency will be to conclude, essentially, that the Popular Front did not mark a significant watershed in French colonial practice and that by the end of 1938 it was pretty much 'business as usual'.

However, if we ask some rather different questions from the two posed above, the conceptual framework we shall need to adopt will be rather different. The key element, which underlies the contributions published here, is French attempts to come to terms with possession of an empire. In this it is possible to see structural continuity from the inter-war period lasting at least until the 1950s. The colonial reform project elaborated by the Popular Front and its subsequent failure were part of a pattern that had its roots in the very acquisition of empire in the previous century. By the First World War, France, like the other major colonial power, Britain, found itself in possession of a vast global empire. The question confronting all subsequent governments was what to do with this empire. Thus, while it is true that the inter-war period was, on one level, the apotheosis of empire – the 8 million people who visited the Colonial Exhibition of 1931 are testimony to the growing enthusiasm for empire – on another level, this period is the one during which the questions posed by the possession of empire first had to be confronted with real urgency. How should the empire best be developed economically, for the benefit of both the metropole and the colonised populations? What were the appropriate political arrangements for governing this vast empire? Out of these questions arose the crucial one of the ultimate aim of colonisation. Was it assimilation into the metropole, whatever that might mean in actual practice? Or was it to maintain as far as possible the cultural identity of the colonised populations within a framework of gradual social and economic modernisation that risked ultimately destroying precisely that which it sought to conserve and defend?

In retrospect, it is clear that the difficulties faced by both the major colonial powers in seeking adequate answers to these questions were inherent in colonialism and were, in fact, ultimately not soluble within that context. This contradiction, which had confronted previous governments, was

the more acute in the case of the Popular Front government because of its explicitly reformist agenda. Here then,
lies the element of change, although it was unintentional.
By committing itself to reform, as both de Gantès and
Norindr show, the Popular Front government decisively
altered the balance of relations within the empire. This
was to become evident after the war, as governments
struggled in vain to grapple with the increasingly divergent political perspectives on empire of the metropole and
the colonised populations.

Seen in this light, the questions raised above concerning
the different perspectives from which the subject can be
viewed and the appropriate conceptual framework for analysis
of the Popular Front are important. In assessing its significance it is necessary constantly to keep in mind the question of how the perceptions of each may be situated in
relation to the essential contradictions outlined above.

PERSPECTIVES

It is widely accepted that the colonial policy of the Popular Front failed to realise its promise of liberal reform and
in the present collection Coquery-Vidrovitch, Brot and Koufan
all emphasise the timid nature of the colonial reforms proposed by the Popular Front, their limited impact in policy
terms and their lack of concrete achievements 'on the
ground'. This is perhaps not surprising, given that the
Popular Front was so short-lived and that, as one commen-
tator put it recently: 'On the space scale of domestic French
politics in the middle of the 1930s, the colonies had moved
off into a far-off orbit.'[4] Thus while the Popular Front is
seen as marking a significant watershed in domestic French
politics, and this notwithstanding the brevity of its period
in power, it is rarely mentioned as more than an
epiphenomenon in the history of French colonialism.

This failure has been accounted for in terms of Paris'
inability to implement its reform project, the resistance to
reform at lower levels of the colonial administration, the
low priority attached to colonial questions, the lack of any
positive programme and a lack of time.[5] More generally,

this gap between the Popular Front's reformist aspirations and its disappointing balance sheet is seen as symptomatic of the inter-war period as a whole: an 'era of lost opportunities', during which colonial institutions failed to develop along with colonial society,[6] distinguished by 'political stagnation'[7] and 'immobility'.[8] Furthermore, however reformist, the Popular Front government was not anti-colonial, which is not altogether surprising given the climate of the time.

The Colonial Exhibition of 1931 represented something of a highpoint of French colonialism. It was not, however, simply a celebration of empire because behind it lay a clear pedagogical intent. Its organisers wanted to promote 'the imperial idea' among the metropolitan population and to show what the empire had brought to France. The exploits of colonial soldiers who had fought in defence of France during the First World War were celebrated and the economic benefits of empire to France were underlined. By 1936 the empire took a third of all French exports and certain industries found over 80 per cent of their markets there.[9] The overall aim of French colonialism was portrayed as the fundamental 'intellectual, moral and cultural unity' of France with her empire.[10]

Thus by 1936 a tide of metropolitan public opinion favourable to empire had been created. In the face of the growing fascist threat, even those who had hitherto been most implacably opposed to French colonialism, notably in the Communist Party, moderated their stance in the interests of uniting republican forces in the fight against fascism. Many people in metropolitan France were already beginning to look to the empire to 'save' France, much as they had done after the First World War and would do again both during and after the Second World War. As two contemporary commentators put it: 'Imperialism is the only way for mature peoples to avoid descending into irredeemable decadence. It is the only means to compensate for the sacrificing of the birth-rate to the facilities and pleasures of luxury, and to prevent the extinction of the élites'.[11] The future of France, not only economically, but also demographically, militarily and in geopolitical terms as a world power, was seen as inextricably bound up with empire.

The Popular Front sought to 'humanise' colonialism, certainly, but did not in any fundamental sense challenge this prevailing orthodoxy. If anything, its reforms sought to bind France and its empire closer together both for the benefit of France and in the interests of the colonial populations themselves. Yet as Brot and Koufan demonstrate, the changes that occurred in the colonies were modest in nature. Furthermore, although the desire to renew colonial *cadres* in French West Africa for example, and to 'africanise' parts of the colonial administration, was frequently stated, little was actually achieved in this area either. Thus whether from a metropolitan perspective or from that of the colonial administration, little had changed with respect to the empire. In both policy and bureaucratic terms, continuity triumphed over change.

In policy terms, there is much evidence to support the view that the Popular Front did not represent a significant break with what had gone before. The Popular Front's proposals for the economic development of the colonies had much in common with the plan put forward by Albert Sarraut in 1921 for the *mise en valeur* of the French colonies.[12] Its commitment to human rights owed much to the ideas of the network of colonial humanists which Hargreaves calls the 'Africanist International'. Thus, as Wilder, LaCoss and de Gantès point out, the main reform proposals of the Popular Front were largely in place by 1936 and in this sense represented little that was new. If we then add the bureaucratic continuity to which Shipway calls our attention and the fact that by 1936–7 no major political party in France was openly anticolonial, the strong elements of continuity are no surprise.

This should not however lead us to under-estimate the significance of inter-war attempts to reconceptualise the colonial project by reducing it to a contradiction between liberal humanist rhetoric that promised change and a continuity of authoritarian practices. What happens to this verdict of institutional failure if we ask a different set of questions, as do both Wilder and LaCoss in their chapters? In particular, what happens if, rather than focus on the question of whether colonial officials genuinely wanted to reform the colonial system, or whether the reform programme was a cynical attempt to distract attention from the reality of colonial domination, we move our focus to the transformation in the political rationality of government during this period? We shall then need to analyse the failure of the Popular Front's reform project in the context of the long-term transformation of state politics that was taking place in western democracies at this time and to seek continuities between this phenomenon and the inter-war shift in colonial government.

This emphasis on continuity should not however close our eyes to the fact that the Popular Front did innovate in significant respects. The setting up of a commission of inquiry and the appointment to it of such leading intellectuals as André Gide, who had in the past been bitterly critical of French colonialism, bear witness to the Popular Front's commitment to improved human rights in the colonies. As both Coquery-Vidrovitch and Koufan assert, the reformist intent of the Popular Front was genuine, as was its commitment to economic and social modernisation.

Even elements of apparent continuity contained the seeds of change. One such example is the imperial conference of governors-general called by Colonial Minister Marius Moutet in November 1936 to discuss a programme of economic and social reform for the colonies. On one level, this can be seen as yet another in a series of inter-war conferences that led to little that was concrete. On the other hand, the conference did put forward some innovative proposals. These included the indigenisation of certain posts within the colonial administration, which was to become the leitmotif of virtually all post-war colonial reform projects, and an emphasis, for the first time, on investment in agriculture and in small-scale projects that would bring immediate benefits to the rural populations. In addition, a programme of public works was suggested, which was to be carried out by paid, rather than forced, labour.

From the perspective of the colonised, on the other hand, the picture that emerges is rather different. There is evidence, on the ground, that change was in the air. There was a surge of political activity in many different parts of the empire, activity stimulated by the prospect of reform or made possible by early changes. Popular Front committees were formed, trade unions organised openly, groups from among the colonised populations demanded equal pay for equal work and strikes were called to press home these demands. There were also signs that some colonial social movements now conceived of their struggle as having an international dimension and the fact that they sought inter-national links, notably with working-class organisations in France, reveal the opening of new fronts in the struggle for colonial reform, as Colás points out. The scale and nature of the demands being articulated suggest a break with the past.

Furthermore, although the achievements of these various movements were relatively limited in terms of the actual concessions won and the few gains that were made were in any case subsequently reversed under Vichy, the Popular Front nevertheless represented a period of political *ouverture*, during which hopes and aspirations were raised. Even if the lid was subsequently put on these, as a result of the fall of the Popular Front and then the coming to power of the Vichy government, once these hopes and aspirations had been unleashed and found a voice, they could not be stamped out. The clock could not be turned back and, once the political situation again allowed their expression, they would be reasserted. In the very different political circumstances of the post-war period, they were to prove irresistible. What is more, the impact of disillusion with metropolitan initiatives was profound. From this perspec-tive, which emphasises the importance of local agency and in this sense reflects a 'bottom-up' approach, while the actual concessions won were indeed limited, the change in ex-pectations and attitudes among the colonial populations was in many respects profound and its consequences were to be far-reaching.[13]

Against this background, the question of the appropri-ate conceptual framework for analysing the Popular Front and empire takes on a rather different complexion from that suggested by more traditional approaches. These fall broadly into two main categories. The first of these has engaged with the continuity versus change debate and has tended, according to whether its perspective is essentially 'top-down' or 'bottom-up', either to stress the elements of continuity between the colonial reform project of the Popular Front and those that preceded it, or alternatively, in drawing attention to the reactions of the colonial populations in many parts of the empire, to show how these represent a significant break with the past. Within this same general framework, another variant of this approach has suggested that, while the Popular Front actually achieved little concrete change, largely because of the resistance it encountered and the fact that it was so short-lived, it did nevertheless set a new reform-oriented agenda for colonial policy-making after the war. Any return to the colonial *status quo ante* was no longer conceivable. The responsibility of the metropole to undertake the economic, social and political modernisation of the empire was recognised and accepted as the essential premise on which any credible colonial policy would henceforth have to be based.

The continuity versus change debate thus remains relevant to an understanding of the Popular Front's imperial policy. The suggestion is not, therefore that it should be jettisoned, but rather that it must be seen as part of an underlying historical pattern. This pattern has its roots, on the one hand, in the transformations taking place in the political rationality of government, and on the other, in the contradictions inherent in colonialism itself, and in this context the debate over continuity versus change takes on a new dimension. In the first case, the colonies are viewed as a kind of testing ground for the new approaches to government and the new colonial rationality needs to be seen as part of a wider historical process of transformation of state politics in western democracies. In the second, the Popular Front is seen as marking the point when the contradictions inherent in colonialism clearly began to manifest themselves as intractable. While it cannot be denied that there are elements of continuity throughout the twentieth century as France pursued her long search for an acceptable, and sustainable, accommodation with empire, it is equally clear that the Popular Front marks a watershed in that history. The attempts of the Popular Front to reform the relationship between empire and metropole highlighted the contradictions inherent in such a project and marked the beginning of a process of change which led, ultimately and inexorably after the Second World War, to decolonisation. The Popular Front can therefore be seen as both part of a longer history and at the same time representing a decisive moment in that history.

With this in mind, explanations for the failure of the Popular Front's colonial project also take on a different significance. Rather than seeking to account for the Popular Front's failure in terms of, for example, the government's short duration, the resistance it faced and the obstacles it confronted, the failure of the Popular Front's colonial project also needs to be seen in the context of the in-built problems of imperialism itself.

This is not to deny the importance of the obstacles facing the Popular Front government as it sought to implement its, albeit modest, colonial reform programme. Firstly, it was effectively in power for little more than a year. Many of those in the cabinet had little or no government experience and most had little knowledge and no direct experience of colonial matters. Secondly, as both Brot and Koufan show, it had to confront often virulent opposition from metropolitan colonial interests within the colonies as well as more passive, but equally effective, resistance from within the colonial administration itself. Thirdly, the little cash it had available was needed for its domestic reform programme and no new money was available for colonial reform. Furthermore, French dependence on empire for a third of its total export markets represented a strong disincentive to the introduction of any changes that might jeopardise the colonial economy.

The intention here is not to deny the validity of these points. It is rather to suggest that an approach which takes as its starting-point the failure of the Popular Front's policy and then accounts for this failure as a product of the circumstances in which it emerged may not provide the most useful analytical framework. In contrast, a conceptual framework that seeks to understand the failure of the Popular Front's colonial reform project as a product of the contradictions inherent within colonialism itself is actually more fruitful.

Evidence for the existence of these contradictions can be seen at a number of different levels. To illustrate this, just three examples from the many provided in the book will be cited here. Firstly, as Hargreaves points out, members of the 'Africanist International' were humanists and reformers, but they were not anti-imperialists. The contradiction between their liberal values and the inherent violence of colonialism was inescapable. Secondly, colonial reformers sought to 'rationalise' colonial rule. On one level, in improving the welfare of indigenous societies within their own framework, their aim was to maintain the link between indigenous people and the land and thus to preserve traditional society while simultaneously transforming it. However, Wilder goes further than this and suggests that we should see the attempts of these colonial humanists to rationalise colonial rule in a broader context, as part of 'an emergent politics focused on social intervention, social integration and social welfare', in which the colonies become a proving ground for this new politics. Thirdly, these colonial reformers viewed progress in the colonies as a common, shared responsibility, yet they knew that the metropole lacked the resources that would have been necessary to enable it to carry out its responsibilities.

To sum up, the Popular Front represents a watershed in the history of the French empire. It exposed clearly for the first time the contradictions inherent in the French colonial project and the limitations of reform within a colonial context. In so doing, it raised the hopes and aspirations of colonial populations and thereby initiated a long-running dialogue between the government and colonial nationalist movements which, after the hiatus of Vichy, was to be resumed at the end of the War, become intense under the Fourth Republic and culminate in the latter winning the argument and their independence. We shall return to this theme at the end of the introduction.

POLICY FRAMEWORK

Ideological roots

Under the Third Republic, France had been ruled by a series of right and centre-right governments in which the

colonial lobby, the so-called *parti colonial*, had, through its
network of influence both within and outside government,
played a key role in colonial policy-making. As the Third
Republic's first left-wing government, the Popular Front could
thus be expected to mark a significant turning-point, with
the importance of the colonial lobby declining while that
of the political left, trade unions, colonial reformers and
left-wing intellectuals increased. There was certainly an
aspiration to implement a programme of colonial reform.
Colonial policy was largely placed in the hands of a number of individuals who had a reputation as advocates of
reform: the Colonial Minister, Marius Moutet, the former
liberal governor of Algeria, Maurice Viollette, Pierre Viénot,
an independent Socialist who was appointed Under-Secretary
of State at the Foreign Affairs Ministry, and Charles-André
Julien, a historian who had been an outspoken critic of
French colonialism. Also, 18 out of 30 colonial governors
were transferred or replaced, although there were few changes
lower down in the colonial hierarchy and many local officials
remained opposed to change.

However, as William Cohen has shown, the Socialists, who
in the 1920s had seen colonisation as a preparation for
self-government, had abandoned this commitment by 1936.[14]
The Socialists' acceptance of the continuation of the empire and adoption of an assimilationist stance was partly a
pragmatic political move, reflecting divisions within the party
which included both colonialist and anticolonialist groups
and individuals. Thus, while committing itself to colonial
reform, the party at the same time declared that it would
retain the empire, on the grounds that to abandon it might
lead to the colonies being subjected to foreign rule by a
colonial power less benign and progressive than France.
This new stance represented a compromise between opposing views within the French Socialist Party (SFIO) and
it is not therefore surprising that the Popular Front's colonial programme was modest in its ambitions, nor that priority was given to economic and social reforms over political
reform. Colonialism needed to be humanised if the continued possession of colonies was to be justified, and this
meant putting an end to colonial exploitation. If colonisation,
for many on the left, was associated with exploitation, and

'colonialism' and 'altruism' were regarded as opposed concepts, this was the fault of the right. It was therefore the task of the left to change this. Colonialism had to become generous and progressive, and it was this that lay behind the concept of 'colonisation altruiste', as developed by Marius Moutet[15] and the Socialist former Governor-General of Indochina, Alexandre Varenne.

In France, the doctrinal roots of this left-wing colonial reformism are to be found in assimilationism. An inherently ambiguous concept, assimilation could be claimed by both the colonial lobby and humanitarian socialists. For the former, it justified and underpinned the dream of a 'greater France', in which colonised peoples would be christianised and brought under the ambit of European civilisation, whereas the republican tradition of assimilation was progressive, holding out the promise of the extension of republican values of liberty, equality and fraternity to the colonised peoples.[16] For many on the left, assimilation also held out the prospect of extending Socialist ideas beyond metropolitan France.[17] This idea had been offered as a justification for colonialism years earlier by Jean Jaurès, and it was an idea that many Socialists now embraced.

The essential ambiguity of the term assimilation, which made it possible for it to be adopted by both conservatives and reformers, does not stop here, however, because assimilation, even in its progressive guise, took for granted the present inferiority of the colonised, while simultaneously assuming their ultimate perfectibility and implicitly positing France as the model of civilisation to which colonised peoples should aspire. Yet this was itself problematic, because which was the 'true France'[18] to which colonised peoples were to be asked to aspire as a model? Was it the modernising, republican, secular France of the towns and cities, or the traditional, rural, Catholic France of peasant farmers and village-based communities? Certainly, the Popular Front showed no signs of wanting to challenge the traditional colonial 'division of labour' between an industrial metropole and an overseas empire, the main function of which was the supply of primary products. The industrial route to economic and social modernisation thus effectively remained closed to the colonies. As a policy, this may have been perfectly 'rational', at least from the perspective of the metropole, and it was also, as Wilder shows, consistent with the aspiration of colonial reformers to 'rationalise' colonialism. But it is highly questionable whether it was in the long-term interests of the colonial populations and we are thus, once again, at the heart of the contradiction, inherent within colonialism, 'between a desire for colonial development and a political economy that produced under-development'.

As a substitute for assimilation through industrialisation and economic diversification, Popular Front colonial reformers put forward the idea of colonial populations developing and progressing within the context of their own communities. The myth of a peasant-based rural France, based on the family and a simple agricultural life, was a powerful one, and not only for French conservatives. Many of the Popular Front's colonial reformers were only one generation removed from this rural France (Moutet, for example, came from the Ardèche, one of the most rural areas of France) and looked to it as a possible development model for the colonies, the economies of which remained almost entirely agriculture-based. Indeed it was perhaps this that lay behind what LaCoss calls the 'primitivising' of Kanak culture in Popular Front colonial discourse. The myth of the innocent 'noble savage' and the promotion of the primitive can thus be seen as underpinning the social modernism of the Popular Front and providing a bulwark against threats of international fascism abroad and civil war at home.

It is a logical consequence of the above that the Popular Front showed no interest in developing waged labour in the colonies. Rather, for its colonial reformers the first, and essential, step on the road to development was the abolition of forced labour, so as to free colonial peasant farmers to cultivate their own land and enjoy the fruits of their labour.[19] Beyond this, improved infrastructure, better health care and the expansion of education were seen as the necessary pre-requisites for the modernisation of colonial society. However, all of this would have cost money, which the French second chamber, the Sénat, was ultimately unwilling to invest. Within existing budgets, there was nevertheless scope for reform, for example in the field of education, but here again colonial reformers were caught up in the ambiguities of their own assimilationism. If colonial societies were to develop within the context of their own cultures and communities, then the expansion of western education on the French metropolitan model was clearly not appropriate, other than for a small indigenous sub-élite whose main function would be to act as the colonial power's intermediaries. And the role of these intermediaries would remain, as in the past, that of assisting France in the administration of its colonial territories, while at the same time dispensing an 'adapted' education to colonial populations, so as to help them prepare for 'modernisation' within the context of their own societies. Caught within its own contradictions, this programme of colonial reform necessarily did not translate, in practice, into significant policy changes in the colonies, as we shall see.

The international dimension

In seeking to understand the ideological and historical roots of the Popular Front's colonial policy, the international dimension is important. In part, this is because the Popular Front's colonial reformers belonged to an international network of European democrats and socialists committed to colonial development and the 'humanisation' of colonialism. These colonial humanists, whom Hargreaves in his chapter calls the 'Africanist International', kept in touch with each other and were aware of each other's ideas and findings through the international network to which they belonged. They were necessarily reformers but, as we have seen, they were not anti-imperialists. Rather, they were internationalists who saw imperialism as bestowing a shared responsibility on the colonial powers for the development and modernisation of the territories over which they exercised control.

At another level, internationalism was important as an ideological component of the working-class parties that came to power under the Popular Front. French Socialists and Communists claimed that their approach to the colonial question differed from that of the bourgeois parties in that they represented the interests of the colonial working masses. As Colás shows in his chapter, there were two main aspects to this. Firstly, there was the impact on trade unions and social movements in the colonies. For example, there was a dramatic increase in trade union membership in Tunisia, which by the end of 1936 had reached 40,000, three-quarters of whom were Tunisians. In French West Africa, trade unions were authorised for the first time, although full trade-union rights were restricted to that small minority of Africans who had received a French education. There was continuous strike action throughout the empire between 1936 and 1938, some of which was linked to metropolitan social movements. Secondly, there was the political dimension, since the greater freedom of action of social movements and trade unions was often accompanied by political mobilisation, as in the case of Néo-Destour in Tunisia and Messali Hadj and the Parti Populaire Algérien in Algeria, both of which took the opportunity to press for independence.

There was, however, no simple, direct link between social movements in the colonies on the one hand and Popular Front organisations on the other. Each had its own agenda. Colonial trade unions used the limited possibilities opened to them by the Popular Front to pursue their demands for improved wages and conditions, while political movements in some parts of the empire took the opportunity to press their demands for independence. The Popular Front, on the other hand, while rejecting the approach of previous governments and recognising the existence of a 'labour question' in the empire, did not conceptualise colonial labour in the colonies in class terms.[20] Its attempts to deal with labour questions also remained circumscribed within a colonial framework. There was no question of a challenge to this framework, nor of support for autonomist organisations or for groups campaigning for political independence. Indeed, the Popular Front broke up the Etoile Nord-Africaine, one of Algeria's most radical opposition movements, in January 1937, because it was considered to represent a threat to the territorial integrity of the Republic.

To sum up, while the Popular Front's reform project was generous in intent, its proposals remained firmly rooted within a colonial context. It is for this reason that it is

more useful, as both Norindr and Wilder suggest, to analyse
and understand the limitations of the Popular Front's colonial reform project in terms of the contradictions inherent within it, rather than in terms of continuity versus change
and/or the tensions between conservatives and reformers
in parliament, in government and within the colonial administration. The ambiguities of the doctrine of assimilation, what Wilder calls 'the contradiction internal to the
political rationality of colonial humanism itself' and the
limitations of its internationalism, all of these are essential
elements in understanding the 'failure' of the Popular Front
genuinely to democratise and humanise colonial governance.
The continuities with the past should therefore be seen,
not as the result of contradictions, for example between
idealistic programmes and intractable colonial realities, or
between reform-minded metropolitan planners and politicians and authoritarian colonial administrators, or conversely
between reformist administrators and an immobile or in-
different Paris bureaucracy, but rather as an inevitable
outcome of doctrinal limitations and of the contradictions
faced by a reformist project in a colonial situation. These
tensions clearly came to the surface for the first time under
the Popular Front and were to become acute after the war.

DIVERSITY OF POLICY OUTCOMES

Colonial firms, French planters and traders and conservative colonialists feared that the Popular Front's programme
of reform would weaken the empire. They were afraid that
the improvements in wages and conditions for colonial
workers would reduce profit margins and economic viability,
and that its political and social reforms would undermine
French authority. Most historians, on the other hand, have
pointed to the very modest nature of the actual changes
introduced. These perspectives are not mutually exclusive.
As Jacques Marseille has shown, the 1930s mark the period
when the more dynamic sectors of French capitalism began
to lose interest in the empire.[21] At the same time, while the
actual changes enacted by the Popular Front were modest, the
rhetoric of reform, accompanied by the failure to implement

significant changes, provoked widespread disillusionment among colonial populations, and notably among the so-called *évolués*. This had serious potential consequences for French colonial authority, since it was to the *évolués* that France looked to act as their intermediaries with indigenous society and it was in partnership with them that the French hoped to maintain colonial rule. Their loyalty and trust were essential to this project. One result of the failure of the Popular Front to live up to its promises was a long-term breakdown in trust between the government and *évolués*, many of whom came to feel that they could no longer have confidence in the government, even a reform-minded one, to implement a genuine programme of colonial reform.

French West Africa was the colony where the changes brought about by the Popular Front were perhaps most noticeable and where the breakdown of trust was therefore slowest to manifest itself. This was mainly because of the reform-minded Governor-General de Coppet, whose actions ensured that the reforming phase of the Popular Front actually lasted longer here than in France (he was sacked by the new Colonial Minister, Georges Mandel, in October 1938, but until that date had consistently tried to push forward a reformist agenda). However, within French West Africa there were enormous variations in impact, notably between urban and rural areas and between the coast and the interior. In Senegal, for example, the impact was greatest in Dakar, Saint-Louis and the other important centres, where Popular Front committees were formed and trade unions became more active, whereas in the interior, where the number of *évolués* was small and the extent of contact with metropolitan France was much less, the impact of the Popular Front was less significant. In his chapter on Guinée, for example, Brot characterises the impact of the Popular Front as 'very weak'. The only exception to this, he suggests, is in Conakry, where a small number of embryonic trade unions were formed, several strikes broke out between 1936 and 1937, and a section of the SFIO was created in 1938. More generally, there was some lightening of the tax burden and punishments under the *indigénat* reduced after 1936, but Brot questions whether even these modest improvements can be wholly attributed to the Popular Front. Overall, it seems, bureaucratic sclerosis, together with active resistance both from within the administration and from colonial firms, combined to neutralise the modest attempts at reform, especially away from the main urban centres, although these latter did witness an unprecedented effervescence of trade union and political activity during the period of the Popular Front.

In Cameroun, where the colonial administration traditionally worked closely with European firms and where forced labour, which the administration often helped to recruit, was widely used, the Popular Front found itself caught in the logic of colonialism. As a result, as Jean Koufan shows in his chapter, its colonial policy was dictated as much by the needs of French firms as that of its predecessors and, as his survey of conditions and indigenous reactions shows, the impact of reforms in this colony was extremely limited.

The Indochinese context was rather different from that of black Africa. Since the beginning of French colonial occupation of black Africa and Indochina in the 1880s, there was a widespread assumption in French colonial circles of a hierarchy in France's colonial empire, in which Indochina occupied a kind of middle position between metropolitan France and the black African colonies. This was because it was considered that its indigenous civilisation was more advanced than that of black Africa and, partly linked to this, it was considered to have greater economic development potential. There were also other important differences between the colonial context in Indochina and that in, for example, black Africa. The Chinese and Japanese threat, Vietnamese nationalism and also, no doubt, the greater distance from France, all of these contributed to a perception that the French position in Indochina was potentially less secure than in Africa. The colonial administration feared the capacity for political organisation of the local population. The creation of *déclassés*, through introduction of French education, and the potential political threat they represented to French rule, were a constant cause for concern among colonial administrators.

One consequence of this was that there was generally a greater willingness to envisage political reform and to allow indigenous people a role in public affairs than was the case in black Africa. From the very beginning of the French occupation, as de Gantès shows in his chapter, colonial rule in Indochina had been characterised by the alternation of periods of reform with periods of reaction. Already from 1905, Governor-General Beau had sought to 'associate' the indigenous population in the development and administration of the colony; between 1911 and 1920, the future colonial minister, Albert Sarraut, had, as Governor-General, pursued a reformist agenda, as had Alexandre Varenne during the period of the Cartel des Gauches. The appointment of the reformist Jules Brévié as Governor-General in 1936 marked a continuation of this cycle of reform and reaction. And, as De Gantès shows, there were many similarities between the measures proposed by Brévié and those put forward by previous reform-minded governors-general of Indochina.

In Algeria, the reforms proposed by the Popular Front were, as Tostain shows in her chapter, cautious and prudent. The most important measure was the Blum-Viollette bill, which provided for 25,000 (out of 6 million) Algerians to be offered French citizenship. It was brought before parliament in December 1936 but was opposed by the colonial lobby within the National Assembly who did all they could to obstruct its passage. Blum hesitated to confront them directly, with the result that, when the Popular Front came to an end in October 1938, the Blum-Viollette bill fell with it.

Thus, as we can see, the immediate impact of the Popular Front on colonial populations varied from colony to colony, and indeed within colonies. In order to understand these differences, we need to examine the factors that determine this diversity of outcomes. However, in assessing these, there is a need to distinguish between the immediate and long-term consequences of the Popular Front for the empire.

If we are seeking to ascertain the long-term impact of the Popular Front in the empire, there are significant parallels to be drawn between different parts of the empire. The first of these is the theme of disillusionment, both because of the failure to implement the promised reforms and the subsequent attempt to turn the colonial clock back under Vichy. Even in Senegal there was a feeling of disappointment which was fuelled by the tragic events at Thiès in September 1938 when six striking railway workers were killed following a confrontation with the army. De Coppet was immediately dismissed by the new Colonial Minister, Georges Mandel, who encouraged the new administration to take a firm stance against the strikers. As a result, order was restored but the bitter taste left by these events and the memory of the unfulfilled promises was to remain alive among many Senegalese. Despite this, and despite the fact that the feeling of disappointment was further exacerbated by the arrival in power of the Vichy regime, which led to the reversal of many of the limited colonial reforms that had been introduced by previous, more liberal, regimes and instituted a new period of repression in many parts of the empire, black African *évolués* were at this stage prepared to keep faith with France. This was much less the case in Algeria and Indochina, where the feeling of discontent was more profound and widely felt.

The political consequences of this disillusionment were significant. Throughout the empire the political reforms, albeit modest, that were introduced by the Popular Front opened up a political space in which political movements were able to emerge and become active. The coming to power of the Popular Front had raised hopes among colonial populations of substantive change and led to an upsurge in political activity. This stalled with the change of government in 1938 and was brought to an abrupt halt by the arrival in power of the Vichy regime in 1940. However, the genie, once out of the bottle, could not be put back: expectations had been raised and failure to live up to them was bound to result in disappointment. The delays in implementing reform during the period of the Popular Front and subsequently the end of the Popular Front and the coming to power of the Vichy regime, with its attempt to turn back the colonial clock, led to widespread disillusionment, especially, but not only, among the colonial political élite. This was not to be forgotten when the war ended and the opportunity for political movements to emerge and become active was once again present. In Indochina and

Algeria, the result of these developments was to give a substantial boost to the nationalist movements in these territories. Even in French West Africa, where the modern nationalist movement emerged rather later, there was an intensification of anti-French feeling once the lid was taken off political activity following the Liberation of North Africa by the allies and the replacement of the Vichy Governor-General Pierre Boisson by the Gaullist Pierre Cournarie in 1943. The pent-up political frustrations of 1938–40 now expressed themselves all the more vehemently. It was in part in recognition of this that the Provisional Government instituted a period of colonial reform by calling the Brazzaville Conference in 1944. The significance of the role of the Popular Front in paving the way for this should not be under-estimated.

In highlighting the continuities in colonial personnel and doctrine between 1936 and 1944–6, Shipway and de Gantès add another dimension to our understanding of the growing frustration felt by many colonial *évolués* from 1936 onwards. Bureaucratic continuity within the colonial administration was accompanied by political continuity at ministerial level (Marius Moutet, who had been Colonial Minister under the Popular Front from 1936–8, returned to the post in 1946). This, combined with the *esprit de corps* that derived from the fact that the great majority of colonial officials had trained at the Ecole Coloniale (renamed in 1934 the Ecole Nationale de la France d'Outre-Mer), served to reinforce the impression of a divorce between the rhetoric of change in Paris and the lack of it 'on the ground' in the colonies.

The most important result of these developments was, as Tostain and de Gantès show for Algeria and Indochina respectively, a loss of confidence in the French Republic to bring about reform. The Popular Front and its aftermath marked an end of the belief among the colonial élite in the possibility of reform being implemented through 'top-down' political action initiated from the metropole, and the emergence of the realisation that substantive change would only come about through their own initiative. The one partial exception to this was black Africa, although here too, as we have seen, there was an upsurge in political activity. In French West Africa, for example, where Marius Moutet was the first Colonial Minister to visit the colony in 1936 and where the socialist Governor-General de Coppet initiated a number of reforms, many *évolués*, while intensifying their campaign for reform, nevertheless maintained their belief in the possibility of reform in partnership with the French, at least until after the Second World War. This was because, for the time being at least, the belief persisted that, if reform had not come about, it was not the fault of the Republic, which genuinely wanted reform, but because of the bad faith and feet-dragging of local *colons* and colonial officials. The decision by the Provisional Government after the war to allow all of French black Africa to elect deputies to the French National Assembly in Paris, albeit with a very restricted electorate, served to maintain this faith in the Republic, at least for a further few years, until it rapidly became obvious that no French government, however well-intentioned, was ever going to be able to meet the growing political, social and economic aspirations of Africans within the context of colonialism.

*   *   *

Overall, then, the Popular Front's achievements were limited. Its historical significance lies elsewhere. The Popular Front can be seen as a defining moment in the history of French colonialism, when the contradictions inherent in the colonial project first became clearly visible. It articulated a colonial humanist project and asserted the need for economic, social and political modernisation as the essential pre-requisites for colonial development and progress. In so doing, it raised far greater hopes and aspirations than previous reform projects and the disappointment was thus all the greater. Indeed, one may wonder, in retrospect, whether the Popular Front did not represent the last chance for the colonial humanist project. This, of course, begs the question as to whether the colonial humanist project would ever have been able to go far, or fast, enough to satisfy the demands of the colonial populations. Nevertheless, its failure certainly taught colonial peoples the lesson that you cannot depend on the imperial power, even one led by a well-intentioned government, to carry out reform. And after the war, the demands for colonial reform, which had been articulated during the Popular Front period, could no longer be resisted, due to the weakened position in which the metropole now found itself. The Popular Front can thus be seen as marking the beginning of French decolonisation, and it is perhaps only the rapid onset of the Second World War that has hitherto prevented it from being seen in this light.

Notes and References

1. See, for example, J. Jackson, *The Popular Front in France* (Cambridge University Press, 1988) p. 288.
2. For example, Julian Jackson, in his book *The Popular Front in France*, op. cit., only dedicates five pages to treatment of the Popular Front and empire; the focus of Anthony Adamthwaite's *Grandeur and Misery* (Arnold, 1995) is France and Europe: barely two pages of the book are devoted specifically to the empire; Eugen Weber, in his book on the 30s in France, *The Hollow Years* (Norton, 1994) has nothing to say about the empire and its importance for France; and Maurice Larkin, in his chapter on the Popular Front in *France Since the Popular Front*, 2nd edn (Clarendon Press, 1997) makes no mention of the empire.
3. For a discussion of the post-war Left's implication in France's colonial project and the problems and conflicts to which this gave rise in the Algerian context, see M. Evans, *The Memory of Resistance* (Berg, 1997) pp. 33–8.
4. R. F. Betts, *France and Decolonisation, 1900–1960*, (Macmillan, 1991) p. 29.
5. W. B. Cohen, 'The Colonial Policy of the Popular Front', *French Historical Studies*, VII, 3 (1972) pp. 368–93; H. Deschamps, 'France in Black Africa and Madagascar Between 1920 and 1945', in L. H. Gann and P. Duignan (eds), *Colonialism in Africa 1870–1960*, vol. 2 (Cambridge University Press, 1970), p. 232; C. Coquery-Vidrovitch, *La colonisation française 1931–1939*, in J. Thobie, G. Meynier C. Coquery-Vidrovitch, C.-R. Ageron (eds), *Histoire de la France coloniale 1914–1990* (Armand Colin, 1990), p. 265.
6. W. B. Cohen, *Rulers of Empire: The French Colonial Service in Africa* (Hoover Institution Press, 1971), pp. 108–43.
7. H. Deschamps, op. cit., p. 244.
8. J. Suret-Canale, *Afrique Noire, L'Ere coloniale 1900–45* (Editions Sociales, 1962), p. 199.
9. J. Marseille, *Empire colonial et capitalisme français* (Albin Michel, 1984) pp. 44, 54.

10. H. Dubief, *Le Déclin de la IIIe République, 1929–1938* (Seuil, 1976) p. 39
11. P. & M. Clerget, *La France dans le monde* (Payot, 1938) p. 8.
12. A. Sarraut, *La Mise en valeur des colonies françaises* (Payot, 1923).
13. See, for example, N. Bernard-Duquenet, *Le Sénégal et le Front Populaire* (L'Harmattan, 1985), p. 226.
14. W. B. Cohen, 'The Colonial Policy of the Popular Front', art. cit., p. 374.
15. See for example, Marius Moutet's development of this idea in his introduction to Mérat, L., *L'Heure de l'économie dirigée d'intérêt général aux colonies* (Sirey, 1936).
16. Cf. R. F. Betts, *Assimilation and Association in French Colonial Theory 1890–1914* (Columbia University Press, 1961).
17. Cf. Marius Moutet who, as Colonial Minister under the Popular Front stated before the National Assembly: 'I am . . . the missionary of revolutionary France', Assemblée Nationale, *Debats*, 15 December 1936, p. 3626.
18. This is the title of a book on French national identity by H Lebovics, *True France*, (Cornell University Press, 1992).
19. Marius Moutet, in Assemblée Nationale, *Débats*, 15 December 1936, p. 3626.
20. Cf. speech by Marius Moutet to the French National Assembly: 'Our whole colonial, programme is based on the indigenous peasantry and whatever we can do to make the work of the black or yellow peasant easier represents the true task of colonisation', ibid.
21. J. Marseille, op. cit., p. 279.

Part 1 Theory and Background

1 The Politics of Failure: Historicising Popular Front Colonial Policy in French West Africa[1]

Gary Wilder

RETHINKING 'FAILURE' THROUGH POLITICAL RATIONALITY

The Problem

In a speech on 'Republican colonial policy', made soon after he was appointed the Popular Front's Minister of Colonies, Marius Moutet affirmed France's commitment to a 'colonial policy of liberation' and a 'policy of humanism' that would be 'loyal to freedom, justice, humanity', and to 'the most beautiful traditions of liberalism and friendship between races'.[2] However, the concrete reform programme he then outlined was restricted to campaigns against famine and disease, and the creation of labour protection laws. He maintained, 'colonial action cannot remain on the level of pure politics, of demands for rights'.[3] As his bureau later reported, 'the Popular Front in the colonies has applied itself to improving the physical, economic, and cultural lives of our *protégés*'.[4] Elsewhere he summarised his aim as: 'to help the ensemble of colonial populations live and live better'.[5]

Moutet's socialist humanism focused on native 'social and economic evolution'. Despite the language he used, his programme differed from a Western liberalism that had always been concerned primarily with individual civil and political rights, guaranteed by a common law.[6] So how are we to account for the way the Popular Front's 'colonial policy of social action' (as Moutet phrased it to the students

33

of the Ecole Coloniale in 1937) privileged social improvement over political enfranchisement?[7] Was this another version of the longstanding colonial refusal to extend rights to racialised subjects? The Ministry of Colonies, after all, believed that the 'change in political orientation initiated by the new [Popular Front] government' would be 'particularly delicate in the colonies, because of the weak degree of natives' political maturity and the disorders that could be created by hastily elaborated reforms.'[8] Or was the new concern for native welfare simply a matter of translating Blum's social programme of 'Peace, Bread, Freedom' to the colonies?[9]

My argument is that the Popular Front's concern with indigenous colonial development and native social welfare was part of a much broader transformation in the rationality and strategy of metropolitan and colonial government in the early twentieth century.

It is generally accepted that the colonial policy of the Popular Front failed to realise its inflated promises of liberal reform in French West Africa, whether due to poor planning in Paris or bureaucratic intransigence in the field.[10] This perceived failure of implementation is then taken to exemplify interwar colonial policy as a whole: an 'era of lost opportunities' and 'political stagnation'.[11] The interwar attempt to reconceptualise the colonial project is thus reduced to a contradiction between a rhetoric of reform and the reality of unchanging colonial violence.

But what happens to this verdict of institutional failure if we regard Popular Front colonial policy through a broader optic and begin by asking a different set of questions? It then becomes not so much a matter of whether Moutet's colonial officials sincerely wanted to improve the lives of colonial subjects (but were prevented from implementing their reforms in practice), or whether the reform programme was a cynical ideology designed to mask the reality of colonial domination. But, rather, a matter of the possible continuities between this interwar shift in colonial government and the long-term transformation of state politics that had been taking place in Western democracies. And of the relationship between the post-First World War emphasis on colonial development and the development, in the early twentieth century, of another phase of global capitalism that required new political strategies and entailed a series of social consequences. In other words, rather than evaluate the Popular Front's legislative record, I suggest we historicise the interwar reform movement and try to account, in broad terms, for the transformation of the colonial government's *political rationality* during this time period.

Thinking Through Political Rationality

I use 'political rationality' in the sense formulated by Michel Foucault.[12] He is interested less in institutions and ideologies than in 'examining how forms of rationality inscribe themselves in . . . systems of practices . . . because . . . "practices" don't exist without a certain regime of rationality'.[13] Foucault defines Western political rationality as 'governmentality', a form of domination whereby 'the state has essentially to take care of men as a population. It wields power over living beings as living beings, and its politics, therefore has to be a biopolitics'.[14] As population becomes a political problem and life a political object, this governmental rationality follows the injunction that 'happiness of individuals is a requirement for the survival and development of the state. It is a condition, it is an instrument, and not simply a consequence'.[15] The new political rationality thus entailed the state management of a population of living, labouring beings whose welfare and happiness was its responsibility. Foucault locates the emergence of this political rationality in the sixteenth century. But a fully developed governmentality, in his account, only became possible after a number of social transformations beginning in the late eighteenth century meant that the promotion of population displaced the power of the sovereign as the privileged means and end of government.[16]

Foucault recognises that there was a mutually constitutive relationship between the productivist dynamic of capitalism and the normalising character of this new political rationality. Following economic development and demographic growth, 'methods of power and knowledge assumed responsibility for the life processes'; just as capitalism 'would not have been possible without the controlled insertion of bodies into the machinery of production and the adjustment of the phenomena of population to economic processes'.[17] But rather than recognise bio-power as immanent to capitalist social relations, he sees the relationship between governmentality and capitalism as one of *adjustment*: an external power contributing to the functional regulation of production.[18]

Yet Foucault's own writing suggests that modern political rationality did in fact possess an instrumental specificity. His conception of governmentality focuses on its economising logic: 'the art of government . . . is essentially concerned with answering the question of how to introduce economy . . . into the management of the state'.[19] There seems to be an economising, maximising rationality intrinsic to governmentality that works instrumentally to correlate means with ends.

So, how can Foucault's conception of political rationality, as I have outlined it, help us analyse the transformations in colonial politics that took place in France after the First World War? His non-humanist account of the emergence of 'welfare' politics as an abstract form of state power between the sixteenth and nineteenth centuries, provides a model for historicising political rationality that neither slips into idealism, voluntarism, nor economism. Analytically, 'political rationality' provides a way to grasp the play of continuity and discontinuity between distinct but intrinsically related modern political forms in time (from one historical conjuncture to another) and space (between metropole and colony).[20]

More importantly, 'political rationality' allows us to think about the complex interdependence of political forms with respect to other dimensions of modernity (namely, capitalism). It allows us to conceptualise political forms as participating in the larger structural order of a common modernity, while recognising that they also contain their own properties, regularities and periodicities which require them to be analysed on their own terms. In other words, Foucault's account of governmentality implicitly suggests that in any given historical conjuncture, there is a dialectical relationship between the dynamic of capitalism and the character of political rationality. This understanding, I would argue, can help us to historicise the interwar shifts in colonial government without restricting them to questions of individual implementation and the institutionalisation of reform.

Accounting for the Transformation

Popular Front colonial reforms were part of a more pervasive reconceptualisation of the political rationality of colonial government in French West Africa after the First World War. Briefly, we can understand this emergent 'colonial humanism' as an attempt to reconcile colonial autocracy with republican principles; to liberalise and humanise colonial rule. As one prominent reformer declared:

> What is needed are new methods, so that administration can be born again, vitalized by a spirit of humanism . . . governing means not acting as a specialist, but as a humanist . . . the territory is not just raw material for finance, commerce, the army and the administration to work with. . . . It is a living body, and we must enter into relations with it if we are to govern it.[21]

This colonial reform movement was characterised by three interdependent objectives, each of which was supposed to enable the others: the preservation of indigenous social relations, the improvement of native social welfare and the promotion of colonial economic development.[22]

Historians have sought to account for these transformations in colonial rationality by focusing on short-term events within French West Africa: a corps of better trained and more sensitive individual administrators, local resistance to governmental policies and the failure of economic development plans.[23] I will argue, however, that during the interwar period, the emergence of colonial humanism transcended the benevolent intentions of individual administrators, was as much a feature of transformations in the form of state power in Western nations as it was a response to local politics, and was intrinsically linked to development policy.

After the First World War, conditions within French West Africa created pressure to reform the precepts and practices of colonial rule. These included the administration's pragmatic recognition that direct domination of massive territorial entities was politically ineffective and financially insupportable; the acknowledgement that France owed a so-called 'blood debt' to colonial soldiers who, in return for having proved their loyalty during the war, were seen to deserve better treatment; and, paradoxically, local African resistance to military and labour recruitment during the war, as well as the gathering conviction that progressive native policies were necessary to counteract the growing social disorder that was the legacy of previous French colonial policies. All this developed in the context of a growing international anti-imperialism fueled by Lenin and Wilson's different reasons for supporting the rights of colonial peoples to self-determination.

Corresponding to these colonial conditions was the development of a new imperial consciousness within France itself. After the First World War, French public and political opinion focused on the empire as a key to national renewal and international stature. The colonies were no longer seen as mere *sources* of manpower, materials and markets, but as intrinsic features of French power, prestige and prosperity. There also emerged a new colonial nationalism, focused on the image of Greater France that maintained that the colonies were in some fashion integral parts of an expanded French nation, even if most colonised populations continued to be legally and politically excluded from the national polity.

In short, this was a moment when French national and colonial histories were as entwined as they had ever been. After the First World War, in both metropolitan and overseas France, there were public debates – about the proper relationship between the empire and the republic, the most ethical and effective form of colonial government, and the juridical status of colonial subjects – out of which developed colonial humanism.

But the development of more liberal colonial policies during the interwar period was more than a matter of moral payback, international legitimation, or practical administrative calculation. Two related determinants of this shift in the rationality of colonial government were significant: first, the emergence of welfare politics as the new organising rationality of the French republican state, beginning in the late-nineteenth century; and secondly, transformations in colonial political economy, and the relationship between interwar native policies and concurrent attempts to promote economic development in French West Africa.

HISTORICISING COLONIAL POLITICS

'Welfare' Rationality and Republican Politics

Over the course of the nineteenth century, the 'social question' came to dominate republican politics, 'solidarity' became the political rationality of the metropolitan state, and 'society' became its target. After the collapse of the Second Republic, as the tension between democratic political equality and capitalist social hierarchy became unmanageable, republicanism began to ground its legitimacy on the state's ability to guarantee social integration, promote social progress and prevent class war. This new political rationality was institutionalised under the Third Republic in reformist social legislation organised around newly legitimised 'social rights'.[24]

The transformation in the political rationality of the state was characterised by the growing prominence of 'administration' within a progressively rationalised governmental apparatus. Charged with the paradoxical responsibility of protecting both individual freedom and social order, the state became increasingly concerned with the general management of society. After 1870, as 'states increasingly penetrated social life' and 'civil society was further politicised', government became further bureaucratised.[25]

By the early twentieth century, according to these accounts, the new political rationality of solidarity corresponded to a changing relationship between state, society and economy.[26] In the 1920s, there emerged a sizeable, if not dominant, movement in France that sought to link state politics with a strong administration – autonomous and effective, scientific and technical – devoted to national public service.[27] A network of business managers, engineers, civil servants, socialists and trade unionists sought to rationalise the national economy through scientific management. After the global depression reached France in the 1930s, they called on the state to correct the cyclical crises of the unregulated free market through economic and social 'planning'. Their goal was to promote both productivity and social solidarity; to perfect, rather than abolish capitalism.[28]

These proto-technocrats also wanted to translate developments in industrial rationalisation and scientific management into a national programme of state rationalisation and comprehensive social management. The 1928 passage of a compulsory national social insurance programme in France, for example, was a watershed in the development of welfare politics.

The new form of French state power extended into the colonial space. Given that French West Africa was increasingly interpellated within the imperial nation-state by the interwar period, the changing form of colonial government was largely determined by the changing character of the republican state. I argued above that Popular Front colonial reforms must be located within the broader transformation of colonial rationality that characterised the interwar French empire. Here I want to suggest that we must take another step and locate colonial rationality within the longer-term reconfiguration of metropolitan government that began in the late nineteenth century.

Colonial humanism also entailed a new form of biopolitical state intervention into the living, labouring lives of its colonial subjects. Its target was indigenous society, its modality was scientific knowledge and its object was native welfare. This new form of colonial politics also entailed state-funded rational planning conceived and executed by an administrative élite of progressive technocrats. It was no coincidence that metropolitan reformers defined the ideal relationship between capital and labour with the same concept that colonial reformers conceptualised the ideal relationship between administrators and subjects: *association*.[29] Interwar colonial reform must therefore be analysed in terms of a broad transformation in the strategy of republican politics, form of state power, and character of capitalist social relations in the early twentieth century.

On the one hand colonial politics were continuous with metropolitan politics. Empire and republic, during the inter-war period, shared a common political rationality organised around: a rationalised administrative apparatus, reformist administrators and scientific planning; 'society' as the privileged site of political intervention; population as the target of that intervention; and social welfare as its objective. On the other hand, given the racialised and autocratic 'rule of colonial difference' that characterised French colonial society, metropolitan politics were also radically discontinuous with their imperial counterpart. Metropolitan and colonial states were not identical with one another; colonial politics were not mechanically derived from republican politics. Rather, metropolitan and colonial forms of government participated in an interdependent but non-identical relationship, characterised by a complex play of continuity and discontinuity; they mirrored each other in distorted ways. Nevertheless, they were constituted by overlapping socio-political fields and participated in the same crisis-defined historical conjuncture.[30]

The Welfare State and Capitalist Society

The relationship between capitalism and the state is enormously complex. Capitalist social relations developed together with the institutions of the modern state; not only alongside one another, but 'entwined' with one another.[31] While neither of the two can be logically or historically reduced to the other, they cannot be separated from one another either. This relationship was as often antagonistic as it was mutually reinforcing. Jessop discusses these two features of modern society as functionally autonomous structures that, in their co-evolution, are 'structurally coupled' and 'strategically coordinated' to one another. In other words, hegemonic projects undertaken by states correspond to specific regimes of capitalist accumulation.[32]

It should not be surprising then, that the reorganisation of republican state power around welfare politics, beginning in the late nineteenth century, corresponded to the reconfiguration of capitalist social relations during the same time period. By the 1870s, as liberal capitalism was being eclipsed by monopoly capitalism and the free market failed to maintain an ordered equilibrium between production, distribution and consumption, a strong state undertook new forms of social intervention in order to ensure the reproduction of social labour required by this new scale of capital accumulation. This expanded state power both sought to stimulate capitalist development and compensate for its negative effects (through welfare concessions). As the interventionist interwar state sought to expand rationalised production, scientific management and social regulation on a national scale it also undertook greater social and cultural projects. In other words, there was a simultaneous and interdependent transformation in economic rationality (state monopoly capitalism) and political rationality (welfare politics).[33]

THE POLITICAL ECONOMY OF COLONIAL HUMANISM

Building on this conception of the entwined relationship between governmentality and political economy, we can now turn to the second structural determinant of interwar colonial rationality. Focusing on the changing character of the colonial economy after the First World War and the emergent strategy for colonial development, will enable us more fully to account for the new humanist native policies formulated in French West Africa during this period.

The Interwar Colonial Economy

Except for a brief move toward free-trade for its colonies in the 1860s, the political economy of French empire until the First World War continued to resemble the mercantilist *pacte colonial*, organised around the idea of complementary, non-competitive economies and relations of exclusive commercial exchange. Fixed in a relationship of economic dependency to the metropole, autonomous colonial development (such as industrialisation) not directly in the service of national needs was prohibited.[34]

By 1914, the consolidation of empire, the intensification of imperial trade, and the creation of a genuine national economy in France all contributed to the closer integration of metropolitan and overseas economies in the period leading up to the war. In the years immediately following the First World War, metropolitan commerce and capital were increasingly redirected toward the colonies as France lost access to most of its overseas investment sites and increasingly protectionist European states withdrew into their national economies.[35] Although the colonial economy remained organised around the old neo-mercantilism, there was a new public and political perception that the colonial economy would become an engine of national economic growth and political security.[36] Instead of simply improving practices of colonial extraction, exploitation and domination, the new objective would be to create a living, functioning, colonial economy which would become integral to a dynamic national economy.

The principal formulation of this new developmental strategy was the Sarraut plan, presented as a legislative proposal in April 1921. Drawing on contemporary ideas about industrial rationalisation and scientific management, Sarraut proposed that colonial production be organised around specialised and functionally interrelated regional nodes of economic growth. He recognised that a self-sustaining colonial economy would require the state to finance colonial infrastructure construction and direct development plans. Such plans would also have to include social welfare measures, because colonial development would require a healthy, minimally educated and stable native population able to reproduce itself.[37]

This was an integrated vision of a single imperial entity in which the growth of the national economy would depend on the vitality of a colonial economy. It would entail a co-ordinated policy of rationalised interdependent production, directed by the metropolitan state, and guided by technocratic administrators. But despite the modernist inflection of Sarraut's comprehensive plan, it remained within neo-mercantilism and made provisions neither for overseas industrialisation nor the creation of balanced regional economies.

Although the 1920–21 economic crisis prevented Sarraut's plan from ever being voted on by parliament, it set the agenda for economic development policy through the interwar period. The tension within the plan between progressive planning and restrictive economic structures expressed itself between the wars in the political economy of French West Africa, marked by the growing prominence of finance capital, on the one hand, and by 'monopoly, mercantilism, parasitism and stagnation', on the other.[38]

The defining feature of the West African economy was France's initial decision to leave most land in native hands to be cultivated by a 'free' peasantry rather than to concentrate it into wage–labour plantations. All of colonial policy was refracted through this need to persuade natives to produce export crops. Major obstacles to economic development were presented by regional conditions that included large distances, underdeveloped infrastructure and low population density, creating labour shortages exacerbated by Paris' demand for military recruitment in the colonies. Colonial governments were thus preoccupied with building roads and railways to link newer hinterlands with older coastal ports and create viable outlets for tropical products.[39]

The federation's economy was fuelled primarily by monoculture: groundnuts and palm oil, as well as coffee, cocoa, bananas and timber. But the economic desire of interwar planners was directed at cotton and the fantasy of developing the Sahelian interior through large scale, state managed and funded projects. These would entail scientific planning, public works, native resettlement, peasant credit systems and forced labour.

An alliance of colonial reformers, modernising engineers and business interests (banks, chambers of commerce, financiers, importers) imagined a West African Egypt (with the Niger as the Nile) that would supply a struggling metropolitan textile industry with French cotton, so that the nation would no longer depend on foreign imports for such high-demand products. The massive irrigation and resettlement project supervised by the Office du Niger – a semi-autonomous public body created in 1932 after 13 years of preparation – marked a victory for modernist planning, but failed to realise the promise of greatly expanded cotton production.[40]

The expression of deep contradictions in the colonial economy, this failure was both structural (the paradoxical pursuit of macro-modernising development within the unchanging framework of colonial commercial capitalism) and conjunctural (grandiose state-planning schemes in the context of economic crises, for example, those of 1920–21 and 1930–31).[41]

During the 1930s' depression, West African commodity prices dropped 60–70 per cent. Less money flowed into colonial budgets from the French state (itself struck by the depression) or from tariff and tax revenues. Local administrations compensated by putting more tax and labour pressure on already over-burdened colonial subjects. The depression thus accentuated the most repressive aspects of the West African colonial economy, even as the presence of empire cushioned the effect of the crisis on the national economy. Although the colonial economy turned around, the prosperity of 1934–37 continued to be accompanied by growing native immiseration.[42]

The economic crisis forced French policy makers to choose between economic restructuring and national protectionism. On the one hand, in order to remain competitive in the global market after the depression, it would be necessary to modernise the national economy. On the other hand, the empire, supported by declining metropolitan industries, allowed France to defer, if not avoid, engaging in this process of reconfiguration.[43]

During the 1930s, there were a number of attempts to define an official development policy, including a 1932 ministerial report, a 1934 Colonial Economic Conference, and Moutet's 1936 Governor-General's Conference.[44] On the one hand, each of these interventions called for coordinated colonial policies at the national level that would require public investment, direct state intervention and even colonial industrialisation. On the other hand, they all, finally, retreated into neo-mercantilism by equating colonial development with export production and sought colonial profits within the framework of monopoly trade. By the mid-1930s, this affirmation of protected markets, commercial capitalism and colonial dependency (supported by cotton interests, declining industries and reformist administrators) became hegemonic. Serious colonial industrialisation was never pursued.[45]

Ultimately, interwar policy was trapped within the contradiction between the need to improve colonial production and a refusal to modernise the social and technological
organisation of production; between a desire for colonial
development and a political economy that produced under-
development. The economic crisis had reinforced the
interwar belief that the future of the national economy would
depend on colonial development. But, by favouring the
most backward sectors of French capitalism, the imperial
economy actually impeded the modernising restructuring
necessary for global competitiveness. Moreover, neo-mercantilist structures meant that genuine development – balanced
economies, indigenous industries, local competition, free
international trade – would be impossible. Yet without such
development, it would be unlikely that colonial productivity
could expand fast enough to fuel the national economy.[46]

The government of French West Africa found itself in a
bind. On the one hand, *la mise en valeur* remained a primary objective for the new colonial humanism. On the other
hand, the administration feared that colonial development
could undermine colonial authority. Industrialisation, it was
thought, would either lead to greater local autonomy from
metropolitan control or to greater social instability (due to
urbanisation and proletarianisation). Yet the attempt to
expand production within the mercantilist protectionist
structures worked to exacerbate native impoverishment.
Deteriorating living conditions in turn increased the possibility of social unrest. Colonial authority, in other words,
could be equally threatened by modernising colonial development and neo-mercantilist underdevelopment. Colonial
humanism's new native policies must be understood as an
attempt to address this dilemma.

The Interdependent Contradictions of Political Economy and Political Rationality

The interwar preoccupation with colonial economic development was founded on two organising assumptions; first,
that the empire should service metropolitan industry, rather
than become a site of local industrialisation that could pose
competitive challenges and secondly, that metropolitan needs

would best be served by stimulating colonial demand. Protected markets would maintain elevated prices for tropical products. Growing native purchasing power would thus create a growing and exclusive market for metropolitan manufactures.[47]

The strategy was to create a 'virtuous circle' of imperial economic growth.[48] The expansion of African agricultural productivity would lead to rising native incomes and greater consumption of metropolitan manufactures, which would stimulate industrial production. At the same time, as more indigenous resources were placed in export over alimentary products, natives would become more dependent on the money economy, and demand for industrial products would continue to rise while the need to cultivate cash crops would simultaneously grow.

But this mechanism would depend on providing natives with incentives to produce export products, persuading them to consume metropolitan imports, and progressively integrating them into the modern money economy. Because African production depended on a system of free-holding peasant proprietors, liberal native policies were necessary to secure their consent to participate in the system. The colonial government had a stake in improving native welfare – focusing on health, hygiene, sanitation, vocational training, education, family relations and incomes – to ensure the social reproduction of colonial cultivators and the quality of their labour. Promoting native welfare and protecting native society would keep colonial subjects enmeshed in the village milieu and guarantee social peace, both prerequisites for colonial development. In turn, economic development would itself work to improve native welfare.

But, as sound as this economic rationality appeared, the virtuous circle was not self-sustaining in practice; it had always to be maintained. So, for example, when prices for Senegalese groundnuts dropped 70 per cent during the 1930s' depression, the system unravelled: production decreased, local purchasing power diminished, imports from France fell, medium-sized commercial houses began to fail, the colonial budget shrank, and public investment in colonial productivity and infrastructure plunged.[49] There were structural and conjunctural pressures that worked to transform the imperial virtuous circle into a vicious circle. This was a paradoxical moment: precisely when colonial development became a national issue, economic crises made such development almost impossible.

During the 1930–31 crisis (and less intensely in 1920–21) metropolitan demand for colonial products dropped, prices fell, natives shifted resources away from exports to food crops and colonial budgets shrank. Private capital fled the imperial economy. Volume of trade with the metropole diminished, even while native production continued to rise. The metropolitan state had less money and little will to fund development plans. Although most of the 1920s and 1934–37 were growth years for the colonial economy, indigenous producers never recovered from the crises. Expanding production primarily benefited large commercial houses, and corresponded to growing native impoverishment. African peasants were especially undermined by the vicious circle: they worked harder than ever, but their standard of living continued to fall.[50]

Progressive native immiseration was partly a function of the fact that colonial governments were under greater pressure than ever before to increase productivity and pursue development initiatives, while their tax revenues were diminishing and metropolitan financial aid was disappearing. Responsible for generating their own revenues, local administrations resolved this tension by more efficiently exploiting indigenous labour and raising taxes when colonial subjects were least able to pay them because of their falling export income. At precisely the moment when it was believed that colonial development was crucial for a modernising national economy, the most repressive and archaic aspects of the colonial economy were thus reinforced.

The growing interwar tax burden forced even more land into export production and away from food cultivation. As colonial development proceeded, food reserves diminished, and famines (as well as chronic undernourishment and ill health) became increasingly commonplace. Recurring food crises provided a rationale for the colonial government to organise African natives into mutualist Sociétés Indigènes de Prévoyance. But the famines were features of colonial political economy rather than native improvidence. And these SIPs functioned to rationalise native export production and institutionalise unfavorable terms of trade. By coordinating efforts by both the administration and the trading companies to require peasants to cultivate certain products and force them to be sold at deflated price, they exacerbated the very problem they claimed to address.[51]

Depressed prices led native incomes and living conditions to deteriorate and export production continued to drop and African colonial governments complemented liberal inducements with coercive measures designed to stimulate native production. These included the forced cultivation of export crops, forced population migrations, the suppression of customary seasonal labour migrations and still higher taxes (so that indebted peasants would have to produce cash crops). Ironically, the very development projects designed, in part, to improve native welfare, contributed to native immiseration.

These rising administrative demands diminished the rural labour-pool and put yet more pressure on household heads to work even harder. Labour-shortages were intensified by chronic migration to neighbouring British colonies as peasants fled the new compulsions and declining incomes. Colonial budgets then shrank further, tax and labour demands increased accordingly, and the self-fuelling vicious circle tightened even more. This (under-)developmental dynamic also incorporated greater and greater numbers of African peasants into the imperial market economy. So the decline in native living conditions was accompanied by the progressive breakdown of customary forms of social organisation, the erosion of indigenous political authority, and a population transfer to increasingly overcrowded, class-stratified African cities with minimal employment opportunities since industrialisation was never pursued and administrative jobs were reserved for colonial subjects with formal education.

Once again, colonial political economy was interconnected to the development of political rationality. New governing strategies were required to counteract the unprecedented rural social transformation and imminent urban social crisis, driven largely by the administration's own development

initiatives. In this case, new native policies sought to minimise the consequences of the colonial vicious circle, rather
than sustain the ideal virtuous circle. We can thus recognise
colonial humanism's protection of indigenous society as an
attempt to control rural migration (to colonial cities and
British colonies) in order to keep natives enmeshed in village
productive relations. Its promotion of native welfare was
an attempt to guarantee the social reproduction of native
labour in a context of plummeting living standards. And
liberalising social, judicial, and political reforms were
designed to forestall social unrest (urban criminality, union-
isation, politicisation, and rural resistance to export production, taxation, and forced labour).

Interwar political rationality was entwined with economic
rationality in contradictory ways. On the one hand, colonial
humanism was an integral element of development plans
that worked to persuade a healthy and qualified population of peasant proprietors to focus their labour on export
production: decent living conditions would facilitate greater
agricultural productivity, protected markets would guarantee high prices for colonial commodities, elevated native
purchasing power would sustain metropolitan industries and
national growth and the growing incorporation of colonial
subjects into the imperial market economy would stimulate
indigenous demand. On the other hand, colonial humanism
emerged as a practical attempt to minimise the deleterious
native poverty, social disorder and political instability
produced by that very development policy. Rising demands
for colonial productivity and economic development during
a period of financial crisis and shrinking state support had
created a self-generating vicious circle: the more the colonial government sought to promote economic development,
the more it worked to impoverish natives, and the harder
natives worked to meet the administration's growing
demands, the lower their standard of living, which led the
administration to put even greater direct and indirect
pressure on peasant producers.

A new political rationality devoted to improving native
social welfare helped the colonial government create a situation of social disorder that in turn required a native policy
devoted to social welfare to avoid a general eruption of

social conflict. This circular contradiction was dynamic. The colonial humanist strategy for maintaining political order and generating profits worked to undermine colonial authority and diminish profits, which then reinforced the government's attachment to that same political strategy: promoting economic development, improving social welfare and protecting indigenous society. From this perspective, we can understand colonial humanism to be a hegemonic project corresponding to *la mise en valeur* as an accumulation strategy for interwar French West Africa.

CONCLUSION

The goal of this essay has been to historicise the Popular Front programme for colonial reform. Its policies must be recognised as having participated in the emergence after the First World War of a new form of colonial government. Colonial humanism cannot be analysed as a narrowly colonial and strictly political phenomenon. Locating interwar colonial politics within a broad analytic framework that includes the metropolitan state as well as the colonial economy enables an interpretation of why an administrative strategy organised around promoting colonial development, protecting indigenous society and improving native welfare may have emerged in this way at this time.

Interwar colonial humanism may be accounted for in two respects. First, the development of this form of colonial government must be located within a pervasive reconfiguration of the French republican state, beginning in the late nineteenth century. An emergent politics focused on social intervention, social integration and social welfare characterised both continental and overseas governmental power between the wars. In so far as France was an *imperial* nation-state, we need to recognise colonial and metropolitan politics as continuous, without reducing one to the other. Secondly, this transformation in colonial politics can only be fully understood if it is analysed in terms of related transformations in colonial political economy. Colonial humanism and *la mise en valeur* were neither competing nor successive policies, but were interdependent dimensions of a broader interwar colonial rationality. In the colonies as in the metropole, transformations in political and economic rationality were intrinsically related to one another, even if they cannot be reduced to one another.

I have not provided an exhaustive explanation for the interwar colonial reform movement. As Foucault writes, there are always exist 'a plethora of intelligibilities' alongside a 'deficit of necessities'.[52] I hope only to have provided a broader account of the emergence of a new colonial rationality that is not focused on individual intentions and institutional implementation. Thus we may have more to learn about colonial politics by attempting to make Popular Front colonial policy historically intelligible, than by remaining preoccupied with its failure fully to realise its 1936 reform programme.

Notes and References

1. This chapter is drawn from research and writing supported by the Fulbright Franco-American Commission, Social Science Research Council, MacArthur Foundation, University of Chicago's William Rainer Harper Fellowship and Spencer Foundation. For responses to an earlier draft of this essay I would like to thank Manu Goswami, Neil Brenner, Bill Sewell, Moishe Postone, and the other members of the University of Chicago Social Theory Workshop. I would also like to thank Amanda Sackur for her editorial comments.
2. Marius Moutet, 'Politique républicaine coloniale', (n.d.) PA28 1/1, Archives Nationales de France, section d'outre-mer (ANSOM).
3. Ibid.
4. 'Note sur les principaux actes au Ministre des Colonies depuis l'avènement du Front Populaire', PA28 1/1, ANSOM.
5. 'Bilan d'action politique juin 1936–octobre 1937', PA28 1/1, ANSOM.
6. M. Moutet, 'Politique Républicaine Coloniale', (n.d.) PA28 1/1, ANSOM.
7. M. Moutet, 'Allocution prononcé par Marius Moutet à la réouverture solonnelle des Cours de l'École Nationale de la France d'Outre-Mer le 3 novembre 1937', PA28 1/1, ANSOM.
8. Léon Geismar, 'Note sur la Conférence des Gouverneurs', 17 juillet 1936, PA28 5/149, ANSOM.
9. Paix, Pain, Liberté.
10. W. B. Cohen, 'The Colonial Policy of the Popular Front', *French Historical Studies*, VII: 3 (1972) pp. 368–93; H. Deshamps, 'France in Black Africa and Madagascar Between 1920 and 1945' in L. H. Gann and P. Duignan (eds), *Colonialism in Africa 1870–1960*, Vol. II

(Cambridge University Press, 1970), p. 232; N. Bernard-Duquenet, *Le Senegal et le Front Populaire* (L'Harmattan, 1985); C. Coquery-Vidrovitch, 'La colonisation française 1931–1939', in J. Thobie, G. Meynier, C. Coquery-Vidrovitch and C.-R. Ageron (eds), *Histoire de la France Coloniale 1914–1990*, 2 vols (Armand Colin, 1990), p. 265.

11. W. B. Cohen, *Rulers of Empire: The French Colonial Service in Africa* (Hoover Institution Press, 1971), pp. 108–43; Deschamps, 'France in Black Africa', p. 244. J. Suret-Canale, *Afrique Noire, L'Ere Coloniale 1900–1945* (Editions Sociales, 1962), p. 199.

12. M. Foucault, 'Governmentality', in G. Burchell, C. Gordon and P. Miller (eds), *The Foucault Effect: Studies in Governmentality* (University of Chicago Press, 1991) pp. 87–104; M. Foucault, 'Omnes et Singulatim: Towards a Criticism of "Political Reason" in *The Tanner Lectures on Human Values, Vol. II*. (University of Utah Press, 1981); M. Foucault, 'The Political Technologies of Individuals', in L. H. Martin, H. Gutman and P. H. Hutton (eds), *Technologies of the Self* (University of Massachusetts Press, 1988) pp. 145–62.

13. M. Foucault, 'Questions of Method', in G. Burchell, C. Gordon and P. Miller (eds), *The Foucault Effect: Studies in Governmentality* (University of Chicago Press, 1991) pp. 78–9.

14. M. Foucault, 'The Political Technology of Individuals', op. cit., p. 160.

15. M. Foucault, 'Faire vivre et laisser mourir. La naissance du racisme', *Les Temps Modernes*, 535 (February 1991) p. 43; M. Foucault, *The History of Sexuality, Vol. I* (Vintage, 1978), p. 145; M. Foucault, 'The Political Technology of Individuals', op. cit., p. 158.

16. M. Foucault, 'Governmentality', op. cit., pp. 96–101; M. Foucault, 'Faire vivre et laisser mourir', op. cit., p. 42.

17. M. Foucault, *The History of Sexuality*, op. cit., pp. 140–3.

18. Cf. M. Postone, *Time, Labor, and Social Domination* (Cambridge University Press, 1993).

19. M. Foucault, 'Governmentality', op. cit., p. 92.

20. Cf. A. L. Stoler, *Race and the Education of Desire: Foucault's History of Sexuality and the Colonial Order of Things* (Duke University Press, 1995) pp. 88–9.

21. R. Delavignette, *Freedom and Authority in French West Africa* (Oxford University Press, 1950), p. 151.

22. I analyse the form, content, and contradictions of colonial humanism at length in, 'Subject-Citizens and Interwar France: Negritude, Colonial Humanism, and the Imperial Nation-State' (PhD thesis, University of Chicago, in preparation).

23. Girardet, *L'idée coloniale*, op. cit., pp. 253–4, 268; Cohen, *Rulers of Empire*, op. cit., pp. 83–107. A. Conklin, *A Mission to Civilize: Ideology and Imperialism in French West Africa, 1895–1930* (PhD Thesis, Princeton University, 1989) pp. 187–297. F. Cooper, *Decolonization and African Society: The Labor Question in French and British Africa* (Cambridge University Press, 1996) p. 28.

24. Cf. S. Elwitt, *The Third Republic Defended: Bourgeois Reform in France, 1880–1914* (Louisiana State University Press, 1986); F. Ewald, 'Insurance and Risk' in G. Burchell, C. Gordon and P. Miller (eds),

The Foucault Effect: Studies in Governmentality (University of Chicago Press, 1991) pp. 198–9; J. Donzelot, *L'invention du social: Essai sur le déclin des passions politiques* (Seuil, 1984).

25. P. Rosanvallon, *L'Etat en France de 1789 à nos jours* (Seuil, 1990); M. Mann, *The Sources of Social Power Vol. II: The Rise of Classes and Nation-States, 1760–1914* (Cambridge University Press, 1993) pp. 394–95, 479.

26. Donzelot, *L'invention du social*, op. cit., pp. 121–77.

27. Rosanvallon, *L'Etat en France*, op. cit., pp. 61–92.

28. R. Kuisel, *Capitalism and the State in Modern France* (Cambridge University Press, 1981); Rosanvallon, *L'Etat en France*, op. cit., p. 238. See also D. S. Landes, *The Unbound Prometheus: Technological Change and Industrial Development in Western Europe from 1750 to the Present* (Cambridge University Press, 1969) pp. 359–419.

29. For the use of 'association' in metropolitan discourse, see Elwitt, *The Third Republic Defended*, op. cit., pp. 17–23, 185–203.

30. For discussions of the relationship between the metropolitan and colonial politics see P. Chatterjee, *The Nation and Its Fragments* (Princeton University Press, 1993) pp. 14–34; R. Guha, *Dominance without Hegemony: History and Power in Colonial India* (Harvard University Press, 1997) pp. 1–99; J. Comaroff and J. Comaroff, 'Homemade Hegemony', in J. Comaroff and J. Comaroff (eds), *Ethnography and the Historical Imagination* (Westview Press, 1992) pp. 265–95; A. L. Stoler and F. Cooper, 'Between Metropole and Colony: Rethinking a Research Agenda', in A. L. Stoler and F. Cooper (eds), *Tensions of Empire* (University of California Press, 1997) pp. 1–56.

31. M. Mann, *The Rise of Classes and Nation-States*, op. cit., pp. 1–88.

32. B. Jessop, *State Theory: Putting Capitalist States in Their Place* (Pennsylvania State University Press, 1990) pp. 196–218, 327–31, 358–60.

33. Cf. J. Habermas, *The Structural Transformation of the Public Sphere* (MIT Press, 1989) pp. 141–51; A. Gramsci, *Selections from the Prison Notebooks* (International Publishers, 1971) pp. 206–318; F. Pollock, State Capitalism: Its Possibilities and Limitations', in A. Arato and E. Gebhardt (eds), *The Essential Frankfurt School Reader* (Continuum, 1982) pp. 71–94, and M. Horkheimer 'The Authoritarian State', in A. Arato and E. Gebhardt (eds), *The Essential Frankfurt School Reader* (Continuum, 1982) pp. 95–117; E. Mandel, *Long Waves of Capitalist Development: A Marxist Interpretation* (Verso, 1980) p. 97; E. Mandel, *Late Capitalism* (NLB, 1975) pp. 481–7.

34. S. H. Roberts, *History of French Colonial Policy (1870–1925)*, 2 vols (P. S. King & Son, 1929) Vol. I, pp. 19–63.

35. J. Suret-Canale, *Afrique noire*, op. cit., p. 204; G. Meynier, 'La France Coloniale de 1914 à 1931,' in Thobie *et al.* (eds), *Histoire de la France Coloniale*, op. cit., pp. 69–209; Coquery-Vidrovitch, 'The Colonial Economy of the Former French, Belgian and Portuguese Zones, 1914–35', in A. Adu Boahen (ed.), *Africa Under Colonial Domination 1880–1935* (University of California Press/UNESCO, 1985) p. 162.

36. C.-R. Ageron, *France coloniale ou parti colonial?* op. cit.; Girardet, *L'Idée coloniale*, op. cit.; J. Marseille, *Empire colonial et capitalisme français. Histoire d'un divorce* (Albin Michel, 1984), pp. 154–56, 259–62, 367–70.
37. A. Sarraut, *La Mise en valeur des colonies françaises* (Payot, 1923); Roberts, *History of French Colonial Policy*. op. cit.; Marseille, *Empire colonial et capitalisme français* op. cit.; Meynier, 'La France coloniale de 1914 à 1931', op. cit. and Coquery-Vidrovitch 'La colonisation française, 1919–1931', op. cit.
38. Suret-Canale, *Afrique noire*, op. cit., pp. 199–236; Marseille, *Empire colonial et capitalisme français*, op. cit., p. 154.
39. Roberts, *History of French Colonial Policy*, op. cit., pp. 318–37.
40. Suret-Canale, *Afrique noire*, op. cit., pp. 354–360.
41. Coquery-Vidrovitch, 'La colonisation française 1931–1939', op. cit., p. 232.
42. Coquery-Vidrovitch, 'La Politique Economique Coloniale', op. cit., p. 125; Suret-Canale, *Afrique noire*, op. cit., pp. 355–66.
43. Marseille, *Empire colonial et capitalisme français*, op. cit., pp. 159, 367–73.
44. Ibid., pp. 159–279.
45. Coquery-Vidrovitch, *'La colonisation française 1931–1939'*, op. cit., pp 246–52; Marseille, *Empire colonial et capitalisme français*, op. cit., pp. 332–7.
46. Cf. Coquery-Vidrovitch, 'La colonisation française 1931–1939', op. cit., p. 245.
47. Marseille, *Empire colonial et capitalisme français*, op. cit.; Meynier, 'La France Coloniale de 1914 à 1931', op. cit., p. 140; Coquery-Vidrovitch, 'La colonisation française 1931–1939', op. cit., p. 245.
48. R. Jessop, 'Post-Fordism and the State', in A. Amin (ed.), *Post-Fordism: A Reader* (Blackwell, 1994) p. 253 and 'The Transition to Post-Fordism and the Schumpeterian Workfare State', in R. Burrows and B. Loader (eds), *Towards a Post-Fordist Welfare State?* (Routledge, 1994) p. 15.
49. Marseille, *Empire colonial et capitalisme français*, op. cit., pp. 285–99.
50. Meynier, 'La France coloniale de 1914 à 1931', op. cit., pp. 127, 138; Roberts, *History of French Colonial Policy*, op. cit., p. 337; Suret-Canale, *Afrique noire*, op. cit., pp. 360–84; Coquery-Vidrovitch, 'La colonisation française 1931–1939', op. cit., pp. 227–38; Coquery-Vidrovitch, 'The Colonial Economy of the Former French, Belgian, and Portugueze Zones, 1914–1935', op. cit.
51. Suret-Canale, *Afrique noire*, op. cit., p. 299; Coquery-Vidrovitch, 'La Politique Economique Coloniale', op. cit., p. 124.
52. M. Foucault, 'Questions of Method', op. cit., p. 78.

2 Reforming Reformatory Technologies in New Caledonia*

Don LaCoss

If nothing else, Foucault has taught us to be suspiciously aware of the modern politics of social reform. As the chapters in this book attest, the true measure of reform in the French Empire during the Popular Front era is mediated by the intentions, motivations, beliefs and value systems of those who made the policy, those who enforced it, and those whose lives were affected by it. It would be reassuring to think that the hope and ethics of liberal humanism celebrated during the two years of the Popular Front were unproblematically successful, and that the lot of those living under French colonial rule was improved. But when one applies a Foucauldian suspicion to some of the things done in the name of universal dignity and progress, one may find the historical experience to be less than optimistic.

Clearly, the infusion of scientific objectivity and rationalism did much to stamp out the cruel and arbitrary abuses often found in the administration of the French Empire. For example, the modernisation of public health and social hygiene regulations enacted by the French in their colonies in the 1930s eased the misery of countless lives. However, when one moves beyond the ends of these reforms and examines the means, one can often detect a different ledger of cost to human life. Powerful examples of the insidious fusion of modernising techniques with the purposes of power can be found in the study of colonial science, particularly in the field of medicine.

At the centre of my contribution to this anthology is a report on New Caledonian leprosy reform policies in the year of the Popular Front's electoral victory. The authors of this report couch their findings in the historical moment of Frontist humanism and civilisation, but what I suggest is that this is just a snapshot of a trend that had been going on in the decades before the Popular Front's formation and which continues in France and its possessions today: the legitimation of oppression under the banner of scientific progress.

The purpose of this chapter, therefore is not to determine whether the report was an accurate account of life in New Caledonia. On the contrary, I suspect that their narrative was a whiggish history of leprosy in New Caledonia from 1914 to 1936 staged for a reading audience that did not share a techno-cosmopolitan view. What can be charted, however, is the trajectory of the representational economy of New Caledonian colonial medicine. Those who formerly had been withheld from the public gaze were now being projected large as educational lessons that were absorbed by all. Simply stated, I use the case of leprosy reform in New Caledonia as a symptom of a long-term condition of French society. These changes were not just a flash in the pan of the Popular Front, but rather were part of a broader current of controlling life through the rational structures of the physical sciences. Whether one is discussing the economic planism of the 1920s, the scientific management of factory assembly lines of the 1930s, the 'apolitical' social-scientist administrators of Vichy's National Revolution, de Gaulle's technocratic élite of 1958 or the physicists of the thermonuclear proving grounds in present-day French Polynesia, the force with which the future of France has been implemented into the present has been intrusive and dehumanising.

TOMORROW LAND

At the 1939 New York World's Fair, Ministre des Colonies, Georges Mandel, announced that French 'modern-minded empire-builders' had rejected 'policies of exploitation', preferring a union of 'emancipation, association, and assimilation'. According to another French Exposition official, imperialist 'national unity' was 'a close collaboration between diverse elements . . . very different from fusion', because 'the fusion of colonial elements with the pristine forces of the mother country would give rise to serious dangers for the latter'. The wisdom of the French colonial policy was apparent in 1939, the official assured, and evident in 'an imperial unity as rational as it is solid and harmonious'.[1]

A testimony to this rational colonialist harmony was filed that same year with the International Leprosy Association. The author reported that the French war on leprosy had been a victorious crusade for modernity. 'The measures . . . employed have as a base the application of modern scientific principles and conceptions imbued with liberalism,' crowed a lieutenant-colonel of the French colonial medical corps. Specifically in New Caledonia, 'much progress has been made' against leprosy thanks to 'definite improvements [that] have been brought about in the existing institutions'.[2] Colonial medical officers M. Kervingant and J. Baré confirmed these findings. As of 1936, New Caledonians had begun to overcome their instinctive repulsion toward the disease' and show an increased concern for the leper's misery, the authors said. They forecast a promising future for the colony and praised the efficacy of modern methods of leprosy prophylaxis.[3]

One could not ask for better evidence of a 'rational, solid, and harmonious collaboration' between coloniser and colonised than the narrative provided in Kervingant and Baré's review. Historically, the island's authorities had a disgraceful reputation for its treatment of the Melanesian population, especially its lepers. In comparison, the situation in 1936 was an optimistic improvement: the officers' show-and-tell of leprosy taxonomies, treatment-strategy maps and statistical tables were convincing credentials of progressivist collaboration. It appeared as if the Popular Front's ideals of humanist reform had integrated nicely with the well-intentioned didacticism of the New Caledonian anti-leprosy campaign. But the point I make in this chapter is that the rational imperial harmony touted by Mandel in 1939 was actually the reinscription of New Caledonians as medicalised objects of knowledge through public health surveillance.[4]

I argue that as a primary source document, Kervingant and Baré's assessment of sanitary reform reveals a different set of conditions, namely the deeper extension of state power in *la plus grande France* into everyday life. Cloaked as colonial public health humanism, anti-leprosy regulations in New Caledonia during the Popular Front were not as much an alleviation as a reinvention of colonial authority, making it more modern and totalising rather than simply brutal and arbitrary; Kervingant and Baré's visual aids illustrate the double-helix of public order ideologies and medical technologies that had been mobilised for control in New Caledonia. Critical to my reading is the way in which defending society against leprosy was no longer a matter of compulsory quarantine, but more accurately the technical management of daily life.

From 1936 to 1939, lepers who would have once been confined to a restricted zone of unspoken punishment, neglect and shame by medico-military authorities were now programmed to broadcast a different set of messages about power and knowledge relations on the island.[5] Modernist social hygiene had become the means for articulating, developing and circulating new economies of power. Power was not reformed but re-formed.

In this piece, I fix Kervingant and Baré's findings within the context of French colonial science, specifically the effect that colonial science had as a form of cultural control. In the project of enculturating the aboriginal populations of the French empire, pedagogical devices based on forms of volunteerism facilitated the internalisation of ideology. Science was one such mechanism, especially under the guise of public health research aimed at creating values that were said to enhance civil society.[6] When read through this Gramscian lens, Kervingant and Baré's report on leprosy and anti-leprosy strategies in New Caledonia excavates the 'grid of intelligibility' used by colonial administrators to secure their control over the island. Situated in the broader field of colonial science, the Popular Front's platform of medical reform in New Caledonia was neither a political turning point nor a contradiction of policy, but rather a single moment in the strategic application of historical, demographic, ecological and social tools on a colonial population and its milieu.[7]

SANITARY MEASURES

Beginning in 1935, colonial administrators in Paris and
Nouméa instituted a series of widely publicised public hygiene
projects designed to rescue the Melanesian Kanaky from
extinction.[8] Among the new controls governing curfews,
immigration and public nudity were a series of reforms
aimed at treating leprosy in the colony. One Parisian champion of this anti-leprosy campaign was Dr Emile Marchoux,
a Pasteur Institute professor with an international reputation in colonial antimalaria research.[9] In 1932, Marchoux
had been appointed president of a newly created commission in the Ministry of Colonies charged with implementing the most recent findings of international leprosy research
organisations, such as the Leprosy Commission of the League
of Nations.[10] Marchoux's aggressive approach was a departure from the previous administrations' policies of sequestering lepers away from population centres and denying
Melanesians treatment. In its stead, he wanted to create a
technical environment for leprosy treatment that could turn
leprosaria from medieval prisons into modern centres for
hygienic instruction. A crucial part of Marchoux's public
health policies was an emphasis on prevention rather than
on removing contagious agents from the social body.[11]

Marchoux objected to the belief that the only way to control
the disease was to limit direct contact through incarceration.
Historically, the leprous body had always been the object
of organised social exclusion in the public's interest, whether
it was banished to the outskirts of the village or herded
into squalid leprosaria. Since the Middle Ages, however,
leprosy quarantine had extended beyond disease control
to use as a police tactic. Many non-infected persons found
themselves accused of leprosy by their communities as an
excuse for ostracisation. It was in these cases that the
antileprosy restraints became instruments that enforced
religious, moral, legal and political programmes as much
as they were meant to prevent the spread of bacillus.
Marchoux opposed the perpetuation of such prejudices on
the grounds that such practices would contaminate the
leprosarium's efficiency in regulating colonial disease.
Speaking for the Academy of Medicine, Marchoux implored

society to defend itself not from the leper, but from 'the germ he carries.' Leprosy needed to be normalised as a biological infection and not a spiritual one, and it was the duty of colonial services to inculcate the public with scientific findings about the causes, effects and treatment of leprosy. The 'horrible social evil that desolates the best of our overseas possessions' was not leprosy, said Marchoux, but was in actuality the belief that leprosy was a sociomoral affliction. He demanded that the aura of superstition and shame that surrounded Hansen's disease be dispelled, and colonial peoples be 'instructed with regard to protecting themselves,' presumably against the disease and their own stupidity. 'It is to dissipate ignorance that we must today apply all our efforts.'[12] In order to accomplish this, the ravages of leprosy must no longer be a source of shame and locked out of sight. Instead, they must be responsibly exhibited for public instruction.

In order to be effective in the negation of superstition, educational propaganda had to be scrupulously grounded in technical accuracy. Social-science fetishes like statistics and flow charts were deployed to influence all segments of the population, not just Kanaks or lepers. Advances in the cataloging of leprosy's forms and stages, as well as changes in archiving patients' medical histories, provided hygiene officials with a more precise means of engineering public-health reform to be pre-emptive rather than reactive. During Marchoux's tenure, the leprosy records kept by the Ministry of Colonies became more precise and more concerned with preventive medicine. Medical officers carefully tracked the number of new cases as opposed to tallying the total number of lepers within a population as they had previously done. Regulations were revamped to acknowledge 'the differences' existing among 'the administrative regime of the peoples and their degree of social evolution', meaning that leprosy cases were now cross-referenced by gender, race and country of origin.[13]

Marchoux's rationalised disease management translated into sharpened methods of clinical detection and surveillance. These programmes provided hitherto unrealised access for a specialist élite into the private lives of tens of thousands. Their power lay not in the brute power to make lepers disappear, but rather in their skill to render them more visible by differentiating, classifying, organising and narrativising leper typologies for public instruction. Quarantine was no longer the physical extraction of a targeted people, but a scientific separation of the populace into discrete administrative units intended for taxonomic display. In Marchoux's proposed *milieu, mesures sanitaires* had literally become sanitary measurements; his prophylactic propaganda changed segregation from a technique of isolation into one of exhibitionary control through instructional surveillance and display. Stated another way, the formerly punitive regime of sequestering lepers was eclipsed in the mid-1930s by a complex of consensual *'dépistage'* logistics. In practice, the empire's population was transformed into a mass more transparently knowable (and thus, more governable) through rationalised administration.

Marchoux's propaganda tactics represented the disease as a medical condition that could be handled with science rather than a moral one to be corrected with punishment. The benevolent *largesse* of humanist biomedicine encouraged communities to discuss the disease among themselves and use government resources to provide rationally for its prevention. Through this kind of public-relations engineering, anti-leprosy ideology was no longer a blunt weapon wielded by the coloniser against the colonised, but rather a more subtle manifestation of state power for all to see, identify with and interiorise. Increased medical surveillance through preventive medical propaganda meant that more control could be exercised over the population under Marchoux's jurisdiction, as is evidenced by the number of those who voluntarily presented themselves to colonial authorities for regulation, classification and biomedical confinement.[14] In 1934 Marchoux was able to cite more than 400 cases of leprosy in the colonies that had turned themselves in since the loosening of policies of mandatory confinement of lepers and increasing educational and promotional programming.[15]

Marchoux's public health interventions resonated strongly with a loose group of similarly minded interwar French social modernists who have been identified as 'techno-cosmopolitans'.[16] These social scientists and functionaries proposed the regulation of life through a deliberately modernist manipulation of politics and aesthetics. Techno-cosmopolitans prescribed scientific restrictions on specific population groups, activities and private interactions with a grammar of public safety, industrialisation and bureaucracy. These social modernists envisioned saving France from itself by synthesising metropolitan, provincial and colonial cultures into a vibrant and progressive political grid. They sought to steer populations with pedagogic broadcasts, advanced communication networks (telephone, telegraph, roads), water and sanitation services, centralised agricultural programmes and rational housing developments. Many of these schemes relied upon colonial territories as proving grounds, and their perceived successes were projected back to Paris as templates for a progressive domestic French modernity.[17]

MODERN PRIMITIVES

Techno-cosmopolitanism is a helpful means for examining Kervingant and Baré's 'La Lépre en Nouvelle-Calédonie en 1936'.[18] What emerges is not just a record of how leprosy prevention measures affected the 1369 patients held at ten leprosy facilities, but rather an attempt to synchronise the lives of all the island's 55,000 inhabitants. Anti-leprosy regulations were instruments used to calibrate Melanesian lepers with each other, with white lepers, with non-lepers in Nouméa and with the broader concerns of Popular Front Paris. Kervingant and Baré's presentation indicates that colonial reform in the shape of rationalised leprosy *'dépistage'* served two functions. Its most apparent use was the effective detection of the disease and those afflicted by it. But this surveillance and broadcast network served another purpose by suturing the leper colonies within the colony closer to the French empire. Kervingant and Baré's report is both a historical account of and a prescription for the fine tuning of expansionist rule in New Caledonia. The tactics for the control of Kanaky had therefore evolved from barbaric genocidal destruction to the 'civilised' spectacle of medicalised objectification.[19]

One way this had been accomplished was through a modification of attitudes through prophylactic public instruction. Kervingant and Baré reported that newspaper articles and posters proudly proclaimed the changes being made in the administration's management of leprosy. Public relations included the erection of a charity ball and raffle social circuit in Nouméa, and the appointment of the colony's governor-general as titular president of the central anti-leprosy fund-raising group. Clergy were asked to recruit settlers in the cause through orchestrated acts of Christian goodwill. The goal was to have all inhabitants overcome their loathing of the disease and to take a greater humanitarian interest in the misery of the afflicted.

Central to Kervingant and Baré's teleology of humanist progress is their discussion of the socio-spatial reforms made at the Ducos leper colony. Kervingant and Baré suggest how the redesign of New Caledonian quarantine camps from dank prison blocks to modern, hygienic sanitoria could be used as educational publicity. If people were informed as to how the leper colonies had changed, then the prospect of treatment would be less frightening and shameful. As a consequence, more inhabitants would turn themselves in to medical inspectors, which was an ideal scenario in Marchoux's gospel of preventive sanitary measures.

The leper colony at Ducos was segregated geographically into three valleys, the Undu for Kanaky patients, the Nimbo for immigrants, and N'Bi for Europeans. Not surprisingly, the whites-only N'Bi compound had the most 'civilised' amenities, with electricity and telephone service on a par with what was found across the bay in the capital. Public-works programmes had repaired the roads between Nouméa and the N'Bi valley, and the island's revamped health service had provided a broad range of recreational activities to make patients' stay more pleasant.[20] Other infrastructural reforms came in the form of increased medical staffing under the watchful eye of the Gaston Bourret Laboratories in Nouméa, with a new medical school and visiting-nurses service planned for the future. In keeping in line with French techno-cosmopolitanism's rhetoric of social defence through self-regulating welfare, the majority of orderlies at the N'Bi valley camp were themselves patients.

Clearly, the report assures the reader, the N'Bi sanitarium was a long way from its grim beginning as a French military penitentiary in the mid-nineteenth century.[21]

In contrast to the N'Bi compound of the 1930s, the Kanak *'quartier'* of the leper colony was less impressive. Kervingant and Baré assumed that this was because Melanesians found its ambiance too European and too penal. This was understandable, they wrote, since the Undu compound 'in no way corresponds with tribal life'. The solution was a complex of agricultural collectives for Kanak lepers. This new network was not to be confused with the 'isolation village' dumping grounds once favored by the French in New Caledonia. Rather, these planned collectives were 'traditional' spaces modelled on Melanesian clan life. The *'villages agricoles pour Hanseniens'* promoted hard work, balanced diets, self-sufficiency and a sense of pride in contributing to the future of the colony. Some modifications to the traditional clan spaces of the *villages agricoles* were necessary, such as French schoolhouses, churches, European clothing, farming tools and fishing tackle. Walking paths were rerouted for a grid of roads and supply lines that would rotate goods and medical surveillance officers to agri-lazarets. As in Ducos, the Bourret Laboratories was the centralised hub for the medical *contrôle* of the Kanak agri-lazarets. The facility was an obvious choice for its archive of medical surveillance of immigrant labour communities in New Caledonia and of Kanak reservations.

Yet in spite of all these laudable reforms, the statistical tables provided by Kervingant and Baré indicate that leprosy cases had increased in the colony. The officers explain this as an illusion caused by the new algebra of modernist *'dépistage'*: there was not an increase in lepers, they assured, only more accurate statistics (*'l'état actuel'*). The numbers were a testament to the power of reformed medico-military surveillance: enlightened, educated families no longer shamefully hid their infected relatives, but now voluntarily turned in suspected lepers for the public good.[22] Meanwhile in the *brousse*, the report claimed that the superstition and suspicion that Kanak chieftains once had for lepers and for colonial leprosy treatment had all but vanished thanks to humanist pedagogical programmes. Kervingant and Baré concluded their presentation on an optimistic note: in spite of the numbers, leprosy among whites had in fact diminished under the Popular Front, while among the native Kanaks and non-European immigrants, leprosy's advances had stabilised.

It is difficult to tell without further research if Kervingant and Baré were converted disciples of Marchoux's modernity, or if they were just astute careerists in the colonial caste system of French public service administrators.[23] In practice, these motivational distinctions are not exclusive and frankly inconsequential. Furthermore, there exists no easy connection that can be made linking Marchoux directly to other so-called Frontist 'Young Turk' politicians who embraced social hygiene as a means for consolidating state power. Such affinities, however, are unmistakable, and show up again and again in French government, from the bureaucratic reform of the technical experts of the Vichy civil service to the post-Second World War *énarque* aristocracy whose scientific management skills were meant to compensate for the irrationalities of French political parties.[24] Medical reform in New Caledonia was not a rupture of liberalism during the salad days of the Popular Front, but actually a continuation of sharp colonial intervention in the South Pacific. We can continue to follow this line right up to the present day by connecting those instances when 'reason' is deployed in order to neutralise opposition under the guise of common-sense consensus. After all, how could any reasonable human being oppose policies engineered for the public good?

THE ANTIDOTE FOR CIVILISATION

Whereas the once-secret shame of the leper had become a billboard promotion for interbellum social regulation in the 1930s, another kind of billboard advertisement appeared in Paris in December 1995 attesting to the latest incarnation of colonial rationalism in New Caledonia. Rather than depicting the island anchored in the cartographic crosshairs of modernist surveillance, these images portrayed a magic kingdom of colour-saturated tropical lagoons choked with lush green vegetation. A small white outrigger of modern design could be seen in the foreground, just above the words '*Nouvelle-Calédonie*'. Although on the other side of the world, the legend at the top of the billboard assured viewers that 'Paradise is not as far away as all that'.[25]

The same week that those billboards promoting tourism to New Caledonia appeared, the French government detonated its fifth thermonuclear weapon in three months at the Mururoa atoll, another idyllic South Pacific island not far from New Caledonia, estimated to be about one and a half times more devastating than the plutonium bomb dropped by the US on Hiroshima.[26] At the 1939 World's Fair, the Ministry of Colonies had released a self-congratulatory statement about how France had avoided 'the fusion of colonial elements with the pristine forces of the mother country' that inevitably led to 'serious dangers'. In 1995, Franconesian 'fusion' had another connotation in the form of 130-kiloton nuclear fusion reactions at Mururoa and Fangataufa.

President Jacques Chirac had described the French-occupied South Pacific as 'the centre of the world in the twenty-first century', bristling with cutting-edge technological progress that included a French satellite tracking centre, underwater mining research stations and, of course, nuclear weapons laboratories.[27] French technology, however, is bad for business; the resumption of fusion weapon testing in the South Pacific precipitated a dramatic drop in French tourism to the '*terre d'avenir*'.[28] The 1995 billboard advertisement was part of a broader public relations campaign engineered to turn that trend around by smoothing over top-secret French experimentation with an exhibition of benevolent tourism. In addition to such spectacular advertisements of exoticised fantasy, the New Caledonian tourist infrastructure worked hard at diverting attention from thermonuclear warheads; Club Méditerranée announced plans to extend its recreational empire beyond Nouméa and build a hotel further up the coast in Hiengheine.[29] The abominations of advanced technology could be swept away by a romanticised stereotype of tropical idyll, presented as an antidote to 'civilization'.

According to a press release from the French Ministry

of Defence, the series of detonations on this secluded island paradise were necessary experiments of France's 'modern and secure arsenal' in preparation for 'future laboratory tests'. I have suggested that France's Pacific colonies have long been a site for laboratories of the future.[30] Popular Front leper colony reform in New Caledonia was not a turning point in liberalising colonial rule there, but rather a single episode in a protracted exercise of organising displays of power for internal identification under the rubric of 'public good'. In the 1930s, leprologists identified the disease as 'the inescapable responsibility of the governments concerned' to the point that 'children born of leprous parents should be removed immediately after birth and brought up under healthful conditions'.[31] I argue that this paternalism is a genealogical ancestor of Chirac's televised pledge in January 1996 that 'the security of our children has been assured'.

In his 1994 satire *Rushing to Paradise* British novelist J. G. Ballard tells the tale of environmentalists who occupy a Pacific Island used by the French to test nuclear weapons. After chasing off the military, the sanctuary of the environmentalists is invaded by explorer–executives of the French and Japanese tourist industry who threaten the island with a new kind of modernist contamination. As the businessmen try to negotiate resort rights with the island's charismatic leader, her right-hand man, Neil, dreams like a shaman about the deserted blockhouses, runways and camera-towers of the test site, 'forgotten totems of the nuclear age that seemed more ancient than any Easter Island statue'. British atomic weapons tests in Australia had fatally irradiated Neil's father, yet the Eniwetok and Bikini lagoons fascinate Neil as 'sacred sites of the twentieth-century imagination'.[32]

In Ballard's fictional world, as in Chirac's, progress is regressive and modernisation primitivises. Instruction, edification, domination and entertainment collapse into an ugly and cynical use of force in the Pacific that rivals the imperialist excesses of the previous century. In New Caledonia, the policing of leprosy in the mid-1930s was given the moral veneer of reform, thereby sugar-coating the deep internalisation of French colonial rule. The thermonuclear detonations of 1995 were justified in shockingly similar terms.

Colonial dreams of rational leper colonies, high-tech proving-grounds and fashionable resort communities provide an architecture of French modernity that eludes historical specificity.

Notes and References

* I would like to thank Amanda Sackur for her hard work and guid-ance in organising my chapter and the stimulating conference from which it came.

1. The thoughts of Mandel and of André Demaison appear in *France: New York World's Fair, 1939* (Higher Council of the French Section of the New York World's Fair, 1939) pp. 24, 85.
2. H. Delinotte, 'The Fight Against Leprosy in the French Overseas Territories: Rôle of the *Commission consultative de la lèpre* of the Ministry of Colonies in the Organisation of Antileprosy Prophylaxis', *International Journal of Leprosy*, 7:4, 1939, p. 530.
3. M. Kervingant and J. Baré, 'La Lèpre en Nouvelle-Calédonie en 1936'; reprinted in *International Journal of Leprosy*, 7:2 (1939), p. 200. See also J. Baré, 'Le Service de la lutte contre la lèpre en Nouvelle-Calédonie', *Annales de médecine et de pharmacie coloniales*, 37:1 (Jan.–Mar. 1939) pp. 165–200.
4. My reading of leprosy as a discourse of both bacteriological and ideological origins is in no way meant to trivialise the experience of this severe condition nor to condemn the work done to alleviate and contain the suffering of those afflicted. Rather, my intention here is to track the broader implications of the strategies engineed to manage the disease, implications that deeply affected the lives of a large mass of people. See also Z. Gussow, *Leprosy, Racism and Public Health: Social Policy in Chronic Disease Control* (Westview, 1989), and M. Vaughn, 'Without the Camp: Institutions and Identities in the Colonial History of Leprosy', in M. Vaughn, *Curing Their Ills: Colonial Power an African Illness* (Polity Press, 1991).
5. This analysis of the New Caledonian antileprosy campaign is in-debted to Tony Bennett's work on the histories and politics of Western museology. Following Foucault's 'lesson of the scaffold', Bennett explains how power is present in certain techniques of public edu-cation and moral discipline, such as those found in museums, trade fairs, and world's expositions. He argues that these institutions did not 'map the social body in order to know the populace by render-ing it visible', but chose instead to exhibit 'the power to command and arrange things and bodies for public display'. The populace, newly educated by these displays, made themselves into 'the sub-jects and the objects of power, knowing power and what power knows, and knowing themselves as (ideally) known by power, interiorising its gaze as a principle of self-surveillance and, hence,

self-regulation'. See Tony Bennett, 'The Exhibitionary Complex', in *New Formations*, 4: 1988, pp. 73–102. A more sustained discussion can be found in Bennett's *The Birth of the Museum: History, Theory, Politics* (Routledge: 1995). See also Paul Greenhalgh, 'Education, Entertainment and Politics: Lessons from the Great International Exhibitions', in P. Vergo (ed.), *The New Museology* (Reaktion, 1989) pp. 74–98.

6. In 1937, for example, Mandel's predecessor at the Ministry of Colonies and his colleague in the Popular Front cabinet, Marius Moutet, told a conference that the key to colonialist harmony was scientific experimentation. Not only was colonial laboratory research 'an urgent necessity' for French economic development but also 'a civilized duty, a beacon to shine'. For more on this, see C. Bonneuil, *Des Savants pour l'empire: la structuration des recherches scientifiques coloniales au temps de 'la mise en valuer des colonies françaises', 1917–1945* (Seghers, 1991); and M. A. Osborne, *Nature, the Exotic, and French Colonial Science* (Indiana University Press, 1994).

7. P. Rabinow, 'Ordannance, Discipline, Regulation: Some Reflections on Urbanism', *Humanities in Society*, 5:3–4 (Summer/Autumn 1982) p. 272.

8. Kanaky were the target of some of the most atrocious treatment in the French empire, brutalised by disease, racism, alcoholism, slave labour, murder and a militarily-defined reservation system. In 1901, the native population had plummeted to 60 per cent of its number in only 14 years, and dipped even further following the First World War. During that decade, it had been predicted by French social scientists that the Kanaks would be 'successfully exterminated'.

9. An excellent account of the 'Pasteurisation' of the French Empire can be found in A. Marcovich, 'French Colonial Medicine and Colonial Rule: Algeria and Indochina', in R. Macleod and M. Lewis (ed.), *Disease, Medicine, and Empire: Perspectives on Western Medicine and the Experience of European Expansion* (Routledge, 1988).

10. This commission was proposed in the summer of 1931 by Lasnet, Surgeon General of the Colonial Health Service. The Commission's 11-member advisory board of prominent administrative, medical, pharmaceutical, and relief officials met for the first time in late January 1932 under Marchoux. As a member of the Academy of Medicine's Permanent Commission of Hygiene and Exotic Pathology, Marchoux's advisory role to the Ministry of Colonies was extended to research work on other (primarily African) imperialist health concerns, such as dysentery, typhus and measles. He also provided public hygiene counsel to the Belgian colonial administration. For more on the links between Belgian tropical medicine and imperialism, see Maryinez Lyons, *The Colonial Disease: A Social History of Sleeping Sickness in Northern Zaire, 1900–1940* (Cambridge University Press, 1992).

11. See Marchoux's comments in *Report of the Leprosy Commission: The Principles of the Prophylaxis of Leprosy*. (League of Nations Publications, 1931).

12. E. Marchoux, 'La Lutte contre la lèpre dans les colonies françaises', *Bulletin de l'Académie de médecine* 26:118 (6 July 1937) pp. 16–22.

13. One officer reported that the 'special regulations' needed for 'the old colonies (Guyana, Antilles, India, Réunion, Sénégal) were not very different from those in New Caledonia, yet the regulations on that island were to be markedly different than those prescribed for Indochina, Madagascar, French West Africa, French Equatorial Africa, Togo, and the Cameroons. See H. Delinotte, 'The rôle of the Commission consultative de la Lèpre au Ministère des Colonies in the Organization of Antileprosy Prophylaxis', *International Journal of Leprosy*, 7: 4 (1938) 517–47.

14. Marchoux's fascination with strategies of prevention mirrors concerns expressed by other architects, planners, and government officials working at this time who believed that prevention was the best cure. As anthropologist Paul Rabinow has written of colonial urbanism projects, '*prévoyance* was no longer the individual moral virtue par excellence, to be inculcated by discipline and surveillance but rather a normalizing administrative function guided by science and operating on an entire population. The transition to technocratic modernism would be completed when the population's norms of health became functions of the instruments of measurement themselves'. See P. Rabinow, *French Modern: Norms and Forms of the Social Environment* (MIT Press, 1989) pp. 344–5.

15. E. Marchoux, 'La Lutte contre la lépre dans les colonies françaises', *International Journal of Leprosy*, 2:3 (Aug.–Oct. 1934) pp. 311–14.

16. The term 'techno-cosmopolitanism' is Paul Rabinow's. He uses it to describe the administrators, scientists and functionaries of Third Republic France who instrumentally deployed the operations of local history, society and culture as discursive devices in order sociologically to blueprint politics, art and science. Rabinow's argument is best illustrated in his study of the kind of urban planning that emerged as a self-conscious modernist discipline in the French colonies between 1900 and 1930. See also Rabinow, 'On the Archaeology of Late Modernity', in R. Friedland and D. Boden (eds), *Now Here: Space, Time and Modernity* (University of California Press, 1994).

17. Unfortunately, lengthy discussions about such projections on the *métropole* are beyond the scope of this chapter. I suspect that this line of inquiry could be especially fruitful in a discussion of the regulation of gender and sexuality in Paris, especially around the ways in which leprosy was frequently elided with syphilis. See Marchoux's comment on the case of the female leper who had been 'secretly infecting' Paris: 'until now, the leper appeared as a danger to the colony, and now, little by little, she has become *un danger pour la métropole*'. See Charles Flandin and Jean Ragu, 'Origine, mode de contagion, durée d'incubation de la lèpre dans 95 cas dont 6 contractés dans la région parisienne . . .', *Bulletin de l'Académie de médecine*, 11:117 (16 March 1937) pp. 337–44.

18. For the interwar *mise-en-valeur* projects, see R. Aldrich, *The French*

Presence in the South Pacific, 1842–1940. (University of Hawaii Press, 1990) pp. 105–38.

19. For more on the medicalisation of colonial subjects, see F. Delaporte, *The History of Yellow Fever: An Essay on the Birth of Tropical Medicine* (MIT Press, 1991).

20. The *Bulletin quotidien du Ministère des Colonies* reported in October 1938 on the impact that the new recreational activities (motion pictures, gardening, cocktail parties, outings, hunting expeditions) had on patient morale.

21. At this time, flying alongside the French *tricolore*, the New Caledonian colonial flag was emblazoned with an image of a French convict and a Melanesian native united with the motto 'Civilise, produce, rehabilitate'. See Jean-Marie Tjibaou, *La Présence kanak* (Éditions O. Jacob, 1996) and Isabelle Merle, *Expériences coloniales: La Nouvelle-Calédonie, 1853–1920* (Belin, 1995).

22. This is also the explanation given by those running the leprosy ward at the Saint-Louis Hospital in Paris, where cases of leprosy increased from 4 to 95 during 1934–7. Officials claimed that the much-publicised new approaches to leprosy treatment had brought patients forward who would have otherwise gone untreated. See Flandin and Ragu, 'Origine, mode de contagion . . .', op. cit.

23. See G. Wright's masterful reading of French specialists who made a career of balancing modernisation and local cultural continuities in *The Politics of Design in French Colonial Urbanism* (University of Chicago, 1991). An excerpted version appears as 'Tradition in the Service of Modernity: Architecture and Urbanism in French Colonial Policy, 1900–1930', *Journal of Modern History*, 59:2 (1987) pp. 291–316.

24. *Énarque* is a term used to denote graduates of the prestigious Ecole Nationale d'Administration and, by extension, the pervasive attitudes inculcated there.

25. 'Le paradis ne doit pas être si loin de ça'.

26. The 1995 blasts at the Mururoa atoll occurred on 5 September, 2 October, 27 October, 21 November and 27 December. Ironically, by the time of the third H-bomb test, there had been a series of considerably smaller explosions by the post-colonial bombers of the Groupe islamique armé in the Paris *métro*.

27. Interestingly enough, that latest series of fusion weapon tests led to more talk of 'invisible threats' as frightening as the leprosy scares of the 1930s. This time, however, the concern is for radiation poisoning; an environmental impact statement is expected in 1998 that will assess the radioactive contamination levels from France's South Pacific test site.

28. At the 1931 Colonial Exhibition, the commissioner for the French-occupied Pacific pronounced New Caledonia worthy of French care and welfare. Commissioner Auguste André went on to praise the archipelago's adminstration for making 'la méthode française' the most liberal and humane colonisation project in the Pacific. The 1931 Exhibition's official New Caledonia pavilion was a French

architectural parody of a Kanak *'grande case'* that housed traditional artifacts of clan authority, as well as relief maps, planispheres, charts, diagrams, photographs, economic tables and dioramas displaying French schemes for modern nickel and chrome mines and plantations of coffee and cotton. It was this spectacular symbiosis of the primitive and the modern that made New Caledonia 'la terre d'avenir'. See A. Demaison, 'Nouvelle-Calédonie et dépendances', in A. Demaison, *Exposition coloniale internationale de Paris: Guide officiel* (Éditions Mayeux, 1931) p. 51. Meanwhile, at the other end of Paris, the Melanesians who had been imported to represent New Caledonia were exhibited as exotic man-eating animals at the Bois de Boulogne zoo. See S. Henningham, '"The Best Specimens in All Our Colonial Domain": New Caledonian Melanesians in Europe, 1931–2', *Journal of Pacific History*, 29:2 (1994) pp. 172–87.

29. This choice of location is remarkable. Like the Ducos compound in the 1930s, I suspect that the proposed Club Med. resort will require an intensive public relations campaign in order to free it from historical connotation: during a particularly fragile political moment in 1984, ten Kanak nationalists were murdered there by settler vigilantes. For three years following the Hiengheine massacre, political tensions escalated to a civil war pitch.

30. One could add New Caledonia's role as a laboratory for DOM-TOM policy experimentation. See J.-Y. Faberon, *La Nouvelle-Calédonie laboratoire de statuts de territoire d'outre-mer* (Société d'études historiques de Nouvelle-Calédonie, 1992).

31. 'The Classification of Leprosy', *International Journal of Leprosy*, 6:3 (1938) p. 406. See also E. Marchoux and M. Chorine, 'La sensibilité au virus lépreux n'est pas plus grande chez les jeunes que chez les adultes', *Annales de l'Institut Pasteur*, 57:6 (1936) p. 583.

32. J. G. Ballard, *Rushing to Paradise*. (Flamingo, 1994) p. 33.

3 The Africanist International and the Popular Front

John Hargreaves

CONTEXT

My approach to the history of the Popular Front is that of a historian of Africa concerned to set the end of colonial rule in an international context. One of the first to attempt this was the *émigré* German scholar M. J. Bonn. In 1932 Bonn, observing post-war 'uprisings for national independence' in Ireland, Egypt, India and in 'nearly all European dependencies with the exception of backward Africa', declared: 'All over the world a period of counter-colonization began, and decolonization is rapidly proceeding.'[1] Recognising the weakness of nationalist movements within Black Africa, Bonn emphasised the support for colonial freedom offered by the League Against Imperialism, launched in Brussels in 1927; and the overseas initiatives of the Popular Front government have often been assessed as if they were intended to advance the cause of colonial liberation, but failed to do so.

But few historians of decolonisation would now give such prominence to the initiatives of European anti-imperialists. Despite the moral commitment mobilised by the League Against Imperialism, it seems clear that Comintern sponsorship of this body was motivated less by informed concern for the immediate future of African populations than by tactical priorities of Soviet policy. Archives recently opened in Moscow should permit closer study of the methods used by its paymasters to maintain control of a useful front organisation. They suggest that the colonial priorities imposed by the Comintern were not always those of the French Communists.[2]

Despite its affirmations of solidarity with colonial peoples, the Parti Communiste Français seems to have felt a patriotic prescriptive right, not wholly free from racism, to primacy in the revolutionary cause. French Communists complained bitterly about the nomination of Lamine Senghor as a Vice-President of the League Against Imperialism; French public opinion, they claimed, would not accept an unsophisticated Senegalese postman to represent what they proudly called 'the second colonial power of the imperialist world'.[3] Instead of advocating the emancipation of the French empire, Communists urged the League Against Imperialism to concentrate on sins of other imperialists in China or Mexico, or of the British in Egypt. Although willing to endorse civil rights protests in Syria and North Africa, they preferred to support Gide's attack on the Congo concessionary regime:

> It would permit us to formulate a negative and sentimental critique, always acceptable to the 'generous pacifists' in our League. Note that in that region, where no national revolutionary movement is present, we would not be obliged to demand immediate independence.[4]

The 'generous pacifists' had more influence on the Popular Front through the Section Française de l'Internationale Ouvrière (SFIO). While few advocated colonial independence, a significant minority of French, as of British, socialists was dedicated to improving the material conditions of colonial peoples and extending their political rights. Marius Moutet, Blum's colonial Minister, had himself been active in the League Against Imperialism. But Marseille's use of Moutet's papers shows the limits of his *politique altruiste*. Ever anxious to gratify *'le tisseur des Vosges'*, Moutet continued to believe that the interests of French workers could better be reconciled with those of African farmers through existing patterns of colonial exchange than by diversification, which some businessmen and officials were beginning to favour:

> It would be a grave error to precipitate our colonies towards an ill-considered industrialisation. We must not create a proletariat which, exploited and discontented, would rapidly become a danger to French sovereignty.[5]

Marseille does indeed see seeds of decolonisation being

sown in the 1930s, not by any ideologists of the Popular
Front, but by French capitalists and technocrats, undertaking strategic re-appraisals of their long-term interest in
the context of the Depression. But this is the *longue durée*.
Although grounds already existed for an eventual divorce
between French capitalism and colonial empire, no suit had
yet been filed in 1936. Neither from above nor from below
was there, during the 1930s, any effective pressure to terminate colonial rule in Africa.

This is no surprising conclusion. Marseille's view of Moutet
echoes the contemporary critique of Daniel Guérin of the
Gauche Révolutionnaire. Guérin believes that not only his
radical anti-imperialism, but the generous if poorly informed
democratic impulses of other French socialists, were frus-
trated by bureaucrats committed to maintaining the interests
of capitalists and *colons* in the name of law and order. Serving
on the unwieldy Commission which the Front Populaire
programme of January 1936 promised would consider
applying the Rights of Man in Africa, Guérin saw well-
intentioned reformers becoming seduced by reactionary
bureaucrats. Germaine Picard-Moch refused to contemplate
votes for illiterate Algerians; Hubert Deschamps discounted
the value of Malagasy petitions; Charles-André Julien warned
against conceding freedom too quickly in North Africa.[6]

Whether or not the Commission had such effects on its
members, it clearly made little impact on policy. French
governments seem never to have understood as well as British
the art of constituting committees in such a way as to produce desirable and practicable recommendations – certainly
not in the colonial field, where the colonial Inspectorate
provided an effective and less ostentatious instrument for
preparing policy reversals. Bureaucratic influence is less
easy to trace in French than in British archives; clearly,
many high officials, both in the Rue Oudinot and in Africa,
were extremely reactionary. But others, who staunchly upheld French control, could be more radical than the politicians – as discussions over industrialisation show. The most
that any Frenchman could offer their African colonies in
the 1930s was reform, in the spirit of what Girardet calls
colonial humanism; and our problem is to identify the
sources of reforming impulse.

This article suggests that during the 1930s French colonial humanists became part of a wider network, which linked limited groups in European civil society who were concerned about African rights and welfare with some of those responsible for their government. The effects of the Depression obliged all those responsible for colonial administration to re-think their objectives. Students of British policy will recognise how easily younger officials in the Colonial Office such as Andrew Cohen, Sidney Caine, Kenneth Robinson, as well as many serving in Africa, fit into Girardet's pattern of 'colonial humanism'. Their concerns were sharpened by a growing awareness of scientific studies of African realities in such fields as public health and nutrition, which emphasised the need to change the economic, if not the political, basis of colonial relationships. I suggest that those informed individuals and groups who were advocating practical reforms or ameliorations became sufficiently widespread in western Europe to merit description as an 'Africanist International'; and that the role of the Popular Front government was to give some ideological 'spin' to modest re-orientations of policy, induced by the impact of the Depression.

AFRICANISTS

It was geographers who invented the concept of the 'Africanist'. Kenneth Robinson has noted how the word was applied to the Sixth International Geographic Congress of 1895 (in which a number of men with official experience participated).[7] But the first body actively to promote an inter-disciplinary focus on African problems was the [Royal] African Society, a predominantly British body founded in 1901 in memory of Mary Kingsley. John Fage's interesting analysis suggests that this was a rather diffuse group of individuals, in which academics were less prominent than persons who were practically engaged in guiding the economic and political future of the tropical colonies in intelligent and humane directions.[8] Fage also discerns a sub-text of Liberal politics, which is less evident in the International Institute of African Languages and Cultures (IAI), founded in 1926.

In this case, the initiative came from Christian mission-aries, ecumenically organised through the International Missionary Council, who were clearly interested in the study of African languages (an essential tool of evangelism) and of African cultures. Their natural partners were anthro-pologists, still the only academics deeply interested in African studies, whose links with missions were as close as those with colonial governments. But J. H. Oldham, a shrewd and tireless agent of the ecumenical movement in its secular relationships, was also concerned to influence policy. Besides lobbying unobtrusively against the political pretensions of Kenya settlers, Oldham had in 1923 been instrumental in establishing the Colonial Office advisory committee on education, where missionaries and educationalists were well represented. Oldham saw the IAI not simply as an academic society concerned to disseminate information, encourage vernacular literacy and standardise practice in such matters as orthography and bibliographical reference, but as a means of bringing persons knowledgeable about African conditions into close relations with those responsible for policy and administration.

The IAI had no obvious political ideology. It was spon-sored financially by the Laura Spelman Rockefeller Fund, an early example of support for African studies from the great American foundations. Initially it was run by repre-sentatives of 28 constituent associations, and another eight were invited to join. The International Missionary Council and the Conférence des Missions Catholiques en Afrique had plural representation. There were six affiliated bodies in UK: five in Germany; four in France; three each in Austria, Italy, South Africa and USA; two in Spain; one each in Belgium, Egypt, Norway, Portugal and Sweden. These were mostly universities, museums and learned societies, with a few semi-official representatives from bodies like the Colonial Office advisory committee. First Chairman of Council was the colonial veteran Lord Lugard; the first joint Directors were Professor Diederich Westermann of Berlin, a former missionary, and Governor Maurice Delafosse, sometime Directeur Politique at the Colonial Ministry, a remarkable pioneer of African historical and cultural studies. When the latter died he was succeeded by another scholarly

French administrator, Henri Labouret, a man who deserves a biography.[9]

Not only was the IAI not a political pressure group; it developed no ideology comparable to the 'Orientalism' so mordantly criticised by Edward Said. Early Africanists were not trying to restructure and dominate old civilisations as a climax to centuries of co-existence and conflict; they were struggling to understand a complex of apparently much simpler entities, towards which most of them felt considerable attachment, or indeed affection. Apart from a few anthropologists, their intellectual pretensions were modest: to accumulate empirical knowledge which might make colonial paternalism more effective: or, as Lugard once expressed it, to do something practical for Africa.[10] The IAI's research programmes, its encouragement of African writing, most of all perhaps the informal exchanges in the margin of its council meetings, were all intended to make the colonial system more responsive to the historical needs of the continent. Twenty-five years later, Labouret was to depict colonialism as one stage in a *longue durée* of African history which would eventually terminate in some form of decolonisation.[11] These Africanists were all in some degree reformers, conscious of the shortcomings of colonial regimes and anxious to improve agriculture, health and education; but they were not anti-imperialists, for they could envisage no truly independent African future until European paternalism had completed its necessary work.

They were also, within the constraints of patriotic duty and loyalty, internationalists. Labouret seems to have provided most of the French material for Lord Hailey's *African Survey*; and in November 1933 Hilda Matheson, secretary to the Survey, suggested that he might be commissioned to prepare a short introductory book on the French colonial system:

He was throughout most friendly and helpful and discussed a number of general points: e.g. the French lack of interest in anthropology and native life and customs generally; their distrust of indirect rule; the different manifestations of colour feeling among French and English; the absence in French territory of any experiment in education like

Achimota; the complete absence of comparative studies
and the lack of contact between neighbouring colonies who
make no attempt to pool experience or compare methods.[12]

Soon afterwards Labouret helped to facilitate the one
semi-official comparative study of the 1930s: the somewhat
eulogistic survey of education in Algeria and Afrique
Occidentale Française by W. B. Mumford and Major Orde-
Brown.[13]

There is, I think, a wider dimension to this readiness of
early Africanists to exchange ideas. Many whom we must
call imperialists had always seen Africa's development as a
shared European responsibility.[14] Contrary to the widespread
myth, the Berlin Conference of 1884–85 had been a last
attempt to avoid partition by regulating the intrusive interests of capitalist states on a continental basis; and even
after partition many with knowledge of African realities
continued to favour such an approach. Such attitudes were
more common in Britain than in France. The IAI's modest
office was in London, and its influence was strongest in
the English-speaking world.[15] French contributions, though
qualitively important, were at first less conspicuous than
those of German Africanists, anxious to restore their country's
colonial reputation. Interest in Spain and Portugal, where
African empire was associated with reactionary nationalism, was weaker than that in some non-colonial states. But
Belgium, despite the rather different economic and ideological foundations of its colonial policy, became a notably
active participant in Africanist debate.

Belgium's first representatives on the IAI Council were
G. Van der Kerken, of the Colonial University at Antwerp,
and E. de Jonghe, of the Institut Royal du Congo Belge,
founded in 1928 to sponsor research in natural, applied,
and social sciences and 'organize colonial propaganda'. In
1932 Van der Kerken was succeeded by Pierre Ryckmans,
a devout Catholic lawyer from a well-connected middle-
class family, who very clearly bridges the worlds of African
studies and policy-making. After serving in the East African military campaign Ryckmans resolved to dedicate his
considerable talents to colonial administration; before his
thirtieth birthday he was in charge of the whole mandated
territory of Rwanda-Urundi. On returning to Brussels in

1928 Ryckmans became in effect a freelance Africanist, combining legal practice with writing, university teaching, consultancy and public lectures; his collected writings, published as *Dominer pour servir*, are a standard text of Belgian colonial paternalism. His very active participation in the work of the IAI (and the Institut Colonial International, based in Brussels since 1894) had the effect, as his biographer puts it 'of broadening considerably his view of the African world'.[16] Although decolonisation had no part in even the longest vista of Belgian colonial policy, this involvement in the Africanist International meant that, as a British official noted in 1956, Belgian practice came to share 'a great deal of common ground' with France and Britain – in contrast to Italy, Spain and Portugal, whose contacts lapsed during the war.[17]

During the 1930s the British Colonial Office began to incorporate the advice and experience of African specialists in its policy-making. Some were employed as specialist Advisers, others appointed to Advisory Committees. Younger officials, in Whitehall and in Africa, began to take more interest in Africanist writings than the senior 'dinosaurs'.[18] Directly or indirectly, the Africanist International was influencing the formation of British policy. Did it have a comparable influence on the Ministère des Colonies?

POPULAR FRONT

Raoul Girardet has shown how Catholic theologians and lay apostles of the Rights of Man joined with reflective practitioners in seeking in 'colonial humanism' a new moral basis for the Imperial mission so flamboyantly celebrated in 1931. Anthropologists like Marcel Griaule had undermined the old justificatory myth of 'African barbarism'; in 1930 the Société des Africanistes was established, again by ethnologists, linguists and adminstrators. In Girardet's words: 'colonial ideology [found] itself constrained to seek other legitimisations, to appeal to different value-systems'.[19] Although the IAI was more widely supported in the UK than in France, its first plenary Congress, as well as two meetings of its executive, took place in Paris in 1931, on the margin of the Exhibition. The near-legendary Lyautey presided over the Congress; and Paul Reynaud, as Colonial Minister, declared that his Ministry attached great value to 'expert advice' such as the IAI could offer.[20]

Unlike their British counter-parts, French administrators had an institutional focus in their search for a new code of responsibility: the Ecole Coloniale. One is immediately struck by the role of administrator-Africanists in raising its intellectual standards from their utilitarian origins. Its Director in 1926 was Georges Hardy, formerly director of education in AOF and in Morocco, a distinguished pioneer of colonial history. The most respected teacher, until his death in 1926, was Maurice Delafosse; from 1929 this status was assumed by Labouret, who remained joint director of the IAI.[21] Under the Popular Front, the name was changed to Ecole Nationale de la France d'Outre-Mer, and the 40-year old Robert Delavignette, a member of Moutet's *cabinet*, became Director. A devout Catholic, Delavignette had already acquired an international reputation for his celebrations of patiently humane work carried out for Africans by European administrators in the bush: his *Service Africain* was later published in English by the IAI. Delavignette's evocation of the rewards of paternal authority sometimes verges on the sentimental; but he was respected within the service, and his preferment testifies to the growing influence of the new colonial humanism.[22]

How was this process affected by the formation of the Popular Front? Calls for reform from practising Africanists seem to have influenced the work of all governments during the Depression. But in the UK, the code of civil service neutrality meant that reformers could operate without partisan attachments. This is not to say that British officials were uniformly Conservative, or even conservative; sympathisers wihin the Colonial Office, such as Sidney Olivier and J. N. Green, advised the Labour Party on colonial issues. But the Fabian Colonial Bureau, which became the most effective channel of communication between socialists and policy-makers, was not founded until 1940.

In France there was no such curtain between colonial administration and party politics. In Algeria and in the old colonies (including the Senegalese communes) political intervention was often direct. After Moutet's official visit to Dakar, government influence assisted the unification of French and African supporters into a Senegalese section of the SFIO, aimed at capturing the parliamentary seat from Galandou Diouf.[23] Party influence was also used in appointments within the colonial service; those of Brévié and de Coppet as Governors-General of Indochina and AOF are frequently cited. A particularly interesting example of interaction between colonial service, Africanist discourse, and party politics is the career of Hubert Deschamps, who in 1936 was appointed to Blum's *cabinet* while on leave from administrative service in Madagascar.

Deschamps' highly readable memoirs depict a liberated young socialist displaying his effortless superiority by preparing a massive Sorbonne doctorate on the Antaisaka while establishing his reputation as a humane and progressive administrator. In the 1960s, as a leading figure in the movement to develop a truly Afrocentric historiography, he was to act as the French 'Consultative Director' of the IAI. But the younger Deschamps made no secret of his political commitment; socialism required serious attempts to apply the revolutionary principle of assimilation to all France's colonial subjects. This, he later made clear in a celebrated debate with Lugard's ghost, involved dissent from the orthodoxy of building upon indigenous African institutions, and from his own teacher Delafosse. In the 1930s, socialism also meant political activism, not only in the 14th Parisian section of the SFIO, but also in a CGT-affiliated trade union, which he pleasantly calls 'the trade union of kings'.[24] Deschamps' duties in Blum's office went far beyond colonial affairs; he was receiving supplicants and monitoring Prime Ministerial correspondence. He later spent a short time in Rue Oudinot, as Moutet's Chef de Cabinet in the Chautemps government.[25]

But what could individuals achieve? Guérin believed that official responsibilities simply meant that socialist reformers became indoctrinated by bureaucratic conservatism, and Deschamps himself does not claim any specific successes for the Popular Front. Another committed socialist, the Algerian-born historian Charles-André Julien, was appointed as Secretary-General of a new Haut Comité Mediterranéen in Blum's office; at least North African policy was now treated at a higher political level, but few lasting reforms could be claimed.[26] It is beyond my competence to evaluate the work of the Front in the wider Mediterranean area, though obviously Viénot's treaty with Syria must count as one of its major successes. One tangible outcome was the establishment in 1936 of the Centre des Hautes Etudes d'Administration Musulmane (CHEAM), to undertake post-experience education for civil and military officers in the Mediterranean territories. The French were more inclined than the British to consider relations with Muslims in a global, rather than purely territorial, context; CHEAM's brief inevitably extended into the Centre des Hautes Etudes sur l'Afrique et l'Asie Modernes which, with a wider brief, continues to provide the Africanist International with access to French policy-makers.[27]

So, although persons associated with the Africanist International enjoyed some enhancement of status and influence under the Popular Front governments, it is difficult to attribute any specific achievements to them. In a wider context, Blum claimed that his government had by its exercise of power 'speeded up the normal course of history'; the most that his Africanist collaborators might claim is that they kept the thrust of French colonialism moving in a progressive direction.[28]

Nor did they help the government to transcend a national approach to African problems; the Spanish Civil War confirmed its distance from Great Britain, the African power with whom it might have found some common purpose. The first brief meeting between French and British colonial ministers, Georges Mandel and Malcolm Macdonald, took place under its successor, in June 1939, and only in response to the imminence of war. Even when the regular liaison which Labouret had hoped for began after 1945, such consensus as could be reached was constrained by divergent political priorities. Co-operation never extended far beyond the technical and practical matters in which the IAI had interested itself, and was in any case short-lived.[29]

During the 1950s the Africanist International expanded rapidly, both geographically and in its academic bases. Many of the younger students of Africa, in North America as well as in Africa, became politically active in the cause of decolonisation. This was never true of the pre-war IAI; even those who, like Labouret, foresaw a time when colonial rule would have fulfilled its purpose rarely suggested how or when this might come about. In the context of 1936–38, the most that I suggest is that those who scrutinise official records should be alert to possible influence from the informed experience of reforming practioners like Labouret and Delavignette, Deschamps and Julien. To Guérin, looking back from the heady 1960s, any such influence could achieve only insignificant deviations from official routine. But the 1960s seem to provide a peculiarly distorting viewpoint for historians of empire.[30]

Notes and References

1. M. J. Bonn in *Encyclopaedia of the Social Sciences*, VII (1932), s.v. 'Imperialism'.
2. J. D. Hargreaves, 'The Comintern and Anti-Colonialism: New Research Opportunities', *African Affairs*, 92: 357 (1993) 255–61. For a fuller account of the LAI, see J. M. Bellamy and J. Saville (eds), *Dictionary of Labour Biography*, vol. VII (London: 1984) pp. 40–50.
3. 'La deuxième puissance coloniale du monde impérialiste'. League Against Imperialism archives, Moscow, 542/16, fos 89–91: Report to the Party Secretary on activity of Ligue contre l'oppression coloniale et l'impérialisme (J. Ventadour: 1927/8).
4. 'Parce que . . . elle nous permettrait une critique négative et sentimentale, toujours facile pour les 'généreux pacifistes' qui sont dans notre Ligue. Il faut noter que là, l'absence de mouvement révolutionnaire national ne nous obligerait pas à nous prononcer pour l'indépandance immédiate.' Ibid.
5. 'Ce serait une lourde erreur de précipiter nos colonies vers une industrialisation irréflechie. Il ne faut pas créer un prolétariat qui, exploité et mécontent, serait rapidement dangereux pour la souveraineté française.' J. Marseille, *Empire colonial et capitalisme français: histoire d'un divorce* (Albin Michel, 1984) pp. 334–7.
6. D. Guérin, *Front Populaire: révolution manquée* (François Maspéro, 1970) pp. 169–78.
7. K. Robinson, 'Experts, Colonialists, and Africanists, 1895–1960' in J. C. Stone (ed.), *Experts in Africa: Proceedings of a Colloquium at the University of Aberdeen*, March 1980, p. 198.
8. J. D. Fage, 'When the African Society was founded who were the Africanists?', *African Affairs*, 94: 376 (1995) pp. 369–81.
9. F. D. Lugard, 'The International Institute of African Languages and Cultures', *Africa*, I (1928) pp. 1–12. For the earlier history of

Africanism in France see L. Delafosse, *Maurice Delafosse: le Berrichon conquis par l'Afrique* (Société française d'histoire d'outre-mer, 1976).
10. Quoted in Lord Hailey, 'The Past and Future of the Institute', *Africa*, XVII: 4 (1947) p. 231.
11. H. Labouret, *Colonisation, Colonialisme, Décolonisation* (Larose, 1952).
12. Rhodes House, Oxford. Perham MSS 674/1. Note by HM, 24 November 1933.
13. W. B. Mumford and G. St. J. Orde-Browne, *Africans Learn To Be French* (Evans, 1935) p. vii.
14. J. D. Hargreaves, *Decolonization in Africa*, 2nd ed. (Longman, 1996) pp. 32, 43, 207.
15. The following figures from a later date are illuminating. In 1963, the circulation of *Africa* was 1785, including 485 copies in USA, 280 in UK: 406 in anglophone Africa (including 67 in South Africa). 72 went to France and 58 to former French colonies: 55 to Belgium and 30 to former dependencies. 56 went to Germany, 47 to Italy, 8 to Portugal, plus 18 to her colonies: 5 to Spain plus 3 to Spanish Africa. 'Report of the Administrative Director, 1962–3', *Africa*, 33: 4 (1963) p. 354.
16. 'D'élargir considerablement sa vision du monde africain', J. Vanderlinden, *Pierre Ryckmans* (De Boeck, 1994) pp. 245–6.
17. Hanrott to Scrivener, 5 March 1956 in D. Goldsworthy (ed.), *British Documents on the End of Empire: The Conservative Government and the End of Empire, 1951–1957*, Vol. I, No. 126.
18. E.g. J. M. Lee, *Colonial Development and Good Government* (Oxford University Press, 1967); J. M. Lee and G. Petter, *The Colonial Office, War and Development Policy* (Institute of Commonwealth Studies, 1982); K. Robinson, *The Dilemmas of Trusteeship* (Oxford University Press, 1965); cf. C. Parkinson, *The Colonial Office from Within* (Faber, 1947).
19. R. Girardet, *L'idée coloniale en France* (Table Ronde 1972) p. 162.
20. Council Reports in *Africa*, IV: 4 (1931) pp. 483ff; *Africa*, V: 1 (1932) pp. 75, 79ff.
21. W. B. Cohen, *Rulers of Empire: the French Colonial Service in Africa* (Hoover Institute Press, 1971) ch. 5.
22. W. B. Cohen (ed.), *Robert Delavignette on the French Empire* (Chicago University Press, 1977). See also R. Delavignette, *Freedom and Authority in French West Africa* (International African Institute, 1950) – a translation of *Service Africain* (Gallimard, 1946).
23. The classic account is R. Schachter-Morganthau, *Political Parties in French-speaking West Africa* (Clarendon Press, 1964) pp. 127–34. See also D. Topouzis, 'Popular Front, War and Fourth Republic politics in Senegal: from Galandou Diouf to L. S. Senghor', unpublished PhD thesis, University of London 1989. For other examples of reaction by overseas SFIO sections see W. B. Cohen, 'The Colonial Policy of the Popular Front', *French Historical Studies*, VII (1972) pp. 389–90.
24. 'Le syndicat des rois'.
25. H. Deschamps, *Roi de la Brousse: mémoires d'autres mondes* (Berger-Levrault, 1975) esp. pp. 129–33, 172–85. See also his well-known

Lugard lecture to the IAI in 1963, 'Et maintenant, Lord Lugard?', *Africa*, 33: 4 (1963) pp. 293–306.

26. C.-A. Julien, *Une pensée anti-coloniale* (Editions Sindbad, 1979) – pp. 102–6 reprints an interview of 1937. There is a sympathetic sketch of Julien's career by André Aymard in *Etudes Maghébiennes: Mélanges Charles-André Julien*. (Presses Universitaires de France, 1964) pp. ix–xv.
27. Cf. C. Harrison, *France, Islam and West Africa, 1860–1960* (Cambridge University Press, 1988) ch. 9.; K. Robinson, 'Experts, Colonialists, and Africanists, 1895–1960', in J. C. Stone (ed.), op. cit., 1980) p. 63.
28. Quoted by J. Jackson, *The Popular Front in France: Defending Democracy, 1934–38* (Cambridge: 1988) p. 275.
29. J. Kent, *The Internationalization of Colonialism* (Oxford University Press, 1992) M. Michel, 'La co-opération inter-coloniale en Afrique Noire, 1942–1950: un néo-colonialisme éclairé?', *Relations Internationales*, 34 (1983) pp. 155–71; cf. Goldsworthy, *The Conservative Government . . .* I, p. 302: memo by Cohen, 20 November 1951.
30. Since this chapter was written, the remarkable study by F. Cooper, *Decolonization and African Society: the Labor Question in French and British Africa* (Cambridge University Press, 1996) has thrown much light on the social theory (as well as the practice) of the Popular Front government. Cooper points up significant differences between French and British approaches, but does not pursue the possible influence of international contacts.

4 The Popular Front and Internationalism: the Tunisian Case in Comparative Perspective[1]

Alejandro Colás

INTRODUCTION

Internationalism has been a central component of socialist politics since the inception of working-class movements in Europe during the nineteenth century. From the outset, the thinkers and activists of these working-class organisations sought to emphasise the international character of proletarian struggles and the universal validity of the principles they espoused. Since the founding of the International Working Men's Association in 1864, this form of political activism has found organisational expression in a number of international associations which managed to keep 'the international' at the forefront of socialist politics during later decades. It therefore seems reasonable to explore the role of internationalism as the principle which ostensibly guided the French left's colonial policy when considering the Popular Front's impact on the French empire.

Drawing on Fred Halliday's formulation, internationalism can be defined with reference to at least three of its basic components. Internationalism can be seen as a *process* whereby the different parts of the world become more closely interconnected in terms of polity, economy, culture and communication. Second, internationalism describes the specific *phenomenon* of social and political organisation of people across national, ethnic or religious boundaries. Lastly, the normative element of the concept presents internationalism as an *ideology* which celebrates the internationalisation of the world as a positive process which unifies the human species in its diversity, thus making conflict, wars, exploitation or discrimination less probable.[2] In this chapter, I shall be focusing primarily on the latter two aspects of internationalism, that is internationalism as a form of political practice and as an ideology. I shall explore the way in which internationalism affected the relations between various Tunisian social movements and their French counterparts during the period of the Popular Front. First, the nature of these relations prior to 1936 will be examined, in so doing briefly pointing out the characteristics of the Tunisian social movements in question. Second, the dynamics of this relationship after the rise to power of the Popular Front will be considered, emphasising the impact on Tunisian politics of international factors such as the rise of fascism, the turn in Comintern policy after 1935 and of course, the developments in the metropole itself. Lastly, some general analytical questions regarding the conjunction of internationalism and the Popular Front will be considered, and the Tunisian experience contrasted to that of Morocco and Algeria.

THE FRENCH LEFT AND INTERNATIONALISM

Until the late nineteenth century, French working-class parties saw internationalism primarily as a mechanism of practical co-operation with their European counterparts in matters relating to strike-breaking, immigration or the homogenisation of working conditions across the continent. It was not until European imperialism reached its peak at the turn of the century that socialist internationalism became inextricably associated with the 'colonial question'. Colonialism was first officially addressed by the French left in 1895, when a resolution denouncing the 'colonial piracies' as 'the worst forms of capitalist exploitation' was passed at the Romilly congress of the Parti Ouvrier Français.[3] The subsequent history of the French left's attitude toward colonialism, however, was to prove much more ambiguous. Following Manuela Semidei's useful classification, we can identify three broad positions on the French left regarding imperialism.[4] In line with the resolution adopted at

Romilly, a considerable number of French socialists remained staunchly anti-colonialist, condemning European imperialism, both in the context of French politics and at the various congresses of the Second International. This 'orthodox' line was gradually contested by a growing number of socialists who, imbued with notions of racial supremacy, celebrated imperialism as a means of extending the more 'advanced' European civilisation among 'primitive peoples' outside the old continent. A third tendency within the French left offered qualified support for colonialist policies. They argued that a 'humane' or 'socialist' colonialism which respected the political rights of the indigenous population and raised their living standard to European levels could benefit both the metropolitan and the colonial working class. Sensitive to their growing electoral success and aware of the increasing role of nationalism in French domestic politics, many socialists saw this option as the most realistic and politically responsible approach to the colonial question.

In this continuing battle among the three tendencies, the bulk of the French left took a 'centrist' position between the anti-colonial left and the imperialist right. The disaster of the First World War and the triumph of the Bolshevik revolution, however, were to bring a realignment in the French left regarding the question of imperialism. At the Tours Congress of 1920 most of the anti-colonialists within the SFIO decided to join what was soon to become the Parti Communiste Français (PCF). As Charles-André Julien suggested, '[the] Socialist Party's formal promise to grant the colonial questions the importance which they deserved' could only be honoured by an adherence to the Communist International.[5] After all, the central impetus behind the founding of the Third International was the recovery of the internationalist spirit which the 'national chauvinists' of the Second International had betrayed. As the eighth of Lenin's 21 conditions for membership of the new organisation put it: 'Every party which wishes to join the Communist International is obliged to expose the tricks and dodges of "its" imperialists in the colonies, to support every colonial liberation movement not merely in words but in deeds . . .'.[6]

The PCF initially took heed of these requirements. In July 1921 it helped to create the Union Intercoloniale (Intercolonial Union), a movement made up of communists from the French colonies which eventually incorporated a number of North African activists. A month later a Comité d'Etudes Coloniales (Committee for Colonial Studies) was set up by Charles-André Julien, in an attempt to report and discuss colonial issues in the communist press.[7] The outbreak of the Rif revolt during 1924–25 prompted a sustained campaign within France in favour of Abd el-Krim, which Georges Oved has thoroughly documented.[8] A year later, the first North African immigrant party and precursor to the Algerian nationalist movement, the Etoile Nord-Africaine (ENA), was established under the auspices of the PCF.

All these examples reflect a genuine, if not disinterested, concern on the part of the French communists for the plight of colonial peoples during the 1920s. As we shall see below, this generally positive attitude was tainted on numerous occasions by the thoroughly chauvinistic – when not overtly racist – positions adopted by French communists.[9] Furthermore, the internationalism of French communists, like that of communists elsewhere in the world, became increasingly subjected to the foreign policy interests of the Soviet Union. Bearing these important points in mind, however, should not preclude recognising the PCF's role in shifting the French left's agenda on imperialism. The diverging attitudes toward colonialism outlined above continued more or less intact into the period of the Popular Front. The anti-colonial tendency within French working-class internationalism, however, had been strengthened by the rise of the PCF, and through the efforts of revolutionary leftists within the SFIO like Robert Longuet or Daniel Guérin. It would be fair to say that by 1936 the terms of debate on the colonial question were significantly modified: those defending the notion of a 'socialist colonialism' were forced to adopt the more guarded language of 'assimilation' as the Leninist endorsement of the right to self-determination gained force among the French left.

THE LEFT IN TUNISIA

The ongoing ideological debates on imperialism examined above cannot be separated from the growing presence of working-class organisations in the colonies. The most vociferous participants in these debates were generally the colonial sections of the SFIO, the PCF or the Confédération Générale du Travail (CGT). These organisations were in turn strongly affected by the emergence of indigenous political movements, generally of a nationalist hue. The interaction between these various movements falls under the first two categories of internationalism as defined above: those referring to the increasing international economic and social interpenetration and the consequent spread of modern forms of social and political association. In order to understand how these two levels of internationalism operated during the Popular Front it may be useful briefly to expound the development of nationalist and working-class organisations in Tunisia prior to 1936.

The first modern political movements in Tunisia emerged from two basic sources. On the one hand, from the first decade of the twentieth century a trend drawing on the reformist legacy of Khayr al-Din (the prominent modernising Prime Minister of Ahmad Bey in the 1870s), set up a number of cultural and educational associations which eventually formed the backbone of the first Maghrebi nationalist party, the Liberal Constitutionalist or Destour Party formed in 1920. On the other hand, a host of metropolitan working-class associations accompanied the establishment of a French Protectorate over Tunisia in 1882. At the outset, the French had intended to create a 'colony for capital' through 'unofficial' colonisation. The long-standing presence of a large Italian immigrant population and a smaller contingent of Maltese and Libyans, however, led to a policy of 'official' colonisation during the 1890s which brought the number of French nationals in Tunisia up from a mere 700 in 1881 to 10,000 ten years later and 91,000 by 1931.[10]

According to Béchir Tlili, a section of the SFIO was already established in Tunisia in 1907, with an official newspaper, *La Bataille*, coming out during a brief period between

1911 and 1912, later to be replaced by *Le Socialiste*. As a prolongation of this activity, the CGT set up a Departmental Union in Tunis in 1911.[11] An independent socialist association grouped around the journal *Le Libéral* and a variety of libertarian and syndicalist organisations completed the picture of working-class movements in Tunisia during the first two decades of the century. With the split in the SFIO at the 1920 Tours Congress, a small section of the Communist International was set up in 1921 at the port of La Goullette, together with its accompanying party organ, *L'Avenir Social,* and the associated trade union, the Confédération Générale du Travail Unitaire (CGTU).

Parallel to this activity among European workers, the Tunisian élites had started to gain some political clout through two cultural associations. The Khalduniya had served since 1896 as forum for disseminating 'modern sciences' like geography, physics or political economy among the Muslim population, while the Association des anciens élèves du collège Sadiki or Sadiqiya, established in 1905 sought to guarantee the continuity of the reformist ideas which had inspired this famous college. The individuals involved in these associations were soon to be dubbed the 'Young Tunisians' by the colonialist press; a name which far from offending their principles, helped to emphasise similarities with other constitutionalist movements in the Muslim world. By 1906 the Young Tunisians presented their political project for the modernisation of the protectorate and in 1907 they began publishing a weekly journal, *Le Tunisien*. Although the movement was proscribed in 1912, and barely weathered the turmoils of the First World War, many of its figure-heads re-emerged in 1920 to form the Destour Party.[12]

A direct off-shoot of this political effervescence was the creation in 1924 of the first Maghrebi trade union, the Confédération Générale des Travailleurs Tunisiens (CGTT). There is no need to delve here into the complex events which lead to the formation of the CGTT.[13] Suffice it to say that it was essentially the result of three factors: the continuing poverty and discrimination experienced by the budding Tunisian working-class; the insensitivity toward this fact displayed by the European CGT; and the growing attractiveness of the nationalist option represented by the Destour. The explosiveness of this combination finally came to the fore when the CGT refused to support a wild-cat strike called by the predominantly Tunisian dockers at the ports of Tunis and Bizerte. With the strike-action spreading across other industrial towns, the leaders of the movement, M'hammed Ali and Tahar Haddad, decided to go ahead with the constitution of a new, nationalist-oriented trade union in November 1924.

The CGTT leadership did not survive the political and administrative onslaught which followed its decision to set up a nationalist trade union. In November 1925, the French authorities tried Mohammed Ali and several other of his comrades, banishing them from Tunisia and thus effectively dismantling the CGTT. Despite its brief existence, the CGTT had demonstrated the relevance of addressing both the needs of the working-class and the aspirations of a colonised population. As Julliette Bessis has observed:

> This purely Tunisian trade union experiment had the positive consequence that it revealed to the Destour, as well as to political and union organizations on the left, the existence of an indigenous working class which was aware, prepared to fight and capable of organising itself.[14]

The legacy of this project was eventually taken up in a different form by a group of young Destourians led by Habib Bourguiba who in March 1934 broke with the old party to create the Néo-Destour. Again, the details of this operation need not retain us here. The Néo-Destour was simultaneously the product of a generational clash between Tunisian nationalists, a regional confrontation between the *beldi* aristocracy of Tunis and the petite-bourgeoisie of the Sahel, and a tactical difference regarding the way nationalists should approach the French authorities. Above all, however, the break-away party was a reaction to the growing role of the masses in Tunisian politics, exacerbated by the onset of the economic crisis in the early 1930s. Its stated aim was the construction of an independent Tunisian state through the mobilisation against colonialism of all sectors of Tunisian society. In this respect, the Néo-Destour effected a double break with the old Destour by replacing the latter's elitism with a staunch populism, and by offering a more pragmatic, although not necessarily more accommodating approach to relations with the French authorities.

This brief overview of the social movements which emerged in Tunisia during the 1920s and 1930s demonstrates that the Protectorate was in the throes of a momentous social and political upheaval. A whole array of political and social organisations – nationalist through to communist – arose as a result of the imperialist penetration and the accompanying colonisation. Internationalism, as defined in the opening paragraphs of this paper was central to this development in at least three respects. Firstly, understood as a process of political and socio-economic integration, internationalism clearly coincided with imperialism; without the French colonisation of Tunisia it is unlikely that modern political movements would have established themselves so rapidly in the protectorate. Secondly, the ideological and organisational parallels between the French and Tunisian social movements reflected an internationalisation of the norms and values of political action. Thirdly, this allowed for the occasional realisation of the ideals of internationalism understood as the political co-operation between organisations across national, ethnic and religious boundaries. In all these senses, internationalism had played a crucial role in the relationship between colonial and metropolitan social movements. With this background, it is now possible to examine how this relationship developed under the Popular Front.

TUNISIA, THE POPULAR FRONT AND INTERNATIONALISM

By all accounts, the triumph of the Popular Front in the French legislative elections of May 1936 was received with excitement and optimism in Tunisia. In a letter to the Secretary-General of the SFIO in Tunisia, Habib Bourguiba emphasised how the Néo-Destour:

is convinced that the left-wing parties that make up the Popular Front really intend to confront the fundamental

problem of Franco-Tunisian relations, and to revise their
methods and doctrines in the light of the facts, in a word,
to reconcile the aspirations of the Tunisian people with
the interests of the protecting power.[15]

There was precious little in the Rassemblement Populaire's
election manifesto to warrant Bourguiba's high expectations. The only reference to the colonies in the Front's
programme appeared in the section on 'Défense de la
Liberté' in which it pledged 'to establish a parliamentary
commission of inquiry on the political and economic situation of, and on the state of mind in, the French overseas
territories'.[16] Beyond this, the Popular Front had not formally committed itself to further policy changes *vis-à-vis*
the colonies. Yet the rise to power of the Popular Front
was accompanied by an explosion of social and political
activity in Tunisia, and by the introduction of several
important political and socio-economic reforms in the
protectorate. Furthermore, for a number of reasons to be
explored below, Tunisia became fully engulfed in the struggle
between fascism and democracy which had inspired the
Popular Front in the first place. Clearly, the preceding years
had prepared Tunisia for a full-blown encounter with both
the principles and processes which characterise internationalism. In order to elucidate this point I shall examine three
aspects of internationalism in Tunisia during this period:
the reforms introduced by the Blum government; the increase in social and political militancy; and the relations
between colonial and metropolitan social movements.

The most immediate result of the new Popular Front
government was the replacement of the reactionary Resident-
General Peyrouton by Armand Guillon, a civil servant known
for his liberal political attitudes and his previous involvement
with the labour movement. Peyrouton had been responsible
for the ferocious repression of the nationalist and working-
class movements over the past three years. Since the
tumultuous events of September 1934, trade-union branches
had been closed, nationalist and left-wing leaders expelled
from the country, and virtually all critical press suspended.
As Mustapha Kraïem has suggested, 'the period of
Peyrouton's Residency was experienced by nationalists and
those of the Left as a dictatorship'.[17]

The arrival of Guillon to the Residency in April 1936 was therefore seen by the left and nationalist forces as heralding the end of a difficult period of clandestine activity. The first few months of the new administration fulfilled this expectation as Guillon proceeded not only to lift Peyrouton's repressive regime but also to extend to Tunisia the progressive reforms introduced by the Popular Front government under the Matignon Agreement of 7 June 1936.[18] The restoration of civic rights of association and expression led to a resumption of political activity inaugurated with a mass demonstration on 14 July 1936 in favour of the Popular Front. A week later, on 20 July 1936, a meeting between trade union and employers representatives led to the signing of the 'Kasbah Accords' whereby three decrees of the Matignon legislation referring to wage increases, paid holidays and eight-hour working-days became applicable in Tunisia.[19]

The second significant initiative launched by the new Blum government was the creation in July 1936 of a parliamentary committee to study the situation in the colonies, as promised in the Popular Front's electoral manifesto. A sub-committee on North Africa, comprising 13 members from different professional backgrounds (civil servants, politicians and 'specialists' of various descriptions) set out to evaluate the state of the colonies under 13 headings, including demography, education, employment, administration and nutrition. The activities of the committee, spread approximately over a 12-month period, displayed a rather ad hoc methodology – including reports, interviews and questionnaires – and produced very disparate recommendations.[20] Perhaps the most fruitful outcome of the exercise was the establishment of direct links between the respective authorities in Paris and the various Tunisian social movements. Admittedly, the largest part of the correspondence received by the sub-committee on North Africa, for example, came from the Popular Front organisations in Tunisia. The Néo-Destour preferred to nurture its good relations with the Secretary of State Pierre Viénot, and viewed the committee's activities with some scepticism.

However, whether through a lack of commitment toward substantial alterations in the political and economic structure

of the Protectorate or because of the limited duration of
its mandate, the Popular Front government failed to institute
major changes in the French colonial policy toward Tunisia.
What it had managed, however, was to transform the nature
of relations between the French administration and the
various political movements representing the colonial
population. It had opened channels of communication and
influence previously closed to most of these organisations.
As Charles-André Julien, one of the notable participants
of this process has testified:

> The Quai d'Orsay and the Hôtel de Matignon ceased to
> be 'high places' where only officials, settlers and busi-
> nessmen could gain entrance. For the first time, Algerians,
> Moroccans and Tunisians had the possibility to express
> themselves freely to the authorities.[21]

While the official colonial policy of the Popular Front had
a limited impact on the social and economic structure of
the Protectorate, the effect at the grass-roots level was much
more pronounced. The importance of the political liberalisation introduced by Resident General Guillon in stimulating the open expression of social and political militancy
has already been highlighted above. But this process was
also the direct result of the tightening links between the
colonial and metropolitan working-class politics brought
about by the triumph of the left in France.

The first indication of this was the creation in the summer of 1936 of a Tunisian Rassemblement Populaire in
the image of the French coalition.[22] This reinforced the
identification of the Tunisian left with the events unfold-
ing in France, and led to a sharp rise in the membership
of Tunisian working-class organisations. The most notable
example of this trend occurred within the labour movement. Before 1936, the membership of the Departmental
Union of the CGT had never exceeded a few thousand; by
the end of 1936 the number climbed to 40,000 members,
three-quarters of whom were Tunisian.[23] All the major
Tunisian industrial centres and some of the agricultural
areas saw the multiplication of local trade-unions which in
some cases extended into previously non-unionised sectors
such as domestic and cleaning workers or bakers.[24] Among

the political parties, both the SFIO and the communists gained adherents as a result of their association with the French Popular Front, although never reaching beyond 1,000 members each. The SFIO had not substantially altered its policy of 'humane colonialism' and continued neglecting the political demands of the Tunisian nationalists. The communists for their part had moved away from their previous anti-colonialism toward an emphasis on the primacy of unity between the metropole and the colonies in the struggle against fascism. Despite these seemingly unpopular stances, both parties managed to increase their influence among the indigenous proletariat and on some occasions, represent the latter's interests before the Regency and the French administration in Paris. The wave of strikes which swept over the Protectorate in the aftermath of the Popular Front victory was a testimony to this. Similarly, the interventions of Tunisian socialists at the SFIO Congress of Huygens in 1936, and their contributions to the Popular Front's commission on the colonies demonstrated a genuine, albeit paternalistic, concern for the socio-economic situation of all Tunisians, whether European or Arab.[25]

What the socialists and communists had failed to register, however, was that by the mid-1930s it was the *political* demand for national independence which preoccupied most Tunisians. The Tunisian left had managed to mobilise the urban working-class after 1936 but had less success with the agricultural workers, the commercial petty bourgeoisie and the large under-proletariat. It was precisely on these social sectors that Bourguiba's Néo-Destour built its formidable ascendance during the Popular Front years. By October 1937 the Néo-Destour claimed 480 cells with approximately 70,000 members across the country. As Mustapha Kraïem has demonstrated, most of the cadres originated from the rural areas of the Sahel and the south (Gabes, Djerba and the Djerid) while its leadership reflected a strong professional and agricultural background: 'On the whole, it was the party of farm-owners and artisan-traders.'[26] Thus, at the peak of their influence, the Tunisian left faced the strongest opposition it had yet encountered in the form of a mass nationalist movement demanding independence. How was the left's internationalism affected by this challenge?

As we have seen, the French left was strongly divided on the question of internationalism, and its role within a left-wing colonial policy. The three tendencies within the SFIO had remained fundamentally intact through the twenties and into the Popular Front. The revolutionary left sector of the SFIO continued its campaign for the 'liberation of colonial peoples' but found little echo in government where Léon Blum, representing the majority 'centrist' position, advocated a policy of 'assimilation' which would bring the colonies closer to France and allow them to benefit from the social reforms and political rights of the metropole. The communists on the other hand, had maintained a relatively consistent anti-colonialism until 1935, supporting the cause of national liberation. Yet by the time of the Popular Front, both parties had come to share a common perspective on the Maghrebi nationalist movements, switching their attention from the 'colonial question' to the question of 'national security'. The reasons for this sudden convergence in the left's position on the colonies are to be found in the very same international conjuncture which gave rise to the Popular Front, namely the rise of fascism in Europe. Thus, internationalism becomes relevant to Tunisia under the Popular Front not only as a principle of political action, but also as a concept which describes the Regency's insertion into the European civil war of the 1930s.

We have examined how in Tunisia, nationalists and socialists suffered equally under the Peyrouton regime and how Bourguiba initially welcomed the Popular Front with a 'favourable disposition' (*préjugé favorable*). The communists in particular were interested in a *rapprochement* with the Néo-Destour which might radicalise the nationalists into a revolutionary position. In the wake of the outburst of popular discontent in 1934, André Ferrat, head of the PCF's colonial section wrote from Tunisia:

> The communists made overtures so that the orders for the general strike should be issued simultaneously by the Socialist Party, the Néo-Destour, the Communist Party and trade union organizations. But Socialist leaders thought that this initiative should come from the Néo-Destour.[27]

International events, however, were to overtake the PCF's

support for colonial insurrection. The rise of fascism in
Europe and in the Far East was menacing to both communist
activity across the old continent, and to the security of the
Soviet Union. In August 1935, the seventh congress of the
Comintern adopted a strategy which it thought could dispel
both these threats: communist parties were to establish a 'united
front' with anti-fascist forces in their own country. The PCF
had no difficulty in embracing the strategy as it had in many
ways originated within the French anti-fascist experience.
Moreover, three months earlier the French and Soviet
Foreign Ministers, Laval and Litvinov had signed a long-
awaited Franco-Soviet Treaty of Mutual Assistance, thus
committing the PCF to the defence of the existing French
regime, Empire included.[28] By the time the Rassemblement
Populaire was formally constituted in January 1936, therefore,
the PCF had clearly endorsed the idea of putting the interests
of the Franco-Soviet Alliance above any ideological commitment
to colonial emancipation. Despite paying lip-service to the
idea of 'the liberation of colonial peoples', Thorez emphasised in December 1937 that, 'Since the decisive issue of the
moment is the victory of the struggle against fascism, the
interests of the colonial peoples lies in their union with
the people of France, and not in an attitude which might
further the aims of fascism and place in Algeria, Tunisia
or Morocco . . . under Hitler or Mussolini's yoke.'[29]

Much historical and political debate surrounds Thorez's
injunction. In terms of the fascist threat in North Africa,
there is little doubt that Thorez was right. The outbreak
of the Spanish civil war in July 1936 had put Spain's protectorate over northern Morocco in the hands of Franco.
Further East, Mussolini used the Italian presence in Libya
and the large Italian population in Tunisia to extend fascist
influence in North Africa. Juliette Bessis has examined in
great detail the methods employed by Mussolini in the
pursuit of this objective, including the Italian consulate and
school in Tunis, the local Italian newspapers and the Arabic
language service of Radio Bari.[30] As regards the pro-fascist
tendency within the nationalist movement, however, Thorez's
concerns were misplaced; the available evidence suggests
that few Tunisians succumbed to the Italian propaganda.
Bourguiba himself had stated as much in response to an

insinuation by the communist Duran-Angliviel that Musso-
lini might attract the nationalist cause: 'No-one in the Néo-
Destour or in our country wants France to be replaced by
Mussolini.'[31]

Nonetheless, it is clear that Bourguiba's initial enthusiasm for the Popular Front began to wane as the Blum
government fell without delivering the substantial reforms
he had anticipated. At the second congress of the Néo-
Destour held on November 7 1937, Bourguiba declared
that:

> the current government has shown by certain of its ac-
> tions its tendency to fall into the old error of using force
> and pressure condemned by its predecessor . . . from now
> on, the Party feels justified in withdrawing its goodwill
> from the present government.[32]

A week later, a general strike was called by the Néo-Destour
in solidarity with the nationalist movements elsewhere in
the Maghreb suffering from a fresh wave of repressive
measures. In the face of worsening relations with the French
authorities – both in Tunis and in Paris – and fuelled by
the need to distance himself from the old Destour after
the arrival in Tunisia of its charismatic leader 'Abd al-Aziz
Thaalbi, the Néo-Destour radicalised its opposition toward
the French administration. The first months of 1938 witnessed a number of serious riots and bloody demonstrations which culminated in the massacre of 9 April, where
112 demonstrators were killed and 62 were injured. The
following day, Bourguiba and 29 other Néo-Destourian
leaders were arrested and the nationalist organisations
outlawed. The Popular Front era in Tunisia had come full
circle.

CONCLUSIONS: THE TUNISIAN EXPERIENCE IN COMPARATIVE PERSPECTIVE

The foregoing discussion has indicated that internationalism
in its manifold analytical and political expressions had strong
implications for the way in which the Popular Front impacted
upon Tunisia. In this closing section I shall try to schematise

the experience of internationalism in Tunisia during the Popular Front by drawing some general contrasts with the Moroccan and Algerian cases. I shall do so by returning to the three aspects of internationalism outlined at the beginning of this chapter: internationalism as a process, a practice, and a principle.

In the Maghreb, imperialism unfolded in very different ways over a century of conquests from the invasion of Algeria in 1830 to the establishment of the French protectorate over Morocco in 1912. All three North African colonies experienced a violent subjection of the indigenous population, an economic transformation geared to the needs of the metropole and an extensive process of colonisation which created a privileged minority of European settlers and immigrants and vast majority of pauperised Muslims. On the other hand, the varying legacy of pre-colonial cultural, political and social structures, and the changing requirements of the metropole meant that each colony developed distinct political and socio-economic characteristics. There is no space to explore these here and it will therefore suffice simply to point out that the different paths of colonial development greatly conditioned the way in which each of the three colonies responded to international events during the Popular Front years. Thus, for example, the mass migration of Algerians to the major French cities in the aftermath of the First World War eventually led to the politicisation of immigrants which was to play a crucial role in the forging of North African nationalism during the 1920s and 1930s. This phenomenon was not as common, and therefore not as influential in Tunisia and Morocco. Similarly, the historical presence of Italians in Tunisia clearly affected the Regency's politics during the fascist ascendancy in Europe, as we saw above. Both these examples reflect the importance of identifying the different patterns of colonial rule when considering the impact of international events on the Maghreb during the mid-1930s.

The particularities of imperialist penetration become more readily apparent when we consider the differences among the internationalist political organisations in the Maghreb. In all three colonies, working-class organisations were first established by Europeans. Nonetheless, the rate of indigenous incorporation into the labour movement varied enormously

from Algeria and Tunisia which had experienced the mass
influx of French capital and the consequent emergence of an
industrial proletariat, to that of Morocco, where capitalist
investment was confined to the mineral extraction sector.
Immigration, again, created a situation whereby most of the
Algerian proletariat was actually located in France, in comparison to a limited Tunisian emigration to the metropole.
This may explain why North African trade-unionism arose
first in Tunisia, despite having a class structure similar to
that of Algeria. From a political perspective, the fact that Algeria
was administratively a part of the *Hexagone*, encouraged
Algerian activists to attach themselves to the existing metropolitan parties as opposed to creating their own. It is noteworthy, for example, that even allowing for differentials in
the total population, the Parti Communiste Algérien (PCA)
could claim 5,000 members in 1936 while the Tunisians,
as we have seen, barely came close to 1,000.[33] The closer administrative ties to the metropole may also have been responsible
for the success of the Congrès Musulman (Algerian Muslim
Congress, the Algerian version of the Popular Front) as opposed
to the elusive Tunisian effort examined above. In short,
although internationalism as an organisational principle
flourished among Tunisian social movements during the
Popular Front, there is no doubt that its distinct administrative
status and the early formation of an élitist nationalist party
marked it off from the Algerian experience.

It was in its ideological formulation that Popular Front
internationalism displayed greatest uniformity across the
Maghreb. As a guiding principle for policy, the Blum government applied the same 'assimilationist' logic to all three
countries: the political and socio-economic benefits of
metropolitan capitalism were to be extended to the colonies. In the case of Morocco and Tunisia, this promise was
partly realised as sections of the Matignon Agreement became
applicable and much of the repressive political legislation
was lifted; the historical *élan* of the Popular Front was
certainly felt in all three colonies as social and political
activism soared across the Maghreb. The Blum–Violette Plan
to extend citizenship to some 25,000 Algerians was perhaps
the only concession to the *political* demands of the colonial
population. Similarly, the dissolution of the Etoile Nord-

Africaine by the Blum government in January 1937 was the earliest expression of the left's staunch opposition to any nationalist agitation in the colonies in the face of fascist advance in Europe. Beyond this, the Popular Front's colonial policy stuck to the 'centrist' line advocated by Blum both outside and inside government.

As regards the position taken by the communists, there was again no fundamental contrast in their attitudes to the three North African colonies. Until 1936, the PCF had supported the anti-colonial struggles of various Maghrebi social movements and had sought to implant itself among the indigenous proletariat. Following the united front policy into the colonies, the communists attempted to co-operate with both Messali Hadj's Etoile and Bourguiba's Néo-Destour. In fact, in the aftermath of the ENA's dissolution the new secretary of the PCA, Robert Deloche, was forced to admit that it may have been 'more appropriate to apply the dissolution act to the fascist leagues' rather than outlaw a movement which had joined the Rassemblement Populaire from its inception.[34] But as we have saw above, once the Comintern strategy of anti-fascist Popular Fronts had been laid down, the primary concern of the communists was to defend at all costs the existing democratic regime against fascist aggression.

This necessarily brief and sketchy contrast between the way internationalism operated in Tunisia and the other two French North African colonies reveals some interesting nuances. By and large, however, Popular Front internationalism produced similar results across the Maghreb. The emergence in the colonies of modern forms of political action over the preceding decades resulted in the explosion of social and political militancy from 1936 to 1938. During these two years, the tensions inherent in the different expressions of internationalism played themselves out with great intensity. Sections of the left remained loyal to the 'orthodox' anti-colonial internationalism and joined forces with the respective nationalist movements. The majority of French socialists followed the tradition of a 'humane' colonialism, most notably from within government, and welcomed the nationalist forces only when they focused on socio-economic issues. The various nationalist organisations for

their part, supported the Popular Front and allied themselves with its representatives in anticipation of eventually
gaining independence. When these expectations were left
unmet, nationalist disenchantment turned into a definitive
break with the French left. Whatever the historical consequences, internationalism in its various guises had played
a key role in the relationship between the Popular Front
and this part of the French empire.

Notes and References

1. The author would like to thank Frank Cass and Co. for permission
to publish sections of this chapter which draw on material published in 'Internationalism in the Mediterranean, 1918–1942', *Journal
of North African Studies*, Vol. 1, No. 3 (Winter 1996) pp. 211–33.
2. This summary is drawn from F. Halliday, 'Three Concepts of Internationalism', *International Affairs*, LXIV: 2 (1988) pp. 187–97.
3. As cited in M. Rebérioux and G. Haupt, 'Le socialisme et la question coloniale avant 1914: l'attitude de l'Internationale', *Le Mouvement
Social*, XLIII (1963) p. 9.
4. M. Semidei, 'Les socialistes français et le problème colonial entre
les deux guerres (1919–1939)', *Revue Française de Science Politique*,
XVIII: 6 (Dec. 1968) pp. 1115–53.
5. Cited in Ibid., p. 1126.
6. Cited in D. Joly, *The French Communist Party and the Algerian War*
(Macmillan, 1991) p. 25.
7. See M. Hamed, 'L'Union Intercoloniale: première école d'activité
politique des immigrés coloniaux en France au lendemain de la
première grande guerre', *Les Cahiers de Tunisie*, *162–3* (4ème semestre
1991–1er semestre 1992) pp. 59–65.
8. G. Oved, *La gauche française face au nationalisme marocain*, 2 vols
(L'Harmattan, 1983) Vol. 1.
9. The most infamous example of this was that of the Sidi-bel-Abbès
section of the Communist International reporting back to Moscow
in that 'the natives of North Africa are currently mostly made up of
Arabs who resist all social, intellectual and moral progress' ('. . . les
indigènes de l'Afrique du Nord sont présentement composés en majeure
partie d'Arabes réfractaires a l'évolution sociale, intellectuelle et
morale . . .'). Trotsky subsequently accused the supporters of this motion
of having a 'slave-dealer mentality'. See F. Alexandre, 'Le PCA de
1919 à 1939-données en vue d'eclaircir son action et son role', *Revue
Algérienne des sciences juridiques, économiques et politiques*, XI: 4 (Dec.
1974) p. 179. For a detailed examination of the Sidi-bel-Abbès affair
see E. Sivan, *Communisme et nationalisme en Algérie 1920–1962* (Presses
de la Fondation Nationale des Sciences Politiques, 1976) ch. 8.

10. J. Martin, *L'Empire Triomphante, 1871–1936*, 2 vols (Editions Denöel, 1990), Vol. 2, p. 103.
11. B. Tlili, *Crises et mutations dans le monde islamo-méditerranéen contemporain (1907–1912)* (Publications de l'Université de Tunis, 1978) p. 289.
12. For the Young Tunisians and their predecessors see, C.-R. Ageron, 'Le mouvement "Jeune-Algérien" de 1900 à 1923' in Anon, *Etudes Maghrébines: Mélanges Charles-André Julien* (Paris: 1964) pp. 217–43; K. Guezmir, *Les Jeunes Tunisiens* (Editions Alif, 1986); A. Mahjoubi, *Les origines du mouvement national en Tunisie 1904–1934* (Tunis: 1982); N. Sraïeb, *Le Collège Sadiki de Tunis 1875–1956: Enseignement et nationalisme* (Alif, Editions de la Méditerranée, 1995); and A. Abdessalam, *Sadiki et les sadikiens* (Cérès Productions, 1974).
13. For a detailed account of the formation of the CGTT see E. Ahmad and S. Schaar, 'M'hammed Ali and the Tunisian Labour Movement', *Race and Class*, XIX (1978) pp. 253–76.
14. 'Cette expérience syndicale purement tunisienne a comme consé-quence positive le fait d'avoir fait découvrir aussi bien au Destour qu'aux organisations politiques et syndicales de la gauche l'existence indéniable d'une classe ouvrière autochtone, consciente, combative, et capable de s'organiser', J. Bessis 'Le mouvement ouvrier tunisien: des ses origines à l'indépendance', *Le Mouvement Social*, IMIX (1974) p. 91.
15. [e]st convaincu que les partis de gauche qui forment le Front Populaire . . . auront à coeur d'aborder le problème fondamental des rapports franco-tunisiens, de réviser les méthodes et les doc-trines à la lumière des faits, en un mot de concilier les aspirations du peuple tunisien avec les intérêts de la puissance protectrice.' Cited in M. L. Chaibi, 'La politique coloniale du Front Populaire en Tunisie (1936–38): Essai d'évaluation', in *Actes du 3e Séminaire sur l'histoire du Mouvement National: Les mouvements politiques et sociaux dans la Tunisie des années 1930* (Ministère de l'Education, de l'Enseignement et de la Recherche Scientifique, 1985) p. 549.
16. '[la] constitution d'une commission d'enquête parlementaire sur la situation politique, économique et morale des territoires français d'outre-mer . . . .' Cited in A. Nouschi, 'La politique coloniale du Front Populaire: le Maghreb', *Les Cahiers de Tunisie*, XXVII (1979) p. 144.
17. 'La période de Peyrouton fut ressentie par les nationalistes et les forces de gauche comme une dictature', M. Kraiem, *Le mouvement so-cial en Tunisie dans les années trente* (Cahiers du CERES, 1984), p. 105.
18. For a full description of the Matignon Agreement and the Popular Front in France see G. Lefranc, *Le Front Populaire (1934–1938)* (Payot, 1965).
19. See J. Bessis, op. cit., p. 93 and B. López García, *Política y Movimientos Sociales en el Magreb* (Centro de Investigaciones Sociológicas, 1991) p. 61.
20. For details on the Commission see C-R. Ageron, 'La Commission d'enquête du Front Populaire sur les colonies et la question Tuni-sienne' in *Actes du 3e Séminaire sur l'histoire du Mouvement National:*

Les mouvements politiques et sociaux dans la Tunisie des années 1930 (Ministère de l'Education, de l'Enseignement et de la Recherche Scientifique, 1985) pp. 103–25.

21. 'Le Quai d'Orsay et l'Hôtel de Matignon cessèrent d'être des hautes lieux où seuls les officiels, les colons et les hommes d'affaires pouvaient accéder. Pour la première fois, Algériens, Marocains et Tunisiens eurent la possibilité de s'expliquer librement devant les pouvoirs publiques.' Ch.-A Julien, *L'Afrique du Nord en marche: nationalismes musulmans et souveraineté française* (René Juillard, 1952) p. 84.

22. See J. Bessis, *La Mediterrannée Fasciste:L'Italie Mussolinienne et la Tunisie* (L'Harmattan, 1984) p. 181.

23. J. Bessis, 'Le mouvement ouvrier', op. cit., p. 94 and B. López García, op. cit., p. 63.

24. For further details on the trade-unions during this period see Kraiem, op. cit., ch. 2 and R. Liauzu, *Salariat et mouvement ouvrier en Tunisie: crises et mutations (1931–1939)* (Editions du CNRS, 1978).

25. See Nouschi, op. cit., and B. López García, op. cit.

26. 'C'était en gros le parti des agriculteurs-propriétaires et des commerçants-artisans', M. Kraïem, 'Le Néo-Destour: cadres, militants et implantation pendant les années trente', in *Actes du 3 Séminaire sur l'histoire du Mouvement National: Les mouvements politiques et sociaux dans la Tunisie des années 1930* (Ministère de l'Education, de l'Enseignement et de la Recherche Scientifique, 1985), p. 46.

27. 'L'organisation communiste fit des tentatives pour que le mot d'ordre de la grève générale soit lancé à la fois par le parti socialiste, le néo-Destour, le parti communiste et les organisations syndicales. Mais les dirigeants socialistes estimèrent que cette initiative devait revenir au néo-Destour.' Cited in J. Moneta, *La politique du Parti communiste français dans la question coloniale, 1920–1963* (François Maspero, 1971) p. 97.

28. For an excellent account of this process and the international context of its genesis see J. Haslam, *The Soviet Union and the Struggle for Collective Security in Europe, 1933–39* (Macmillan, 1984) chrs 3 and 4; J. Haslam, 'The Comintern and the Origins of the Popular Front 1934–1935', *Historical Journal*, 22:3 (1979) 673–91; J. Néré, *The Foreign Policy of France from 1914 to 1945* (Routledge & Kegan Paul, 1975) ch. 11.

29. Cited in M. Rodinson, *Marxism and the Muslim World* (Macmillan, 1978) p. 98.

30. J. Bessis *La Mediterrannée Fasciste*, op. cit.

31. 'Personne au Néo-Destour ni dans notre pays ne veut que la France cède la place à Mussolini', cited in ibid., p. 217.

32. 'le Gouvernement actuel a montré par des actes précis sa volonté de revenir à la vieille erreur de la politique de force et de contrainte condamné par son prédécesseur . . . le parti s'estime fondé à retirer dès maintenant au Gouvernement actuel le préjugé favorable . . .', H. Bourguiba, *La Tunisie et la France* (René Juillard, 1964) pp. 153–4.

33. Figures taken from López García, op. cit., p. 41.

34. Cited in Rodinson, op. cit., p. 97.

5 Protectorate, Association, Reformism: the Roots of the Republican Policy Pursued by the Popular Front in Indochina

Gilles de Gantès

Albert Sarraut, the most ardent advocate of colonial administration founded on liberal principles, explained that he arrived at his doctrine after reflecting on the contradiction between the need for action and humanist ideas.[1] Although he explicitly referred to the criticisms voiced by the radicals against colonial expansion in the 1880s, one can detect in what he wrote an echo of the heated debates which took place in Parliament during the reports by Maurice Viollette and Messimy, on the basis of which Sarraut had been appointed Governor General of Indochina in 1911.

Although they had opposed colonial expansion, when the radicals, and later the socialists, came to power, they had no choice other than to set about governing a colonial empire. This involved them in having to resolve a contradiction: how were they to reconcile the republican principles of equality and freedom with the possession of colonies? This contradiction concerned all the colonies, but before 1914 most of the theorists who favoured 'humanist' colonisation, concentrated on Indochina. Foremost among these, of course, was Sarraut but his views were shared by Maurice Viollette and Marius Moutet. As these two men played a major role at the time of the Popular Front, it is interesting to observe what Indochina provided by way of a model of a liberal policy before 1914.

It is hard to decide upon the right word to describe the

policies that served as a model to those who played a part
in the Popular Front: Reformist? Humanitarian? Progressive? Liberal? Republican? I would tend to opt for the last
of these adjectives;[2] it seems to cover all the contradictions of the type of relative liberalism practised in the colonies. In fact three common features characterise the
successive republican policies in Indochina, from that of
Jean-Marie de Lanessan (a Protectorate policy) to that of
Jules Brévié, via that of Paul Beau (Association), Albert
Sarraut and Alexandre Varenne. In the first place they were
opposed, hotly at times, to the policy of 'domination' which
relied for the most part on the military balance of power
and on the retention by the French of everything – no
matter how minor – to do with the running of the colony.
The second common feature was that the native population
occupied a central place in their deliberations; this meant
that they constantly sought to win the co-operation of the
people by offering them certain compensations. It should
be noted, incidentally, that, in the case of Indochina, the
native people referred to by the theorists were essentially
the Annamese, as the French called the Vietnamese at this
time: the Cambodians and the Laotians were held to be
less 'advanced'. Finally, for these Republicans the idea of
a 'civilising mission' was not just a hollow expression: to
them the concept was the only one that could justify colonisation. The native whose co-operation they sought, then,
was not the mandarin or the scholar of the past, but the
Vietnamese who had had a French-style education and had
gained 'up-to-date' qualifications. This was what differenti-
ated Varenne from Pasquier (who was an expert on the
Annam of the past and Governor-General in the early 1930s),
Sarraut from Merlin, and Paul Beau from Anthony
Klobukowski. Also, the sharp distinction traditionally made
between 'assimilation' and 'association' does not seem so
marked to me: indeed, while soon abandoning the example
of total naturalisation as was practised until 1850 in the
old colonies (the West Indies, Réunion, India, etc.), the
Republicans were always tempted to apply the philosophy
of the Enlightenment which held that the Vietnamese would
one day raise themselves to the level of the French. It fell
to Jean-Marie de Lanessan to be the first to try to resolve

the contradiction mentioned by Sarraut between deeds and principles; he had to devise a theory and to put it into effect in an effort to win over the Vietnamese.

THE DEVELOPMENT OF A REPUBLICAN DOCTRINE OF ACTION

Protectorate Policy

The birth of the programme that de Lanessan intended to put into effect, owed a great deal to the theoretical debates about colonisation which were widespread at the time of his appointment.[3] Thus it was that, at the International Colonial Conference held in Paris in 1889, there was animated discussion on the subject of the report delivered by Dr Le Bon who criticised the effects on the colonised peoples of assimilationist practices, the destructive consequences of which he roundly condemned.[4] That same year, Dr Jules Harmand explored the same theme of the need for autonomous development for the Annamese people:

> Our duty as conquerors', he declared, 'if we are conscious of the mission which falls to us, consists in resolving to improve the lot of the Annamese people . . . without causing further breaks in the chain of their traditions, their future and their ambitions, which are engraved in the two thousand years of their national history. The Annamese are certainly not children whom it is our task to educate; equally they are not savages on whom experiments can be conducted as if on a tabula rasa. . . . Therefore we must take, as it were, this entire people, with its customs, its institutions, its own values and its superiority in relation to its neighbours in order that we may make of it our . . . associate.[5]

The objective of Association, then, was to reinforce colonial power. Also, since Harmand considered nationalism to be an integral part of the Vietnamese culture, it was essential that, for Association to be effective, and for any risk of revolts to be averted, all control should be in the hands of the French alone.

These views are consistent with the general development of French anthropology in the 1880s. Like their other European counterparts, French anthropologists took a keen interest in colonisation. Like them, they believed in the law of natural selection which apparently explained the evolution of species – including the human race. Many of them thought that it was possible to establish a hierarchy of races, ranging from the primitive to the advanced on the path of Progress. After 1870, however, their theories underwent a change – for three reasons. Germany justified its annexation of Alsace and Lorraine on the grounds of racial theory, which prompted French anthropologists to modify their statements. Moreover most of them were staunch republicans, so they had somehow to reconcile their theories about race with the question of the equality of individual rights. Finally, Lamarck's theories about the heredity of acquired characteristics lasted for a long time. This brief excursion into anthropology would seem to be far removed from Indochina if de Lanessan had not been so closely involved in these debates.

De Lanessan had a theory of his own: like Darwin, he believed in natural selection which eliminates the weak. However, he noticed that certain animal and vegetable species have strategies of association which enable the weak to survive; this he called the Law of Solidarity. Relations between 'races' are subject to the law of solidarity. In the case of colonies, then, the Whites, who are dominant but who cannot adapt to the tropical climate, are in a position of association with the natives. It is not possible, though, to assimilate the natives, owing to the fact of the heredity of acquired characteristics. What the colonisers can do is educate the natives so that they are better able to engage in the struggle for life, but in their own way and in accordance with the characteristics of their civilisation.[6]

This doctrine, then, enabled the view according to which a social hierarchy exists objectively to be reconciled with the wish to apply republican principles. It gave a new and timely legitimacy to colonial policy; the colonial empire had expanded into a region where populations which were widely different had to be administered, and 'assimilation' appeared to be virtually utopian.

The situation in Indochina was anything but propitious when de Lanessan took up his appointment there; the French had been bogged down for over five years in a struggle without respite or lasting success against the monarchist resistance and Chinese incursions.[7] De Lanessan intended to bring an end to the conflict with an original and inexpensive plan to encourage collaboration. For him Vietnamese nationalism was a fact. This was denied by most of his predecessors and changed the attitude regarding pacification: it was a case of confronting not bandits but armed patriots, which explained why there was a great deal of complicity on the part of both villagers and high-ranking Vietnamese. It was necessary, therefore, to respect the self-esteem of the latter so as to convince them that the interests of the colonisers were fully compatible with those of the colonised. Once those of high rank were won over, Pacification could be completed speedily and at little cost. Moreover their co-operation would make it possible to drive out the bands of Chinese which were causing havoc in Tonkin.

What de Lanessan set out to do as Governor was inspired by these principles. On his arrival, he sought the collaboration of both the Court and the cultured élite by treating them with respect and by making concessions to the minorities in the upland region. In establishing the security of Indochina, de Lanessan, from a purely political point of view, was wholly successful. His premature recall was linked to trifling scandals (brought about, as it happened, by the limited freedom of action permitted him by the French government) and to matters concerning domestic policies being pursued in France, not to any failure in the task which had been assigned to him.

His downfall, though, was probably linked also to his success: once he had definitively beaten the monarchist patriots, there was no further purpose to be served by maintaining him in his post. The priority now was to develop the potential of the territory. Théophile Delcassé, who had dismissed him from his duties, was a firm supporter of this approach. In January 1893, in his very first speech as Under-secretary of State for the Colonies, he declared that 'for many years to come the sword is to be merely a means of ensuring protection . . . now is the time for agriculture and the building of roads and bridges to flourish and make fruitful what has been won by the sword. . . . We are now entering a period which will be primarily utilitarian'.[8] Following the departure of de Lanessan as Governor, succeeding Governors-general did not concern themselves with matters to do with the indigenous population, because the colony seemed to be firmly established; they were free to pursue a policy of domination. In order to be able to set his budget on a firm footing, Doumer in particular had to place severe limitations on the prerogative of the Vietnamese and especially of the Court in Hué. This ran counter to the policy pursued by de Lanessan.

Certain specialists, however, were still pondering the need for association with the indigenous people.[9] The Spanish–American war prompted comparative reflection on the respective values of the colonisation measures adopted in the English-speaking world and those in Latin countries.[10] The idea of association was developed in all the post-1900 colonial congresses and by intellectuals such as Durkheim and Arthur Girault.[11] During the debates in the International Colonial Institute in May 1903 (held in London but published in France) much attention was paid to this line of thought, which had a marked influence on official policy from 1905 onwards.[12]

Association

Paul Beau, a diplomat who was a *protégé* of Delcassé, held the office of Governor-General of Indochina from 1902. He was firmly convinced of the need to develop the region, unlike his predecessor Paul Doumer who had dreamed of expansion in China. By 1905 though, he had done very little. It was Etienne Clémentel, who, in February 1905, officially launched the new policy by stating that every effort should be made 'to understand the natives better and to associate them with our interests'.[13]

As was the case during de Lanessan's governorship, the problem to be solved was that of political unrest within Indochina and at the same time the threat of danger from without; in 1905 the Indochinese problem was no less alarming than it had been in 1890. The victory of Japan over the Russians provoked grave misgivings and for a time the French feared that Japan might invade. 'There is only one possible way of defending Indochina: defence by the natives themselves'.[14] Involving the indigenous people in the defence of their own country seemed to be a sound and inexpensive way of tackling any outside attack and of avoiding internal unrest; it required propaganda to persuade the Annamese that they stood to gain a great deal from the French presence, and also provided a few material benefits which boosted the self-esteem of those members of the élite who agreed to take part in the colonial administration of their country.[15]

The involvement of the local people was also vital, in the view of the authorities in Paris, to the development of the potential of the region. Given that refunds on loans depended upon it, there was urgent need for this development. For Jules Harmand it was 'vitally important for us to give back to the Annamese people the drive they once had' if the land was to be colonised. Irrigation schemes had to be undertaken, the Annamese people had to be given tax exemptions and land: 'the only colonisation that really works is colonisation by natives'.[16] Furthermore, Paul Beau hoped to have the whole of Indochina (including Cambodia and Laos) colonised by the Vietnamese at a time when the western boundaries of the French possessions were in the process of being officially fixed. Were that to happen, the Vietnamese, merely by their presence, would deter any threat posed to Indochina by Siam.

For those coming after him Paul Beau has always been seen as the governor who was the champion of the native people: the founder of the University of Indochina and of the Tonkin Local Consultative Forum, the symbol of French liberalism later commended by Albert Sarraut and Alexandre Varenne.[17] These two establishments were certainly the most tangible monuments to the policy of Association. It is worth reflecting briefly on this double reform the features of which were quite distinct and often adopted again later. The proposed development programme for public education was mainly concerned with two different domains: the University of Indochina and, more importantly, primary education.

It was provided in two different institutional settings: native education in the strict sense of the term, and the Franco-Annamese schools. Concerning the 'wholly native schools . . . we are currently endeavouring to move towards a more modern organisation which will better conform to our educational ideas', wrote the Director of Public Education.[18] But the administration concentrated mainly on Franco-native primary schooling. It remained, though, largely undeveloped. Schooling was divided into three different levels, the third of which was the equivalent of the top classes of French primary schools, The ablest pupils continued their schooling in the six post-primary schools.

Above this level, 'the Annamese, at least the upper classes and those who are wealthy, insist on having more. They already send their sons to France and Algeria to study in our *lycées*. A group of local people have recently formed an association in Hanoi to foster secondary and higher education. This move is not without its drawbacks. Although it is desirable that the young Annamese, on completion of their primary education, should go to France to continue their education in our great schools, it must be said that their time spent as boarders in our Lycées has so far not produced very satisfactory results'.[19] There was, then, a 'missing link'. Logically, Paul Beau should have considered filling the gap by importing into Vietnam secondary education modelled on the French system, just as he had organised Franco-native primary schooling replicating that existing in France. This he did not do, as he thought French secondary education would be inappropriate. However, credit must be given to Gourdón for introducing Franco-Annamese secondary schooling, even if only in order to avoid the Annamese organising it themselves. In a sense, then, it was with some reluctance that secondary schooling was introduced.

To satisfy the needs of those Annamese who were educated and eager to acquire western knowledge, Paul Beau founded the University of Indochina in 1906. This had a major impact throughout the whole of the Far East, since it demonstrated that modernisation could be encouraged under colonial rule, as well as in independent Japan and Siam. In Vietnam, where considerable prestige was attached to higher education, the founding of the university was seen as a great benefit afforded to the indigenous population, an alternative to the traditional Chinese style of training. However, things were not quite what they seemed. The new establishment adopted courses which had been in existence for many years (e.g. in the Medical School, the Civil Engineering, and Posts and Telecommunications departments, etc.), something which was not wholly in keeping with its supposedly innovative nature. The limitations of the new establishment, then, were obvious and the wealthy Annamese families who wanted a university education for their children still had to send them to France. Nevertheless the principle behind it and its name were of great symbolic importance, which is why it was able to shrug off criticism and also the verbal caution of its promoters, Beau and Gourdon. This educational reform amply illustrates the essence of the republican philosophy regarding the governing of colonies: educate the indigenous population up to a certain level only, and thus limit access to higher education. Although some opportunities were opened up to the natives, that was merely to prevent them taking matters into their own hands.

Association also meant consulting the Annamese on the governing of their country. As regards native representative institutions, Paul Beau set up a two-tier system. The first tier, set up under the decree of 1 May 1907, was composed of commissions in each province which were meant to assist the French officials. The members of these assemblies were elected by village elders, not appointed as they had been hitherto, and European nationals were not permitted to sit in them. Association had, therefore, a spatial implication since, if taken to its logical extreme, the natives would have been involved virtually unaided in the management of the rural areas, whereas the Europeans would have been confined to the towns. The second tier, established by the decree of 4 May 1907, comprised the Tonkin Native Consultative Chamber which was somewhat the same as an earlier body proposed by Paul Bert.[20] It was divided into three different sections. The first was made up of elected rural representatives at the rate of one per 35,000 taxpayers, the second of elected representatives of payers of business rates at the rate of one or two per province, and the third of appointed representatives from the ethnic minorities. Elections for the first two of the sections were first held in November 1907.

The third element in the policy of Association concerned the law. On 31 July 1905 the fourth chamber of the court of Hanoi was established. Its specific task was to hear appeals brought against native courts, and it naturally represented a certain measure of mistrust of the traditional élites. For this reason it reinforced the criticisms of the colonials, even the most liberal of whom felt that justice was weighted too heavily in favour of the Annamese. Furthermore, it stripped the mandarins of much of their power.

Taken as a whole, it must be said that the effects of the reforms were welcomed by the Vietnamese people to an extent which caused problems even for the French. This at least was the view of the colonial decision-makers in 1908 when several revolts broke out. The Minister for the Colonies, Milliès-Lacroix, was tempted to implement a different plan, proposed by Anthony Klobukowski, which favoured the traditional native leaders rather than the modernist cultured élite.

The debate in France in the years following 1910

Nonetheless, in France the debate concerning colonial affairs and the Republic went on and led to the liberal doctrines being firmly established. The debate was influenced by events taking place in Indochina, and by what was happening on the political scene in France.

The growing power of the Socialist Party under Jaurès gave rise, as far as colonial affairs were concerned, to questions as to the fate of native people, and nudged ministers responsible for the colonies towards reform. Indeed, socialist theories about colonisation were crystallised during that period: the Amsterdam Conference of 1904 prompted discussion on the matter; there followed the publication in 1905 of a book by Paul Louis attacking colonialism, the campaigns of *La Guerre sociale* by Gustave Hervé, which began in 1906, and the firm commitment to the cause by Jaurès from 1907 onwards.[21] Broadly speaking though, the socialists devoted little time to the colonies, and had no clearly defined views on the subject; but they were quick to decry possible scandals or abuses involving citizens of the colonies.[22] Republican activity, in the opinion of one observer, 'would have been considerably slowed down if the radical and radical-socialist party had not had to take its opponents from the far left into account'.[23]

It must be noted, however, that in the debate taking place in the years following 1910, the Comité d'Action Républicaine aux Colonies, set up in 1906, and the Ligue des Droits de l'Homme played a much more active role than did the SFIO. Indeed, the debate on the necessary reforms in the colonies was mainly prompted by Maurice Viollette, who was a member of the former of these bodies, and Francis de Pressensé, the chairman of the latter. The result was that criticism was directed primarily at the failure to respect the rights of individuals, especially in the field of justice. Beginning in 1909, the Ligue des Droits de l'Homme called with increasing insistence for civil rights for the natives, 'in matters regarding elementary rights to life, liberty and property'.[24]

With regard to Indochina, politicians sympathetic to the Ligue were outraged by the minimalist programme drawn up by Klobukowski; it came as a shock to those who sought a guaranteed improvement in the conditions of the Vietnamese people. One of the objectives of a liberal policy was to make doubly sure of the French colonial presence. 'If we succeed in persuading the Annamese of the sincerity of our intentions regarding them, and in proving to them that their cause is closely linked to our own', wrote Messimy in his report of 1910, 'then no matter what agitators may say or do, nobody will listen to them.' Viollette himself spelt out the limits in his speech in the Chamber on 12 July 1911. Advocating the setting-up of native consultative chambers, he saw their role as being to express '[their] views on everything other than purely political matters' and provide the opportunity to 'make observations on the budget, taxes and public works – in short on anything that does not concern sovereignty'.[25]

Debate on reform in Indochina was, in the end, always linked to the development of the country's potential which at that period was really beginning to get under way. As Viollette wrote, 'in the colonies the fate of the natives is the major preoccupation, and this is in the interest of the colonisers. Indeed, if the French nationals in the colonies are to have the means of putting their capital and their industrial skills to good use, do they not need to have on hand an abundant and healthy workforce with the necessary training to enable them to adapt to the demands of modern agriculture and industry?'.[26]

The outcome was that the reforms proposed by Messimy and Viollette met with parliamentary approval, and Messimy took over as Minister for the Colonies on 27 February 1911. His appointment clearly indicated a change of policy and also had a heartening effect on those progressive deputies who had been so critical of the colonial policy of his predecessors.

THE CRYSTALLISATION OF THE REPUBLICAN TRADITION

Sarraut in Indochina

Sarraut was appointed on 1 June 1911 specifically to implement in Indochina the ideas of Messimy and Viollette. The aim was, on the one hand, to streamline the way the colonial administration functioned (the setting-up of financial controls, compulsory learning of the Vietnamese language, reducing staff numbers, etc.) and, on the other, to devote more attention to the indigenous population.[27]

The policy put into effect by Sarraut during his two periods in office was the best possible expression of what a republican colonial policy aspired to be. Also, in what he did he was supported (kept under a watchful eye?) by the Ligue des Droits de l'Homme. Commenting, some weeks later, on a note from Sarraut about the organisation of justice in Indochina, Moutet wrote to him: 'confident of the goodwill that you have shown, we [the Ligue] hope to convince you that there is more to be done, on this and other matters, than you indicate in your note'.[28]

As it happens, Sarraut's first period in office was somewhat disappointing from the Ligue's standpoint even though his views in general were genuinely progressive, bearing in mind the climate of opinion at the time. Sarraut devoted his energies mainly to improving the administration, and going ahead with developing the country's potential; one of the first tasks he undertook was the securing, in June 1912, of a loan of 90 million francs, 19 million of which was allocated to the provision of water supplies in agricultural areas. Moreover he kept fully abreast of events surrounding the Chinese Revolution, especially since Phan Boi Chau, the Vietnamese nationalist, had set up bases in South China. Sarraut later organised an efficient intelligence service based on consuls in the region.

With regard to policies concerning the indigenous population, symbolic measures were of importance. Sarraut systematically exercised his legal right to intervene (*'Appel à minima'*) in cases in which Europeans were punished too leniently by the courts for acts of violence committed against natives. He was also the first to appoint a Frenchman of Vietnamese extraction as an administrator. Similarly, he adopted a certain number of symbolic measures in the field of education, such as the reorganisation of the Medical School in April 1913, the reopening of the University and the updating of the triennial examinations. He also revived the native consultative chamber in Tonkin, which held its first session in October 1913. This reform was limited since, on the one hand, only heads of cantons, one representative per village and graduates were eligible to vote and, on the other hand the assembly could not draw up its own agenda, and fulfilled only a consultative role. The reforms had a distinctly associationist tone 'tending both to separate the French nationals from the natives on deliberative bodies, and to establish Chambers for each of these groups'.[29]

Sarraut's second period in office was more noteworthy. In the field of education in particular Paul Beau's programme was officially readopted in December 1917 although effectively it had begun in Varenne's time. In a speech delivered on 27 April 1919 in Hanoi,[30] Sarraut spoke of future emancipation modelled on that of the British Dominions, and proposed a Charter that would guarantee the Vietnamese people representation on elected bodies which would exercise a measure of control over the colonial power. Moreover he advocated greater freedom of expression for what might be called new Vietnamese élites. Thus financial support was given to the journal *Nam Phong* (founded in 1919) and also to the Association pour la formation intellectuelle et morale des Annamites (AFIMA). As can clearly be seen, this was in line with the views promoted earlier by de Lanessan when he was Governor – the wish to foster the modernisation of Vietnamese society, not by assimilation but within its own framework.

After the period from 1911 to 1920, then, it looked very much as if theories concerning political reforms to be implemented in Indochina had been so constituted and crystallised that they could not develop further.

Sarrautism

In summarising his political philosophy a few years later, Sarraut revealed that he regarded colonisation as being quite simply an act of aggression prompted by self-interest. However, as it had by then become so firmly established, it could be morally justified on the grounds of the effectiveness shown by the colonisers. He expressed the view that the world's riches should be exploited in the most rational way possible: riches belonging not to whatever peoples (Sarraut used the word 'races') might happen to live close to one or several of them, but to humanity as a whole: 'all mankind should derive benefit from all the riches scattered throughout the entire globe'.[31] This amounted, then, to a new interpretation of the development of potential; it was to be the sole justification of colonisation. In short, the colonisers were constrained to develop both people and things in the most rational way possible, or otherwise risk having their domination legally called into question. There was no suggestion that backward peoples should be eliminated, but that they should, initially, be helped to overcome their deficiencies, and educated so as to enable them to participate in the exploitation of the common heritage. What Sarraut was advocating was that natives should be accorded 'the same fundamental guarantee of individual status and personal rights as we demand for ourselves'.[32] They should also have legal protection, education, access to jobs in the public sector and finally freedom of self-expression.

As Sarraut saw it, the maintenance of the high quality of

such colonisation should be carried out on two levels – the international and the local – by the populations under colonial rule. With regard to representative institutions, he considered that the time was not yet ripe to turn them into Parliaments. He went only so far as to favour allowing them a greater say in financial matters, and especially in drawing up budgets. However, he did not think that they should have any choice as to whether taxes should be paid, although taxation could be the subject of open debate. In sum, 'at the very moment when we are asserting that change is possible', Sarraut wrote, 'we assert by the very idea of change that it is not possible to conclude that political and administrative equality are achievable in the immediate future'.[33]

The need for action to be taken meant that, during its gestation period, the requisite work needed safeguarding, especially from the natives until they were sufficiently educated to understand their own interests. This was why Sarraut wanted to develop public primary and secondary education while at the time limiting access to higher education, which he likened to 'a potent wine which quickly goes to one's head'. He pressed the need to the lay sound foundations and ensure that readiness for change in the indigenous population would be as widespread as possible. However, a little later he went on to add that administrative careers should not be barred to well-educated natives, although he felt the time was not yet ripe for them to occupy senior executive posts.

A Progressive Nuance: Alexandre Varenne

The last progressive republican to govern Indochina prior to 1936 was the Socialist, Alexandre Varenne. In some respects he proved to be more radical than not only Sarraut but also Brévié. As was the case with his predecessors, the dominant factor governing what he did was the threefold necessity to satisfy some of the wishes of the indigenous people, to ensure Indochina's security, and to promote the country's development. His appointment was linked to the current political situation in France, as also were the campaigns against him and the constraints upon his actions:

he was severely hampered by the rightward shift in the complexion of the government in 1926.

Varenne had to concern himself with the danger threatening Indochina connected, as during the time of Sarraut, with the Chinese problem. It so happened that, at that time Mikhail Borodin was establishing an alliance in Canton with the Kuomintang (Chinese nationalist party), which posed a threat to the internal security of Indochina. The future Ho Chi Minh arrived in Canton in November 1924, and Jacques Doriot, who was then the chairman of the colonial section of the French Communist Party, introduced the Association Révolutionnaire de la Jeunesse Vietnamienne (Thanh Nien) to the Comintern, following a mission to China in February and March 1927.[34]

Varenne justified opening up administrative posts to natives on the grounds that the defence of Indochina had to be ensured: 'it must on no account be forgotten that we French amount to only a tiny handful among 20 million natives, and that along 1500 kilometres of frontier there are turbulent states the hostility or reticence of whose intentions towards us will be directly proportional to our strength or weakness. This is why we must have the support of the bulk of the natives, and we can no longer disregard the ambition of the Annamese people to take part in the government of their own country'.[35] The defence of Indochina, then, was of vital importance, and as large number of Annamese wanted to have greater influence – a view shared by Varenne – then their wishes had to be granted. As Varenne saw it, 'respect for others lies at the very heart of the Indochinese question'.[36] Moreover, as R. Colonax stressed, Bolshevism had not yet taken control of nationalism, so 'respect for the principles of the Declaration of the Rights of Man would be enough to have a calming effect'.[37]

Varenne completed two periods of office in Indochina: November 1925 to October 1926, and June to November 1927. In the course of the first, according to his own accounts, he brought about reforms in three different fields. In the administrative field (Varenne did not use the word 'political') the advancement of the Annamese in the civil service was promoted, as was their access to civil service grades usually reserved for the French. The representative councils were also reformed. In the social field a range of measures concerning public health were adopted (vaccination, water purification, medical care, etc.) and steps were taken in an attempt to limit the debts of the Vietnamese (a clampdown on usury, and the introduction of gaming laws). Finally, in the economic field funding was provided for major civil engineering schemes (harbour walls in Tonkin, the 400-kilometre stretch of the Trans-Indochina road from Tourane to Nha Trang), land ownership was regulated, and Varenne tried to promote tourism. During his second term of office, he applied himself more resolutely to the social problem. The education system was reorganised and decentralised, agricultural credit was extended to Annam and Tonkin, and labour laws were enacted (October 1927, accompanied by the setting-up of an inspectorate). The decree instituting the credit bank, Crédit agricole, in Indochina was dated 4 September 1926 and was to some extent intended to capture the headlines in France as Varenne was then about to leave.

In all of this there was no political element. For a long time Varenne was, it seems, reluctant to accede to the demands of the Vietnamese to form a political party. He later came to regret this, concluding in the early 1930s that, had there been a moderate party, 'the Annamese would have fought against each other, not against us' and that furthermore, the multiplicity of secret societies would thus have been avoided.[38]

CONCLUSION

Alexandre Varenne, then, proved to have been the most radical of the colonial office-holders, at least in what he said, for he uttered the word 'independence'. The subsequent actions of the Popular Front were somewhat less forward-looking, or at least they harked back to the policies of de Lanessan, Paul Beau and Albert Sarraut. For these men 'Association' had been the catchword. But 'associating' the natives meant involving them in the improving and rationalising of the colonial system – in other words the negation of the very idea of future emancipation, even though the word was frequently mentioned.

The problem which confronted Brévié in 1936 was the same one that his liberal predecessors had encountered. When a measure of freedom of expression was granted, the Vietnamese did not make use of it in the way expected, and this led to the frequent flare-up of nationalism. Under Paul Beau there were revolts in 1908, and the first large-scale demonstrations by the Vietnamese in the streets of Saigon occurred during Varenne's term of office. The only man successfully to 'associate' the Vietnamese was Sarraut, with the Parti Constitutionnaliste. The consequence was that the liberals themselves would probably have been prompted to repeal some of their own reforms if they had not periodically given way to reactionaries.

The Popular Front leaders were, in a sense, even less equipped than their predecessors to understand what was going on around them because they had fallen for their own rhetoric. Indeed, at the outset the theories of Association sprang from the taking into account of Vietnamese nationalism, not from lack of awareness. Harmand, Lanessan, Beau, Sarraut and Varenne had been fully aware of it; they quite simply hoped to put it to good use, Lanessan to counter the Can Vuong,[39] and Paul Beau to populate the Indochinese peninsula. For many reasons, however, when the Popular Front came to power the initial political strategy for the region was gradually forgotten. For one thing Moutet had not had much overseas experience and in particular knew little about Indochina. Also, all visible signs of nationalism inside the country had been stamped out by the police (hence the painful surprises of 1945) and the surviving nationalists were rallying beyond the borders.

The relative failure of the Popular Front in Indochina can be explained by a number of external factors: the political situation as a whole, the withering away of the electoral alliance, budgetary problems, increasing international tensions in Europe, and then the Second World War. But the reforms proposed under the Popular Front coalition were structurally limited by the theory underpinning them. Other factors also played their part: for example, although de Lanessan, Beau, Sarraut and Varenne had wanted to guide the native population along the road to Enlightenment and progress, they had always thought that this would be a long process. Finally, being shorter of ideas than their predecessors, the members of the Popular Front found themselves having to cope with a situation in which the stability of French supremacy had deteriorated because not only were the demands made by the Vietnamese greater, but also because, by the late 1930s, the relative power of France in the world was not what it had been in the 1890s.

Notes and References

1. A. Sarraut, *Grandeur et servitude coloniale* (Editions du Sagittaire, 1931) p. 106.
2. A. Larcher also favours this word 'L'ordre par la concorde: essai sur les réformismes coloniaux en Indochine, 1902–1945', D.E.A. thesis, Université de Paris VII, 1994, p. 11.
3. For a full account see D. Deschamps, 'Les sources scientifiques et la politique indochinoise de Jean-Marie de Lanessan', in P. Le Failler and J.-M. Mancini (eds), *Viêt Nam. Sources et approches, Actes du Colloque international Euroviet*, Aix en Provence, May 1995, Université de Provence, 1996, pp. 279–92.
4. Ibid.
5. 'Notre devoir de conquérants, si nous avons conscience de la mission qui nous incombe, consiste à prendre la résolution d'élever cette race annamite ... sans rompre davantage la chaîne de ses traditions, de son avenir et de ses ambitions, inscrites dans les deux mille années de son histoire nationale. C'est que l'Annamite n'est point un enfant dont nous ayons à faire l'éducation, ce n'est point un sauvage sur lequel on puisse faire des expériences comme sur une table rase.... Nous devons donc prendre, pour ainsi dire, toute cette race, avec ses moeurs, ses institutions, ses valeurs propres, sa supériorité vis-à-vis de ses voisins, pour en faire notre ... associée', quoted by A. Larcher, 'D'un réformisme à l'autre: la redécouverte de l'identité culturelle vietnamienne, 1900–1930', *Etudes indochinoises*, 4 (1995) p. 91.
6. Expressed in many books and articles, including: *La lutte pour l'existence et l'association pour la lutte* (1881) and *Le transformisme. Evolution de la matière et des êtres vivants* (1883). Quoted by D. Deschamps, op. cit., pp. 283–4; see also C. Fourniau, *Annam-Tonkin, 1885–1896. Lettrés et paysans vietnamiens face à la conquête coloniale* (L'Harmattan, 1989) p. 187.
7. See also C. Fourniau, op. cit., pp. 150–56 and 185–96.
8. '... l'épée ne saurait plus être pendant longtemps qu'un agent de conservation ... le moment est venu de laisser l'agriculture, les travaux publics, féconder, exploiter ce que l'épée a conquis.... Nous sommes

entrés dans la période essentiellement utilitaire'. Quoted by A. Neton, *Delcassé (1852–1923)* (Académie diplomatique internationale, 1952) p. 122.

9. G. Leclerc, *Anthropologie et colonialisme* (Fayard, 1972) p. 41.

10. H. Deschamps, *Méthodes et doctrines coloniales de la France* (Presses Universitaires de France, 1947) p. 145.

11. C. Gilbert, 'Les Congrés coloniaux de 1900. Une nouvelle politique coloniale?', Master's thesis, IHPOM, Aix-en-Provence, 1992. See also G. Leclerc, op. cit., p. 44.

12. T. E. Ennis: *French Policy and Development in Indochina,* University of Chicago, 1936. See in particular ch. 5, 'French Administrative Accomplishments', pp. 78–110. The debate regarding Association was not confined to the French. In Great Britain, it was also lively. See R. Albertini, *The Administration and Future of the Colonies* (Doubleday, 1971) p. 38.

13. '. . . [il vaut] mieux connaître l'indigène et l'associer à nos intérêts'. Quoted by C.-R. Ageron, *France coloniale ou parti colonial?* (Presses Universitaires de France, 1978) pp. 189ff..

14. 'Il n'existe qu'une défense sérieuse de l'Indo-chine: c'est la défense par l'indigène', J. Ajalbert, *L'Indo-Chine en péril* (Stock, 1906) p. 14.

15. Letter from Broni (interim Governor-General) to the Department, 15 November 1905. ANSOM Indochina AF c. 9 d. 54.

16. 'Il est indispensable que nous redonnions à la race annamite l'essor d'antan . . . la colonisation par l'indigène est la seule vraiment efficace'. Interview with Eugène Jung, *L' Avenir économique de nos colonies* (Félix Juven, 1908) p. 15.

17. However, in order to discredit the policy of Sarraut and Varenne, those who favoured an 'iron hand' approach repeatedly declared throughout the 1920s that the 1908 revolt was the result of the liberal measures adopted by Beau.

18. '. . . [en ce qui concerne] les écoles purement indigènes, très nombreuses, dont l'institution est antérieure à l'occupation française . . . nous nous efforçons présentement de faire évoluer vers une organisation plus moderne et plus conforme à nos conceptions pédagogiques'. Report of 25 July 1907, AOM GG 7707.

19. 'Les Annamites, du moins la partie riche et élevée de la population, réclament davantage. Ils envoient déjà leurs fils en France et en Algérie pour suivre les cours de nos Lycées. Tout récemment, une Association indigène pour l'encouragement aux études secondaires et supérieures s'est constituée à Hanoi. Ce mouvement ne va pas sans inconvénients. S'il est souhaitable que les jeunes Annamites, alors que leur éducation première est achevée, aillent en France se perfectionner et se spécialiser dans nos grandes Ecoles, par contre leur séjour dans les internats de nos Lycées n'a guère donné jusqu'ici de résultats bien remarquables'. Ibid.

20. Letter to Chailley of 10 May 1907, AE PA 11 vol. 3.

21. See also: C.-R. Ageron, *L'anticolonialisme en France de 1871 à 1914* (Presses Universitaires de France, 1973) pp. 21–32. Two main lines of thought underlay the French socialists' anticolonialism. On the

one hand, in accordance with Marxist doctrine, they rejected the imperialism which prompts nations to conquer others solely for the benefit of the few. On the other, the tradition of 1789 and 1848 – that of the Abbé Grégoire and Victor Schoelcher – stressed the right of native peoples to justice and equality before the law. See R. Thomas, 'La politique socialiste et le problème colonial de 1905 à 1920', *Revue française d'Histoire d'Outre-Mer* (1960) 2, p. 223.

22. *L'Humanité*, the Socialist newspaper gave less coverage to colonial matters than did, for example, the more conservative newspaper, *Le Temps*. See: G. Pio, *Le socialisme français et le phénomène colonial à travers "L'Humanité", 1904–1907*, Masters dissertation, Aix-en-Provence, 1975.
23. '[L'oeuvre républicaine] serait singulièrement ralenti sil le parti radical et radical-socialiste n'avait pas à compter avec ses opposants d'extrême-gauche', C. Devilar, *L'Opinion*, 3 January 1914.
24. '. . . au point de vue des droits élémentaires de vie, de liberté et de propriété', Francis de Pressensé in the Chambre des Députés, 2 April 1909. It is worthy of note that he made no mention of equality, that other basic right. See also C.-R. Ageron, *France coloniale ou parti colonial*, op. cit., p. 154.
25. '. . . [leur] avis sur tout ce qui n'est pas action politique pure [et la possibilité de] présenter des observations sur le budget, sur les impôts, sur les travaux publics, en un mot sur tout ce qui n'est pas attribut de la souveraineté', *JORF, Documents parlementaires* (1911) p. 1709.
26. '. . . dans les colonies la préoccupation du sort des indigènes est primordiale et centrale, et cela dans l'intérêt même des colons. Pour que nos nationaux, en effet, puissent avoir aux colonies le moyen d'appliquer utilement leurs capitaux et leur industrie, n'est-il pas nécessaire qu'ils y trouvent une main d'oeuvre abondante et robuste, des intelligences éveillées capables de s'adapter aux exigences de l'agriculture et de l'industrie modernes?' M. Viollette, preface to the booklet by H. Bobichon: *La Politique indigène dans les Colonies françaises* (Bureaux de la France d'Outre-Mer, 1912) p. 4.
27. J. Ajalbert, *L'Avenir du Tonkin* of 25 May 1911.
28. '. . . c'est en comptant sur une bonne volonté dont vous avez donné des preuves que nous [la Ligue] espérons vous convaincre qu'il y a autre chose et plus à faire que votre note ne l'indique'. Letter of 8 June 1914. ANSOM PA 9c.5.
29. '. . . tendant à séparer les Français des indigènes dans les corps délibérants, et à créer des Chambres pour chaque catégorie'. Indochina Committee, at its meeting of 20 February 1913, ANSOM CFOM R.75.
30. Delivered in front of one of the oldest temples in Hanoi and a symbol of Vietnamese nationalism, this speech seems to have been widely distributed and had a significant influence on the Vietnamese élites. For a detailed analysis of this speech see A. Larcher, *L'Ordre par la concorde. . .*, op. cit.
31. 'L'humanité totale doit pouvoir vivre de la richesse totale répandue sur la planète', A. Sarraut, *Grandeur et servitude coloniale*, p. 111.

32. '... les garanties primordiales du statut individuel, de droit personnel que nous réclamons pour nous-mêmes', ibid., p. 121.
33. '... dans le moment même où nous affirmons une possibilité d'évolution, nous affirmons par l'idée même d'évolution, l'impossibilité de conclure à la réalisation immédiate de l'égalité politique et administrative', ibid, p. 166.
34. See S. Quinn-Judge, 'Ho Chi Minh: New Perspectives from the Comintern Files', Le Failler P. and Mancini J.-M. (eds), op. cit., pp. 171–88.
35. 'On ne peut tout de même pas oublier que nous sommes un nombre infime de Français au milieu de 20 millions d'indigènes, que nous avons sur 1500 kilomètres de frontières des Etats turbulents dont les intentions seront hostiles ou réservées suivant que nous serons plus ou moins forts nous-mêmes. Pour cela, il faut que nous ayons avec nous la masse des indigènes et nous ne pouvons pas ignorer plus longtemps l'ambition du peuple annamite de prendre part au gouvernement de son propre pays', Le Quotidien of 5 April 1926.
36. '... tout au fond de la question indochinoise, il y a cette question d'égards', Chronique de l'Institut colonial français of 30 November 1926. ANSOM PA 28 c.3 d.63.
37. '... le respect des principes de la Déclaration des Droits de l'Homme suffirait à créer l'apaisement', L'impartial français, 5 May 1926.
38. '... la lutte serait livrée entre Annamites et non pas contre nous'. Letter of 1930 or 1931 to Robin (a senior French civil servant in Indochina) in ANSOM PA 28 c.3 d.60.
39. Resistance movement to the French under Emperor Ham Nghi which was active between 1885–96.

6 Reformism and the French 'Official Mind': The 1944 Brazzaville Conference and the Legacy of the Popular Front

Martin Shipway

To what extent did the French colonial administration prepare the end of their empire in Sub-Saharan Africa? The short answer must surely be that this was never the explicit or conscious aim of official French colonial reformers, whether the reforms under consideration are those of the Popular Front in 1936–37, those which emerged from the 1944 Brazzaville Conference (which are the particular subject of the present chapter), or even those which resulted from Gaston Defferre's Loi-cadre of 1956. Colonial reform was designed at every stage to consolidate and rationalise the empire, though the means chosen to achieve these ends in 1936, 1944 and 1956 were presented in humanitarian, social reformist and democratic terms, rather than in terms of imperial efficiency. Thus, however short-sighted, untimely or just plain clumsy it may now appear, the declaration which headed that part of the Brazzaville recommendations which dealt with political reform reflected nothing more than an official, political and public consensus regarding the future of empire, which is to say that it had one:

> Before examining this part of the agenda, the French African Conference at Brazzaville decided to establish the following principle: The ends of the civilising mission accomplished in the colonies exclude any idea of autonomy,

all possibility of evolution outside the French bloc; also
excluded is the eventual establishment of self-government
in the colonies, even in a distant future.[1]

This represented a 'bottom line' to which neither Marius
Moutet, Colonial Minister in 1936 (and again Minister of
Overseas France in 1946–47) nor Defferre and his ministerial
colleagues in the mid-1950s, nor de Gaulle even as late as
1958 would have objected. If, however, the question is
reformulated in terms of the possible decolonising impact,
intended or otherwise, of colonial reformism, a more subtle
and complex answer is indicated. This chapter approaches
this broader question by examining the continuities and
contrasts between the Popular Front's colonial reforms and
those of the Brazzaville Conference which convened less
than eight years later, in January–February 1944. In the
case of the Popular Front, as is argued elsewhere in this
volume, a large part of the answer lies in the disillusionment which resulted from the rapid demise of the Blum
government in France, and the defeat of the expectations
raised by what Catherine Coquery-Vidrovitch calls 'the time
factor'.[2]

But the same is not true for the Brazzaville Conference,
whose recommendations were implemented in one form
or another and formed the basis for French colonial policy
for most, if not all, of the period which led up to independence. To what extent therefore, were the senior colonial
officials who deliberated at Brazzaville inspired by the
precedent of 1936–1937, and in what ways had the agenda
changed in the face of world war, French defeat and
occupation and the emergence of a potential international
challenge to the legitimacy of the French empire? Did the
French empire effectively if unwittingly move closer to African
decolonisation in 1944? Before considering these questions
in relation to the Conference agenda, prior questions need
to be addressed concerning more fundamental bases for
continuity, namely those of personnel and of professional
ethos.

BRAZZAVILLE AND THE *ESPRIT DE CORPS*

Even in the face of world war, eight years is not a long time in the life of a bureaucracy with a strongly defined identity. Continuities in the formulation of policy and its reception between 1936 and 1944 should therefore not surprise us, especially given the fact that the French colonial administration was largely spared the worst of the French *'abîme'* of 1940–44. This is not to deny the significance of the shifts in policy which resulted from the demise of the Popular Front or from the change of regime which every French colonial dependency experienced at least once at some point between the defeat of France in June 1940 and the Liberation. Nor is it to deny the sincerity of their attachment to one or other camp in the internecine rivalries occasioned by defeat. But these changes were experienced by men with a shared background and with a shared outlook and values as administrators which arguably went as deep as political loyalties. Where other than in the depths of the Sahel could a senior administrator write in his annual report, under the heading: 'important political events', that there was nothing to report for 1944?[3]

The ostensible defining principle for membership of the corps of Governors and Governors-General which formed the deliberative body at Brazzaville was loyalty to de Gaulle. Thus, the administrations of the four colonies of Afrique Equatoriale Française (AEF) and Cameroun had all run the gauntlet of 'rallying' to de Gaulle during the so-called 'trente glorieuses de l'Afrique Française' in July-August 1940.[4] Félix Eboué, then Governor of Tchad, was rewarded for his leadership in this process with the post of Governor-General at Brazzaville, and in this capacity chaired the Brazzaville Conference. His Secretary-General at Fort-Lamy, Henri Laurentie, moved with him to Brazzaville, and was largely responsible for organising the conference (although he did so from his new job as Director of Political Affairs in the Colonial Commissariat at Algiers).[5] When Afrique Occidentale Française (AOF) came under Gaullist authority with the establishment of the Comité Français de la Libération Nationale (CFLN) at Algiers in July 1943, only the Governor-General, Pierre Boisson, and four out of seven Governors were replaced. Two of the three remaining Governors attended at Brazzaville, including Governor Toby of Niger already quoted, but a third, Governor Croccichia of Guinée, failed to attend, perhaps unable to stomach the occasion. According to Cohen, only about 20 officials in AOF lost their jobs as a result of the Gaullist takeover.[6]

The relative importance of Gaullism in terms of administrative ethos can thus easily be exaggerated. On the other hand, being in the right place in 1940 served as a boost to a number of flagging careers, including those of Pierre Cournarie, who became Governor-General of AOF in 1943, and Pierre de Saint-Mart, whose career had started alongside Félix Eboué's in pre-1914 Oubangui-Chari, and who became Governor-General of Madagascar in 1944. Both men earned opprobrium at Brazzaville and subsequently as staunch conservatives, condemned by Laurentie as representatives of what the younger man saw as the 'bureaucratic mind':

> ... honest, hard working and ultimately impermeable to any kind of general thinking. ... This obstinate refusal to change or make any kind of revolution, this insistence on maintaining colonial paternalism indefinitely is the most deplorable state of mind there is these days.[7]

If impeccable Gaullist credentials were thus no guarantee of a capacity for innovative or imaginative policy making, a far more significant characteristic of the corps of Governors is revealed by the fact that 18 of the 21 deliberative members (including Laurentie and his deputy, Georges Péter), were graduates of the Ecole Nationale de la France d'Outre-Mer (ENFOM).[8] Sometimes criticised for instilling in its cadets an unthinking conformism, ENFOM nonetheless enjoyed the distinction of being the only one of the French *grandes écoles* at this date (that is, before the foundation of the Ecole Nationale de l'Administration in 1947) whose purpose was to train administrators.[9] Given that the ascendancy of ENFOM dated largely from the 1920s, this was probably the first time that such a majority of 'Colo' graduates could have been mustered at the rank of Governor and above. Brazzaville was thus a significant defining moment for the French colonial service's *esprit de corps*, although this too was to act more as a brake than as a spur to reform.

Was there then any obvious correlation between participation at Brazzaville and sympathy with the reformist
spirit of 1936–37? The exception rather than the rule in
this regard was the case of Félix Eboué. Appointed Governor
of Guadeloupe by Moutet in 1936 but recalled to Paris
after the fall of the second Blum government, Eboué was
then posted by Georges Mandel to the remote and (until
1940) unimportant colony of Tchad, which was seen as a
demotion. As a Socialist party member, freemason, and as
the highest-ranking Afro-Caribbean officer in the colonial
service, Eboué had more reasons than most people to side
with de Gaulle, or at least against Vichy, in 1940. There
were some noted left-wingers at Brazzaville, especially André
Latrille, Governor of Côte-d'Ivoire, whose report on forced
labour practices was one of the conference's undoubted
highlights. The sponsor of Félix Houphouët-Boigny's early
political career in the colony, Latrille reported with glee
in 1945 that his palace at Abidjan was denounced by local
European planters as a 'repaire de staliniens'.[10]

On the whole, however, the service's well-known ex-Popular
Front men were absent from the roster at Brazzaville, largely
because they had failed to attract the attention or approval
of the makeshift administration in Algiers. This was particularly the case of three significant absentees: Robert
Delavignette, who served in Moutet's private office (cabinet)
in 1936–37, and was Director of ENFOM in occupied Paris,
and still serving as Director of ENFOM in occupied Paris;
Louis Mérat, Moutet's Director of Economic Affairs, also in
post in the Ministry in Paris; and Marcel de Coppet, Governor-
General of AOF from 1936 to 1939, who was removed as
Governor-General of Indochina in 1940 after his attempt
to rally to de Gaulle. Hubert Deschamps also, who served
on Léon Blum's staff at Matignon in 1936–37, and whose
wartime career included a succession of Governorships in
Djibouti, Côte-d'Ivoire and Sénégal, was not posted by the
new régime, though he was in Algiers in late 1943 and
contributed a heartfelt defence of assimilation doctrine to
pre-conference briefings.[11] The prevalence of officials who
owed their posts to the often fortuitous circumstances in
which they had rallied to the Gaullist cause led to something
of a backlash after Moutet's return to the Ministry in January

1946. Mérat in particular, appointed Moutet's *directeur du cabinet*, railed against the vacuous and slavish invocation of the Brazzaville recommendations, which, he complained, 'remain the Tablets of the Law, revealed truth, the taboos which may be alluded to but never questioned'.[12] However, the choice between conformism and resistance to the undoubted bandwagon effect of the 'esprit de Brazzaville' was a separate issue from adherence to, or rejection of, its underlying doctrinal principles or policy implications. Any continuities between the 'spirit' of 1936–37 and the revived sense of purpose and innovation (however theoretical) which prevailed at Brazzaville lay, not so much in individual contributions, as in the ethos of the Colonial Corps as a whole. The point is not that senior officials sympathised with Popular Front policy (though many of them had), but that they responded positively to the decision taken in 1943–44, as in 1936–37, to take colonial policy seriously and bring it to some extent into the political limelight. To put it another way around, this is what happened when, in Daniel Hémery's suggests, when the Ministry of Colonies started to show signs of political imagination.[13]

COMPLETION AND INNOVATION: THE BRAZZAVILLE AGENDA

In the preparations for the Brazzaville Conference, its sponsors and organisers said little to confirm or deny continuities between past and present policy. References to the Popular Front, for example in the colonial policy debate which took place in the Consultative Assembly at Algiers in January 1944, may well have been suppressed for fear of rocking the CFLN's rather rickety vessel, held together by a volatile alliance of Gaullists, Communists, Socialists, various resistance groups and opportunists (or the 'simples combattants', 'poètes d'action' and 'politiques' whom de Gaulle identifies in his Memoirs).[14] On the other hand it was considerably more important, both at Brazzaville and in the preceding debate, to stress the innovative nature of the Conference, whose central purpose was to convince an international audience of France's generosity and efficiency as a colonial power: the new French regime must not be seen, either by the peoples of the Empire, or by potentially hostile international opinion, to lag behind the pronouncements of their Allies in colonial matters. As Pierre-Olivier Lapie, a future colonial spokesman for the SFIO, put it in the Consultative Assembly's debate:

> Do I need to draw attention to the terms of the Atlantic Charter? While all around are rethinking the colonial world, France cannot afford to remain silent or absent. It is only just that, following the deeds and declarations of the Americans, the South Africans, and the Australians, France should also make itself heard, and act.[15]

Thus, unlike the Popular Front's efforts eight years before, Brazzaville was staged in large part as a propaganda event, the content of which was largely subordinate to its presentation. Nonetheless, the Conference may be seen as part of an ongoing colonial debate stretching back over the preceding 20 years or more, in which elements of continuity and contrast were offset by genuine efforts to innovate.

There was one obvious way in which the new colonial administration, headed by the CFLN's Commissioner for the Colonies, René Pleven, sought to underline a break with the past. This consisted in an effort to play down what were seen as the essentially economic preoccupations of interwar colonial policy, derived from the grandiose pragmatism of Albert Sarraut's colonial doctrine, but given emphasis by the Depression. As Pleven argued in his opening speech at Brazzaville:

> The fact that economic affairs were given priority in this way reflected the preoccupations of a period dominated by an unprecedented world crisis; in large measure that crisis stemmed from a financial view of the world according to which money was no longer the servant of mankind but an end in itself.[16]

Economic policy at Brazzaville was now to take its rightful place, subordinate to social and political issues. In this sense, the new agenda was considerably more ambitious than the preceding Governors' Conference of 1936, as Pleven was careful to point out.[17] Nonetheless, the economic themes dear to Sarraut and his successors in the interwar years were reiterated in the Conference agenda, including the old chestnut of the *pacte colonial*, which was ritually denounced:

> On the spurious grounds of sharing out the world's resources, nations are quite happy even today to internationalise the old doctrines of the protectionists (or even, some might say, of the slave trade): Africa, or so the story goes, will provide raw materials for the industrialised continents in return for finished manufactured goods.[18]

Calls for a mass social policy to provide an umbrella of health care, education and administrative efficiency were duly debated and reflected in the Conference recommendations. But here as elsewhere at Brazzaville, the governors found their deliberations proceeding along well-worn intellectual grooves. Historians have provided partially overlapping interpretations of the Brazzaville Conference's economic recommendations. For Jacques Marseille, the watchword at Brazzaville was one of caution, as the governors set out modest plans for colonial industrialisation which had already been exceeded in scope by colonial planning under Vichy.[19] More recently, Frederick Cooper has placed the deliberations at Brazzaville in a long line of imperial 'fantasies' which are crucial if we are to understand the 'imagined communities' which the French colonial administration was seeking to establish. The social vision presented by the Brazzaville Conference was thus one in which Vichy's modernising, corporatist fantasy of Africans working in a largely imaginary industrial sector was tempered by a partial reversion to the more traditional colonial view of Africans as peasants tied to the land.[20] Of course, as Cooper further shows, neither vision met the realities of rapid postwar social and political development in French colonial Africa.

The shift in emphasis away from economic considerations was thus largely illusory or, at least, a matter of presentation rather than substance. In most areas, there was little to distinguish either the rhetoric or the content of Conference recommendations from past policy, though the semi-public forum of Brazzaville enabled the Governors to lend freshness to general principles of French colonial policy which were far from innovatory, such as the recommendation that French should be used as the exclusive medium of education. This sounded like a ringing endorsement of French Republican principles applied to the colonies, but in fact reflected nothing more than general practice in Sub-Saharan Africa (but not in Indochina, Madagascar or North Africa, all of which were exempted from the principle).[21] On the other hand, the Governors' relative freedom of manoeuvre at Brazzaville allowed them to cut through some issues of considerable controversy. This was particularly the case concerning forced labour, an issue which went to the heart of liberal aspirations to colonial humanism. As Cooper has argued, the Popular Front government's efforts to bring the French labour regime in line with the ILO's 1930 Convention banning forced labour had foundered on the ingenuity with which the colonial administration and employers were able to disguise or justify recruitment practices. The frankness with which the administration in Vichy-controlled French West Africa (up to November 1942) discussed the necessity of forced labour thus at least had the virtue of allowing abusive practices to be identified, as a first step along the way to reforming them.[22] Even so, the Governors at Brazzaville were relatively cautious in their recommendations, in part because they were committed to maintaining a crippling colonial war effort which would have been unsustainable without the forcible recruitment of African labour. Nonetheless, the Conference welcomed Governor Latrille's report on forced labour in Côte-d'Ivoire, and accepted his five-year plan for phasing it out across French Africa, as well as his proposal for a one-year Service Obligatoire du Travail (Obligatory Labour Service) to replace it (the name of which somewhat infelicitously recalled the Vichy regime's Service du Travail Obligatoire which press-ganged French workers for forced labour in Germany). In the end, the Brazzaville recommendations were superseded on this subject by the law passed in the First Constituent Assembly on 30 March 1946, known as the 'Loi Houphout-Boigny' after its chief sponsor, which brought forced labour to an end 16 years after the ILO Convention had been passed.[23]

The authors of the Conference agenda placed emphasis on two key areas in which innovation was expected: Native Policy ('la politique indigène') and the idea of a new

Federation of the French empire. In neither area did the Conference delegates pass recommendations meeting the expectations invested in them. In the first of these areas, the Conference organisers were to some extent the victims of their own propaganda. Félix Eboué's circular of 8 November 1941, drawn up following a much smaller conference held at Brazzaville, had been distributed by the Gaullists in London under the grand title 'La nouvelle politique indigène', and was widely used as evidence of French new thinking on colonial issues.[24] Elevated to figurehead status, and rather tactlessly cited by Pleven and others as proof of France's lack of racial prejudice,[25] Eboué himself was hardly the right man for the publicity foisted upon him. Nearing retirement, with a dignified career stretching back to 1909, he was unable to participate fully in the Conference owing to ill health and advanced hearing difficulties; he died in May 1944, aged 60, on leave in Cairo. Moreover, Eboué's circular seems to have been intended as an attempt to reinstate and reinvigorate existing colonial practice, rather than to reform it. His authority and inspiration came from the doctrine of indirect rule developed and practised in Morocco by Marshal Lyautey, whom the circular quoted directly, but Eboué seems also to have taken note of the British system of Indirect Rule in Northern Nigeria. In the present context the key point is that Eboué thus took issue with the classic Republican doctrine of Assimilation, and with the policy of Direct Rule associated with it:

> To attempt to make or remake a society in our own image, or at least according to our own mental habits, is to court certain failure. The native has a certain code of behaviour, laws, a nation, which are not the same as our own. We will bring him good fortune neither by applying the principles of the French Revolution, which is our revolution, nor by judging him according to the Napoleonic Code, which is our code of laws, nor by replacing his chiefs with our administrators, who will think for him, but not with him.[26]

As various commentators have shown, however, by declaring his position in a long-running, not to say stale and rather sterile, doctrinal debate, Eboué was overlooking the complexity, or rather the necessary inconsistency, of his own policy proposals. On the one hand, he proposed placing greater reliance on traditional chiefly structures of local rule, although these did not necessarily exist in French Equatorial Africa, or had been substantially eroded or compromised by half a century of French administration. In this way, Eboué was repeating the interventionist errors of his British counterparts, applying principles of indirect rule where they were less appropriate than in the Northern Nigerian emirates from which Lugard had drawn his original inspiration.[27] On the other hand, other key elements of Eboué's policy were classic assimilationism, particularly his idea for a 'Statut des Notables Evolués', which followed in a direct line from earlier attempts, including those of the Popular Front, to extend the rights and duties of citizenship to carefully selected and screened African (or Indochinese, Malagasy, North African . . .) beneficiaries of French education. This was an idea which had been applied already by Eboué in French Equatorial Africa, although by his own admission at the conference it had met with little success: by early 1944 only 125 individuals had been accorded the status of 'notables évolués'. (literally, 'evolved dignitaries').[28]

The debate on 'Native Policy' at Brazzaville revealed further how difficult it was for experienced colonial practitioners to reconcile their own expertise and pragmatism with the need to agree on a fresh-sounding and unequivocal declaratory policy. René Pleven opened the debate by polarising the issues, thus compounding the earlier error of proclaiming Eboué's circular as brand-new:

> He stated that there was a classic controversy between two theses: what one might call the Eboué thesis which argues that natives should develop within traditional institutions, and the thesis to which he would not necessarily wish to attach the label 'assimilationist', but which does in fact argue that, since French civilisation is the most advanced, we should make every effort to bring natives up to its standards.[29]

Although no doubt pulling their punches out of respect for the ailing Eboué, the Governors refused to bow out of the ring. The text of the recommendations reflected some of the spirit of Eboué's ideas, in particular the high-minded but rather unspecific concern with the moral well-being of African families, and his proposal for a 'Statut des Notables Evolués' was adopted. But the Governors expressed a clear preference for the assimilationist 'thesis' which Pleven had clumsily sought to discredit, and which squared so easily with the Republican rhetoric required for domestic consumption. Within the context of a semi-public colonial conference, it would be difficult to fault the logic of Governor Raphaël Saller's restatement of the classic assimilationist defence:

> Evidently, the purpose of our civilisation is to bring civilisation to others. So we civilise, that is to say, we are not content to provide merely a surplus of material well-being, but we also impose moral rules and intellectual development. And by what methods and according to whose example should we do this, if not by our own methods and according to the example of our own civilisation, in the name of which alone we may speak? For what authority would we have to speak in the name of the civilisation whose people we are trying to improve?[30]

Indeed, it was precisely this easy assumption of public rhetorical manners which irritated Léon Pignon, Laurentie's assistant at the Conference and a future High Commissioner in Indochina. As he argued, the fact that the Conference had opted for the solution which had inspired French colonial policy going back to the Revolution was all the more surprising given that the assimilationist stance had been taken, 'not by parliamentarians unversed in colonial matters, but by experienced colonials, in touch with customs and with sociology'.[31] In other words, what concerned Pignon, himself a former brilliant student at ENFOM, was that the Governors were letting the technocratic side down and turning against the logic of their training and experience. What Pignon and his senior but iconoclastic colleague Henri Laurentie were perhaps unprepared to accept was that consensus on this issue was never likely to be possible, as it would have required the resolution of a probably quite fruitful tension between field experience on the one hand, which dictated solutions on the basis of pragmatism and limited resources, and on the other the basic ideological assumptions on which the conception of a French Republican colonial service was founded.

Promotion of the Eboué 'thesis' involved a subterfuge by which it was deceptively presented as a brand-new doctrine, rather than as one term in a long-standing if rather false debate. By contrast, the second key area of the Conference agenda, concerning constitutional reform, centred on proposals which were so startlingly innovative that the corps of Governors stopped short of recommending more than that the issue be taken up by a competent body of constitutional experts. The proposals in question originated in Laurentie's ambitious scheme for a French Federation, according to which the French empire would be transformed into a new federal structure, with metropolitan France at the top of a hierarchy of French dependencies graded according to their capacity for political and administrative autonomy. No doubt the Governors acted properly in postponing discussion of what even Laurentie later disarmingly admitted was 'a brilliant idea lacking any concrete reference to reality'.[32] Nonetheless, the idea was to provide the germ of subsequent French policy leading to the construction of the French Union. As the present author has shown elsewhere, Laurentie's thinking was also to have a profound if multivalent impact on subsequent policy making in the Ministry of Colonies, particularly with regard to Indochina.[33]

The Federal idea falls largely outside the perspective of the present chapter, because it properly belongs to the post-Brazzaville period, but the Governors' dismissal of Laurentie's proposals, which after all had the backing of René Pleven, the CFLN and the Consultative Assembly at Algiers, is nonetheless of relevance concerning the continuities in the administrative ethos thus revealed at Brazzaville, as the Governors rejected not only Laurentie's proposals but also implicitly a key part of the analysis which accompanied them. Laurentie's explication of the internal rationale for restructuring was largely uncontroversial (because vague and general), and indeed much of it was reproduced word-for-word in the truncated constitutional recommendations eventually published:

France's political power should be exercised precisely and rigorously across the whole of the Empire.

At the same time the colonies should enjoy considerable administrative and economic freedoms. Equally, the colonial peoples should be able to express these freedoms for themselves, and their freedom should be developed and extended gradually in such a way that they are involved in the running of their own countries.

Even at this level there was room for misunderstanding: a further paragraph was suppressed, perhaps because it contradicted one of the Conference's most enduring recommendations, which was that the African territories should elect representatives to an Constituent Assembly in liberated Paris.[34] However, there was also a substantial international dimension to Laurentie's analysis, which the Governors chose to overlook. As suggested above, the Brazzaville Conference was in large measure conceived to meet a perceived international challenge to the French empire, occasioned by the defeat of 1940, by the emergence of the two soon-to-be-Superpowers, both ideologically committed in their different ways to anti-colonialism, and by the steps which had already been taken by the Dutch and British to reform their imperial structures. Laurentie's response to this challenge was to think the unthinkable, on the premise that the Empire might collapse or be wound up if sufficient structural reforms were not implemented. Indeed, he subsequently extended his analysis to encompass the nationalist threat to French imperialism in the Middle East and Indochina, and the more diffuse but nonetheless disturbing manifestations of 'colonial crisis' elsewhere in the Empire.[35]

By contrast, the collective response of the Governors was essentially one of presentation. This much was clear already from the position paper prepared by one of Laurentie's senior colleagues at Algiers, Emile de Curton, in the run-up to the Conference, in which he suggested that there were two relevant questions concerning French imperial policy:

1. What is our imperial policy?
2. What is the French imperial policy which we should be declaring to a foreign audience?

Discounting the idea of federation as impractical, his answer to the second question set the tone for the Conference:

> We should adopt whichever definition sounds noblest. We should affirm that we intend unreservedly to grant the most generous of statutes to our colonial possessions. In all international colonial conferences we should show ourselves to be the most liberal, least imperial of nations. But at the same time we should take every opportunity to declare, with no less resolve than General Smuts has shown, that our national sovereignty must remain intact, and that those nations which have had sole responsibility for their colonies in the past must retain that exclusive responsibility in the future.[36]

It was this thinking which was apparently behind the declaration quoted at the outset of this chapter, although the Governors' defiance could no doubt have been couched in a less blunt, more nuanced form of words. Aside from the teasing question of what was in the Governors' minds when they categorically ruled out 'self government', the declaration was in essence a statement to the effect that they would continue to cling to the old certainties, according to which French colonialism was a matter of sole French sovereignty and responsibility.

Continuities between the Brazzaville Conference and the ill-fated reformist efforts of the Popular Front may thus be identified in both positive and negative terms. On the one hand, Brazzaville gave senior French colonial officials, or at least those who found themselves in the right place (politically and geographically) in 1943–44, the opportunity to review and expand upon items on the reformist agenda, including issues of economic reform, on which subject Brazzaville had little new to say, or colonial citizenship (also addressed by the Gaullists in Algeria, which fell outside the Brazzaville Conference's competence). The Governors were also able to move, however cautiously, towards implementing long-delayed humanitarian reforms which the Popular Front had been unable to implement, such as the reform of the labour regime. Crucially, the Conference was a forum in which long-standing debates could be revisited, and a shared set of values reaffirmed, even when the process of reaffirmation brought disagreements to the surface, some of them ill-tempered. Indeed, we should beware of over-emphasising the importance of the doctrinal differences expressed in the ten days of closed sessions at Brazzaville, or of reading history backwards when interpreting the views of iconoclasts such as Laurentie. Brazzaville was not a failure simply because the most radical views on offer were rejected; rather the Conference succeeded in passing the rec-ommendations with which the colonial service as a whole no doubt felt most comfortable. Laurentie remained a colonial liberal and an institutional maverick, and his confidential analysis of France's imperial dilemma remained controversial; indeed, he was ultimately sidelined as a result of some or all of these facts. Nonetheless, he remained a loyal and committed colonial official.[37]

On the other hand, it is difficult to resist the notion that more *should* have changed in the world-view of colonial administrators between 1936 and 1944, and that the continuities between the two reformist episodes should have been less marked. In 1936, after all, the French colonial service could still operate on the assumptions that colonial reform was exclusively an internal affair, that the system of 'European collective security for Empire', as Ronald Robinson has termed it, was still in place,[38] and that the terms of a liberal colonial agenda could still be decided without reference either to the outside world or to colonial public opinion. By 1944, these assumptions were at the very least questionable. And yet the corps of Governors deliberating at Brazzaville largely chose to ignore or deny this new outlook, while insisting on an agenda which would hardly have seemed radical in 1936. Ironically, whilst Pleven, Laurentie and their colleagues wrote Brazzaville off as a partial failure, they were obliged to pretend officially, in keeping with the conveniently intangible 'esprit de Brazza-ville', that the Conference was the *nec plus ultra* of colonial reformism.

In conclusion, it is this cultivated illusion of reformist liberalism propagated by the French administration that perhaps provides part of the answer to the broad question posed at the outset. While the Brazzaville Conference did nothing deliberately to further decolonisation, which was after all an alien concept in 1944, it unwittingly provided some of the building blocks for more substantial progress. Although this would provide the subject of a far wider study than the present chapter allows, the idea may be briefly, and tentatively, illustrated in two ways. First, the Conference's recommendation that the colonies elect representatives to an eventual Constituent Assembly (a practice which was maintained into the Fourth Republic) brought about one of the most distinctive features of the French decolonisation process. In effect, it provided the mechanism by which African and Malagasy politicians could gradually assume a leadership role in French colonial politics, both in Paris and at home, and gain local legitimacy and authority from legislative advances. Thus the Malagasy *députés* were able to take credit at home from the 'loi Houphouët-Boigny' of March 1946 banning forced labour.[39] Secondly, more generally, and borrowing one of the central arguments of Frederick Cooper's recent work, the Conference recommendations established a conceptual and discursive framework by means of which members of an emerging colonial élite could lay claim to the reality behind or beyond the grandiose rhetoric of the 'esprit de Brazzaville'. In other words, the old-fashioned assimilationist doctrines, which Laurentie and his fellow progressives had so criticised, were finally turned to advantage in a transformed colonial and international environment. By adapting to their own ends the Republican arguments of equality and fraternity, Africans could make the case for creating their own political parties, labour movement, social legislation, a large measure of self-government (after 1956) and, eventually, independent statehood.[40] This was surely an outcome which would have bewildered even the most liberal and outspoken members of the corps of Governors at Brazzaville.

Notes and References

1. La Conférence africaine française de Brazzaville, avant d'aborder cette partie du programme général qui était proposée à son examen a cru poser le principe ci-après: 'Les fins de l'oeuvre de civilisation accomplie dans les colonies écartent toute idée d'autonomie, toute

possibilité d'évolution hors du bloc français; la constitution éventuelle, même lointaine de self governments [*sic*] dans les colonies est à écarter.' Ministère des Colonies, *La Conférence Africaine Française* (Ministère des Colonies, 1945), hereafter cited as *Conférence*, p. 32.

2. 'le facteur temps', C. Coquery-Vidrovitch, 'Colonisation ou impérialisme: la politique africaine de la France entre les deux guerres', in *Le Mouvement social*, no. 107, April–June 1979, pp. 51–76.

3. 'Pas de faits particulièrement saillants en 1944' Gouverneur Toby, Rapport Politique, Niger, 1944: Centre des Archives d'Outre-Mer, Aix-en-Provence, Archives du Gouvernement-Général de l'AOF, 2G-44-22 (14Mi1853). As he continued: 'The population has calmly pursued the war effort of the last five years.' (Les populations ont continué dans le calme l'effort de guerre commencé 5 ans plus tôt.')

4. 'thirty glorious days of French Africa' (recalling the 'trois Glorieuses' of 1830)

5. B. Weinstein, *Eboué* (Oxford University Press, 1972). On Laurentie's subsequent career as Director of Political Affairs in the Ministry of Colonies and his role in policy making especially in Indochina, see M. Shipway, *The Road to War: France and Vietnam, 1944–1947* (Berghahn Books, 1996).

6. W. B. Cohen, *Rulers of Empire: The French Colonial Service in Africa* (Hoover Institute Press, 1971), pp. 169–70.

7. 'l'esprit "administrateur": ... honnête, travailleur et à la longue, imperméable à toute espèce d'idées générales... Cette espèce d'obstination à ne pas vouloir changer, à ne vouloir faire aucune révolution, à perpétuer indéfiniment le paternalisme colonial est la plus déplorable disposition d'esprit que l'on puisse trouver aujourd'hui.) Laurentie to Bayardelle, 4 Aug. 1944, Archives nationales (AN), Laurentie papers, 72AJ538. On Saint-Mart, see AOM, Fichier des anciens élèves de l'Ecole Nationale de la France d'Outre-Mer, 39APOM4; on Cournarie, see Denise Bouche, 'La réception des principes de Brazzaville par l'administration en A.-O.F.', in Institut Charles-de-Gaulle & I.H.T.P., *Brazzaville, aux sources de la décolonisation* (Plon, 1988), hereafter cited as *Brazzaville*, pp. 207–08.

8. Those who were not ENFOM graduates were Saint-Mart, Dagain (Sénégal) and Roguet (Tchad): *Brazzaville*, pp. 61–2. Formerly known as the Ecole Coloniale, ENFOM was still knowm informally as 'Colo'.

9. Cohen, op. cit.; for a more critical view see Louis Sanmarco, *Le colonial colonisé* (Editions ABC, 1983) pp. 49–50.

10. Rapport mensuel du Directeur des APAS, no. 395 APS, June 1945, AOM, 2G-45-115 (14Mi2704).

11. Gvr. Deschamps, 'Notes sur la politique coloniale', Algiers, 8 January 1944, AOM, Affaires politiques (AP), 2288/1. See Hubert Deschamps, *Roi de la brousse: Mémoires d'autres mondes* (Berger-Levrault, 1975). He subsequently resigned from the service when Pleven's successor as Minister, Paul Giacobbi, questioned his resolve in resisting Italian threats to Djibouti in 1941.

12. ('demeurent les Tables de la Loi, la vérité révélée, les principes 'tabous' auxquels on se réfère, mais qu'on ne discute pas'). Louis

Mérat, *Fictions . . . et réalités coloniales* (Sirey, 1946), preface by Marius Moutet, p. 25.

13. D. Hémery, 'Aux origines des guerres d'indépendance vietnamiennes: pouvoir colonial et phénomène communiste en Indochine avant la Seconde Guerre mondiale', *Le Mouvement social*, no. 101 (Oct.–Dec. 1977) pp. 4–35.

14. *Journal officiel de la République Française. Supplément. Débats de l'Assemblée Consultative Provisoire* (hereafter cited as *JOACP*), 1944, no. 6, 13 Jan. 1944; Charles de Gaulle, *Mémoires de guerre*, 3 vols (Plon, 1954–59 repr. 1970) t.II, *L'unité, 1942–1944*, p. 182.

15. (Ferai-je enfin état de certains termes de la Charte de l'Atlantique? Dans cette grande reconsidération générale du monde colonial la France ne peut demeurer muette, ni absente. Il n'est que juste qu'après les paroles ou les actes d'Amérique, d'Afrique du Sud, d'Australie, la France à son tour se fasse entendre et agisse.) *JOACP*, 13 Jan. 1944, p. 13.

16. (Cette sorte de primauté accordée à l'économique était le reflet des préoccupations d'une période dominée par une crise mondiale sans précédent, causée largement par des conception financières qui faisaient de la monnaie non plus l'instrument destiné à servir l'homme mais une fin en soi) *Conférence*, op. cit., p. 19. Albert Sarraut, *La mise en valeur des colonies françaises* (Payot, 1923).

17. See J. Marseille, 'La conférence des gouverneurs généraux des colonies (novembre 1936)', in *Le Mouvement social*, no. 101, Oct.–Dec. (1977) pp. 61–72.

18. 'Sous prétexte de répartition des matières dans le monde, on se contente volontiers, aujourd'hui encore, de transposer sur le plan international les vieilles doctrines protectionnistes, pour ne pas dire esclavagistes: l'Afrique, dit-on et écrit-on, fournira les matières premières aux continents industriels qui rendront à l'Afrique leurs articles fabriqués.' Programme général, AOM, AP/2288.

19. J. Marseille, *Empire colonial et capitalisme français: Histoire d'un divorce* (Paris, 1984) 344–46, and 'La Conférence de Brazzaville et l'économie impériale: "des innovations éclatantes" ou des recommandations "prudentes"?', *Brazzaville*, pp. 107–15.

20. F. Cooper, *Decolonization and African Society: the Labor Question in British and French Africa* (Cambridge University Press, 1996) p. 174.

21. See D. E. Gardinier, 'Les recommandations de la Conférence de Brazzaville sur les problèmes d'éducation', in *Brazzaville*, op. cit., pp. 170–80.

22. Cooper, op. cit., p. 153.

23. Ibid., pp. 178–80, 187–94. See also Hélène d'Almeïda-Topor, 'La question du travail forcé', in *Brazzaville*, op. cit., pp. 115–20.

24. Weinstein, *Eboué*, op. cit., pp. 270–4; the circular appears in Jean de la Roche and Jean Gottmann, *La fédération française* (Editions de l'arbre, 1945) pp. 586–627.

25. In itself, the choice of Mr Eboué is a supporting argument for our views on colonial affairs and is a clear indication of our position on racial policy.' ('Le choix de M.EBOUE serait à lui seul un argument

en faveur de nos conceptions coloniales et indiquerait clairement notre position à l'égard de la politique des races.'): Commissaire aux Colonies, 'RAPPORT à MM. les Présidents et Commissaires du C.F.L.N. Objet: Conférence des Gouverneurs d'Afrique [sic]', n.d. (late 1943), AOM, AP/2288/1.

26. ('Faire ou refaire une société, sinon à notre image, du moins selon nos habitudes mentales, c'est aller à l'échec certain. L'indigène a un comportement, des lois, une patrie qui ne sont pas les nôtres. Nous ne ferons pas son bonheur, ni selon les principes de la Révolution Française, qui est notre Révolution, ni en lui appliquant le code Napoléon, qui est notre code, ni en substituant nos fonctionnaires à ses chefs, car nos fonctionnaires penseront pour lui, et non en lui.'). 'La nouvelle politique indigène', in de la Roche and Gottman, op. cit., p. 585. Also quoted in Elikia M'Bokolo, 'French Colonial Policy in Equatorial Africa in the 1940s and 1950s', in Prosser Gifford and William Roger Louis (eds), *The Transfer of Power, Decolonization 1940–1960* (Yale University Press, 1982) pp. 172–92.

27. M'Bokolo, op. cit. On the 'working misunderstandings' which arose from the misapplication of Indirect Rule in, e.g. central Nigeria and Tanganyika, see D.C. Dorward, 'Ethnography and Administration: A Study of Anglo-Tiv "Working Misunderstanding"', *Journal of African History*, XV, 3 (1974) pp. 457–77, and John Iliffe, *A Modern History of Tanganyika* (Cambridge University Press, 1969) pp. 322–4.

28. Conférence Africaine Française, procès-verbal, 3 Feb. 1944, AOM, AP/2288.

29. ('Il montre qu'il y a une espèce de controverse classique entre deux thèses: celle qu'on pouvait appeler "la thèse EBOUE" qui désire l'évolution de l'indigène à l'intérieur des institutions traditionnelles, et celle qu'il a hésité à qualifier de l'assimilation, mais qui, en fait, considère que, la meilleure civilisation étant la civilisation française, nos efforts doivent tendre à en approcher les indigènes le plus possible). Ibid.

30. ('. . . que le but de notre civilisation est de civiliser. Donc nous civilisons, c'est-à-dire que nous ne nous contentons pas d'apporter un surcroît de bien-être matériel, mais aussi une règle morale et un développement intellectuel. Et par quelles méthodes, en proposant quel exemple, sinon les méthodes que nous pratiquons nous mêmes et l'exemple de notre propre civilisation. Nous ne pouvons parler qu'au nom de celle-ci, autrement quelle autorité aurions-nous pour parler au nom de la civilisation des peuples que nous voulons élever?'). Ibid.

31. ('non par des parlementaires ignorants des questions coloniales, mais par des coloniaux expérimentés, très au courant des coutumes et de la sociologie'.) 'NOTE sur l'attitude de la Conférence de Brazzaville à l'égard de la circulaire du 8 novembre 1941', ref.LP/SC, n.d., AOM, AP/2288/5. On Pignon's subsequent career, see Shipway, op. cit.

32. ('une idée brillante à quoi l'objet concret ferait défaut'.) In the report of the Commission of Experts, 'Commission chargée de l'étude

des mesures propres à assurer aux Colonies leur juste place dans
la nouvelle constitution française', AOM, AP/214. On the debates
and findings of this Commission, see Shipway, op. cit., pp. 41–63.

33. Ibid., *passim.*

34. ('On veut que le pouvoir politique de la France s'exerce avec précision
et rigueur sur toutes les terres de l'Empire. On veut aussi que les
colonies jouissent d'une grande liberté administrative et économique.
On veut également que les peuples coloniaux éprouvent par eux-
mêmes cette liberté et que leur liberté soit peu à peu formée et
élevée afin qu'ils se trouvent associés à la gestion de la chose publique
dans leur pays.') Programme général, AOM, AP/2288. & *Conférence*,
op. cit., p. 32. The suppressed paragraph read: ('On ne veut pas
que par une extension arbitraire, les colonies s'entremettent dans
les affaires de la France métropolitaine. On veut encore moins que
les milieux politiques et d'affaires de Paris soient en mesure de
faire pression sur les affaires intérieures des colonies.') The
recommendation ran counter to the spirit of the Federal idea,
although it subsequently became an integral part of French Union
politics (see also below).

35. See Shipway, op. cit., pp. 64–83.

36. (1. – Quelle est notre politique impériale?
2 – Quelle est la politique impériale française que nous devons
proclamer être la nôtre aux yeux de l'étranger?
'... adoptons tout de suite la définition la plus noble. Affirmons
sans réserves notre désir absolu de donner à nos possessions coloniales
le statut le plus généreux. Montrons-nous dans toutes les conférences
coloniales internationales la nation la plus libérale, la moins
impérialiste. Mais proclamons, en toute occasion, avec la même
énergie que le Général Smuts, que notre souveraineté nationale
sur nos colonies doit rester intacte, et que les nations qui ont été
seules responsables de leurs colonies dans le passé doivent en rester
entièrement responsables dans l'avenir') Notes sur le programme
général de la conférence de Brazzaville, 20 Oct. 1943, AOM, AP/
2288/4.

37. By misreading his official role, and by anachronistically equating
'liberalism' with support for decolonisation, J. I. Lewis erroneously
condemns Laurentie as a 'colonial conservative', in 'The French
Colonial Service and the Issues of Reform, 1944–8', *Contemporary
European History*, 4, 2 (1995) pp. 153–88.

38. 'Imperial Theory and the Question of Imperialism After Empire',
in R. F. Holland and G. Rizvi (eds), *Perspectives on Imperialism and
Decolonization* (Cass, 1984) p. 84.

39. See M. Shipway, 'Madagascar on the Eve of Insurrection, 1944–
1947: The Impasse of a Liberal Colonial Policy', *Journal of Imperial
and Commonwealth History*, 24, 1 (Jan. 1996) pp. 72–100.

40. Cooper, op. cit., clearly presents his arguments in a far more nuanced
and elaborate form, and is chiefly concerned with the second and
third items on this list.

Part II   Diversity of Outcomes

7 The Popular Front and the Colonial Question. French West Africa: An Example of Reformist Colonialism

Catherine Coquery-Vidrovitch

The Popular Front government left a limited but nonetheless important legacy in Africa. It came to power in a context in which colonisation was accepted by everyone, with the exception of a very small minority on the radical left. There was therefore no question of the Popular Front government being anticolonial; it was instead, according to Colonial Minister Marius Moutet, a question 'of adapting the saying of President Léon Blum to the realities of overseas France: that is, of establishing a maximum of social justice and human opportunities within the context of colonialism'.[1]

To a certain extent this was not pure rhetoric, at least in French West Africa. Unlike Indochina, where the Popular Front government was obliged by the activities of Vietnamese revolutionaries to adopt a repressive policy, or Algeria, where the cautious reform proposals did not even see the light of day because of the hysterical reaction of the *colons*, the few reforms introduced in French West Africa can be seen in many ways as the first steps on the road to decolonisation.

THE CONTEXT

The anticolonial strand of opinion within the French left in respect of black Africa had been energetically expressed since before the First World War, particularly by progressive Christians such as Pierre Mille and Félicien Challaye

155

in the *Cahiers de la Quinzaine*. As a young man, the former had accompanied the explorer Savorgnan de Brazza on his third mission in 1905 to remedy the abuses in the Congo. In 1936 he was one of the few to express his hostility to capitalist and oppressive colonialism that set out to humiliate the native population, and he asserted his impatience to see the colonised regain their independence.[2] As for Daniel Guérin, who was also a fervent anticolonialist, he was expelled from the Socialist Party in 1937.[3] However, these were the views of a minority within the French left.

The Communists, who were still vilifying colonial abuses in the Chamber of Deputies in 1930, notably on the occasion of the vicious repression of the Baya revolt in Equatorial Africa, had changed their tune since the coming to power of Hitler in Germany. The priority was now the struggle against European fascism since the solution to the colonial problem would follow naturally from the defeat of fascism. But for now the colonies had to unite their forces against the fascist threat in Europe. Furthermore, the 1931 International Colonial Exhibition in Paris had popularised colonialism: 208 exhibitions and conferences were held during this year, a figure which rose to more than 500 by the time of the 1937 Colonial Exhibition and which shows the growing French enthusiasm for the affairs of 'greater France'.

Under these conditions, there was no question of the Socialists challenging colonialism *per se*. The new Colonial Minister, Marius Moutet, was explicit in this respect: 'It is a reality . . . the disappearance of which at the present time would lead to more drawbacks and bring more disadvantages than advantages. It is a fact that we have taken responsibility for certain countries that we call colonies. . . . It is a question of incorporating them into our national life.'[4]

This moderate position can also be explained by the context of the economic crisis from which France was only just emerging: the only French worker to whom the same minister alluded in his inaugural speech to the Conference of Governors-General (see below), was the '*tisseur des Vosges*' (Vosges weaver) who knew that 'his work and productivity [were linked] to the increase in earnings of the Senegalese peasant farmer'.[5]

The Popular Front government coalition did not therefore at any stage question imperialism itself, even in its programme for government. Léon Blum belonged to the most reformist wing of the Socialist Party, which believed that it was not sufficient to promote reforms within the imperial framework but thought that it was necessary to prepare the peoples under French domination for independence. But he remained very cautious in his proposals and in his ministerial statements spoke simply of the great expectations raised by our programme'[6] on French soil: in this, he was thinking particularly of North Africa, where his most spectacular colonial failure awaited him. This was the so-called 'Blum-Viollette' project, which, to the dismay of the *colons*, sought to promote a limited extension of the right to vote to Algerian Muslims.[7]

THE PROPOSALS

The government's proposals for the colonies were therefore limited in scope. They were restricted to the launching of a wide-ranging fact-finding mission to the colonies. The task was entrusted to a parliamentary commission chaired by the President of the Human Rights League, Henri Guernut, a former Radical minister. Its brief was to 'lay the basis for the renovation of the French colonial system [by seeking to establish] the needs and legitimate aspirations of the populations living in the colonies, the French protectorates and the mandated territories' and it was to 'propose any reform that seemed appropriate'.[8]

One of the three sub-commissions was given responsibility for black Africa and Madagascar. The planned enquiry was to be exhaustive, covering everything from population to food supplies, living conditions, standard of living, work and education, and also including administrative and political problems and 'the aspirations of the natives'. But its establishment took time. Although numerous questionnaires were sent out, only two researchers actually set out for the colonies in 1937 (André Gide and André Philip) and, as a result of the decline in popularity of the Popular Front, the commission suspended its activities in 1938.

The commission did not bring its work to a conclusion, but the mass of information it collected is available and provides a treasure house of data for historians. For example, a 202-page report was produced on the condition of women in west Africa, which remains the first substantial report on the subject.[9]

However, while the Socialists did not have any difficulty accepting the existence of the colonial empire, they nevertheless set out, on the one hand to put an end to the abuses to which it had given rise, and on the other, to organise economic and social life better, so as to make it both more humane and more productive.

This was the aim of the second major initiative: to call a colonial conference in order to examine all the problems and put forward solutions. This was not a new idea, as there had been a series of such conferences since 1917. The objective of the first of these had been to draw the Empire into the war effort. More recently, against the background of economic collapse, the government had, in 1933–34, organised the Conférence Economique de la France Métropolitaine et d'Outre-Mer, the resolutions of which were published in full in 1934. The Popular Front government was too short-lived to be able to do the same. But the archives show clearly what the group's intentions were: following so closely after a recent conference on the same theme, the initiative to organise yet another conference indicated a clear willingness to seek out innovative solutions. This was evident particularly in the social sphere, although there was to be no substantial change in economic policy apart from the adoption of certain principles.

It was in its social programme and through its promotion of grass-roots development projects that the Popular Front's plans differed both from those of previous governments and from those of the Vichy government a few years later. In 1931, Edmond Giscard d'Estaing (the father of the future President of the Republic) had, in a report on the economic situation in AOF, recommended that 'priority [should] be given to centres of economic development' – later to be called '*pôles de développement*' – which meant concentrating on 'useful Africa' (the ports and the coast), and abandoning the poor areas of the interior to themselves.[10] The Conference of Governors-General, despite being composed largely of top colonial officials just as its predecessors had been, attached central importance to feeding the population, and thus to the struggle against the widespread famines that were endemic. The recommendation was not only to institute a stocking system and create reserve granaries but, above all, to give priority to food crops over cash crops. From this sprang an interest in local, village-based development projects such as well boring, small-scale engineering projects and grants to cooperatives (called 'sociétés de prévoyance'). In preference to railways and ports, central importance was attached to 'permanent silos, to protect against fire and insects; wells built of cement; the construction of footpaths and permanent bridges with a view to abolishing the odious system of work in lieu of taxation; craft training and rural schools; and the creation of new economic and cultural lifestyles in rural areas'.[11]

The traditional scorn for so-called 'micro-measures', that had been evident since they were first proposed by Albert Sarraut after the First World War, was thus abandoned. Large development projects were rejected: 'out of a fear of proposing projects that were too small in scale, overambitious plans had been adopted'.[12] Serious reservations were expressed about the Office du Niger, a huge agricultural development project that had been launched in 1931 and that swallowed up a third of the entire loan budget for French West Africa in 1937: 'It is a huge project, but it demands great sacrifices of Africans from other regions [and also of those from the area[13]] who, for the most part, do not have the basic necessities'.[14]

Despite the evident similarities, which will be discussed below, the proposals put forward by the Governors-General differed significantly from the recommendations of the previous colonial conference. Prestige projects were rejected in favour of small-scale works that were likely to bring immediate benefits. The aim was to reduce the drain on the budget that experts represented by substituting 'as far as possible the foreman for the engineer'.[15] As far as large scale development projects, port development and railway construction were concerned, caution was recommended; and as for laterite roads, they were preferable to large metropolitan-style roads so as to 'avoid wearing out the population through the imposition of useless demands' and the excessive use of forced labour.[16]

The objective was to base economic growth on expansion of the local market, which essentially represented a transposition to the colonies of the objective of metropolitan social policy for the benefit of workers. There was thus a recognition, for the first time, of the need to reduce the tax burden: as one epithet of the time put it, 'in order to be social, a colony must be fiscal'.[17] This was the first item to be put on the agenda of the Conference by the Colonial Minister. The Minister did not intend to challenge the arguments in favour of taxation on moral and educational grounds – the idea that taxes were 'an incentive to work' – that had traditionally been put forward by the *colons* and the central administration, but he recommended 'prudence' and 'the maintenance of a balance between the needs of society and the needs of individuals'.[18] A substantial reduction in the rate of the head tax was recommended and it was to be replaced by an income tax, the introduction of which had consistently been opposed by the *colons*. But the budget crisis prevented the government from going any further.

Health care, 'an essential instrument of our colonial policy',[19] was recognised as another priority because it was seen as an 'essential complement to food security' and an arm in the battle against the 'demographic problem'. What was new was the means recommended: instead of sedentary health care based in urban areas and focussing on curative medicine, the emphasis was placed on 'mass medical intervention', concentrating on prevention and carried out in the bush by mobile health teams and surgeries which had hitherto only been used in exceptional cases by anti-sleeping sickness teams.

Schools policy was also important, but this was no longer aimed at creating a 'political élite' that risked degenerating into an 'intellectual proletariat', but rather at providing the rural masses with the cultural basis for their economic development. The aim was less to 'instruct' the young than to 'prepare them for their social function'. As a result, the emphasis shifted from general to vocational education, because 'in our colonies, it is often more useful to train good peasant farmers, rural craftsmen and foremen . . . than black or yellow *bacheliers'*. In other words, the assimilationist ideal was being abandoned in favour of English-style pragmatism.

Overall, this health and education programme, which the government did not have time to implement, did not differ substantially from the ideas put forward some 15 years earlier in the second, social section of the Sarraut programme which had since then become the bible of enlightened colonialists, despite the fact that its actual achievements had never lived up to expectations.

This well-meaning socio-economic programme was itself the result of contemporary prejudices against industrialisation in the colonies. Indeed, in line with the 'new deal', an economic programme was announced that was based on 'the command economy run in the general interest', so that 'capital is invested in the colonies, remains there, works there and is put to productive use, instead of constantly seeking to escape in the shortest possible time'. Thus, the idea was developed of 'industrialising' within the framework of 'economic decentralisation' adapted to the new demands of capitalism. In the Minister's *cabinet*, Louis Mérat put forward the idea of colonial 'development', a new word that was more open than the *'mise en valeur'* that had been put forward hitherto, and this development was to be 'without restriction, with the aim of creating, as rapidly as possible, the complex economies necessary to secure their own future'.[20] In Indochina, Paul Bernard, an economist who was an associate of Edmond Giscard d'Estaing, had no hesitation in proposing to resolve the social and political crisis in Vietnam through industrialisation.[21] But AOF had not yet reached this stage. The Bordeaux palm oil traders were too attached to their advantages to agree to relinquish their metropolitan privileges. As for Moutet himself, he was influenced by his conception of rural socialism and had no wish to promote a western industrial model amongst a peasant-based population. The Popular Front's colonial economic policy thus represented a backward step when compared with the technocratic ideal of the industrial economy put forward by the 1934 Conference. The prerequisite for growth was what Marius Moutet called the 'Franco-colonial economy', in other words the expansion of the imperial import market by raising the purchase price for agricultural products so as to increase the purchasing power of the peasant farmers.

The idea of large-scale industrialisation in the colonies continued to raise the fear of proletarianisation of the colonial populations. This was the reason why, ultimately, the Popular Front decided to tread carefully and stepped back from taking such a decision. No overall programme was proposed, although the question of industrialisation was put to the Chamber of Deputies in 1936 and again in 1937. But the *Inventaire économique de l'Empire* published the following year still confined itself to the consideration of commercial ties, mining and agriculture: nothing at all was said about industrial potential.[22] On the eve of the Second World War, imperial policy had taken a considerable step backwards.

OUTCOMES

On the economic front, the Popular Front did not have time to implement its programme. It did not even have the courage, when confronted by Béline, the formidable head of the Office du Niger project, either to modify the Office's programme or to reduce its cost. Nevertheless, despite these limitations, the Popular Front's social programme produced results that were far from negligible.

The most symbolic was the ratification of the Convention on the Right to Work, which had been agreed by the International Labour Organisation in 1930 but over which France had until then dragged its feet, precisely because of the issue of forced labour in the colonies.

The most dramatic measure was without doubt the promulgation in 1936 of the law authorising trade unions.[23] As a result, AOF became the only territory on the continent to allow Africans – the 'natives' as they were called in those days – to join a union. Until then, only informal mutual aid societies had existed, and even they were only just about tolerated under the law. As for professional associations they came under the Code pénal, because it was traditionally considered that the colonial population was not sufficiently educated to appreciate the benefits of labour laws. It should be noted that trade union rights were not extended to AEF, which was considered too backward, or to Indochina, but for the opposite reason: the high level of politicisation of the Vietnamese meant that it was too risky for the government, even a Socialist one, to legalise trade unions.

Following the introduction of the labour legislation, which in theory was applicable only to those people who had received a French education but in practice was granted fairly freely, there was a hitherto unprecedented level of unrest.[24] By the end of 1937 there were, in Dakar, nearly 8,000 union members grouped into 42 trade unions and 16 professional associations. Between 1,500 and 2,000 workers went on strike, starting with dockers in the port of Dakar, then in Rufisque, Saint-Louis and Kaolack, followed by the bakers, the Huileries et Savonneries de l'Ouest, and so on. Their action brought forward the publication of social decrees implementing the eight-hour day (nine in the rest of AOF) and covering such subjects as accidents at work and the working conditions of women and children. There were also plans to reorganise the Inspection du Travail and, most importantly, a whole range of collective agreements were signed with a view to regulating relations between employers and workers in private companies.

But the bell tolled for the Popular Front in 1938 when, in the railway town of Thiès, a railway workers' strike was put down by the army. Official figures showed six dead and 90 injured. The intervention revealed the gulf that was opening up between, on the one hand, the *évolués* – regular waged workers who were covered by the government's policy on collective agreements – and on the other, day labourers or workers who were taken on to undertake specific tasks and who sought, through violence and bloodshed, to challenge the colonial system itself.[25]

The second social initiative, which was adopted in 1937, may appear anodyne. It was nonetheless very popular and enjoyed immediate success because of the extreme unpopularity of forced labour for public works. Under this system, any adult who was physically fit was compelled to work on public projects without pay for an average of between

8 and 15 days per year. The requirement did not in itself
appear excessive, but it was extremely badly organised and
subject to all sorts of abuses: in particular, men had to
travel and feed themselves at their own expense and the
obligation for the most part fell upon the same group of
people, those who were chosen by their chiefs as the most
wretched and least able to defend themselves. The system
was not abolished but became optional and could be avoided
by the payment of an additional tax.

However, they did not go so far as to promulgate the
French metropolitan Code du Travail (although this was
done in Indochina, where forced labour was abolished as a
result). In black Africa, this would have to wait until 1952.
Nevertheless, the speed with which the system of forced
labour for public works disappeared is testimony to the
success of the measure. And the colonial administration
also gained, because the extra tax payments served to pay
the wages of workers whose freely consented labour gave
far greater satisfaction than that of workers recruited under
the previous compulsory system.

There is no doubt that trade union freedoms provided
an outlet for African political expression. But the time for
anticolonial radicalism had not yet arrived, at least in black
Africa. In 1936, the Senegalese Socialist Party had been
created in the Four Communes with a view to the elections and with the tacit approval of the colonial administration, yet in 1936 it was the moderate Galandou Diouf
who was elected to the French parliament against the
Socialist Lamine Gueye. The election campaign took place
in an atmosphere of extraordinary enthusiasm, because this
privileged moment gave the hope of obtaining all the improvements wanted from the colonial regime. But there
were important ambiguities: the politicised élite, brought
up under the French system, confined itself to demanding
partnership with the coloniser, so as to administer themselves, but did not challenge the colonial system itself. This
was in accord with the colonial ideals of the French Socialists. As for those who were not *originaires* of the Four Communes, their aim was above all to gain French nationality,
as this was considered the best guarantee of equality with
metropolitan France.

Their main means of expression was the press, which was subject to strict censorship. For this reason, it was important to find 'assimilated' directors who would enjoy a privileged status and who, ideally, would have French nationality and not therefore be subject to the *indigénat*. One of the most active newspapers was the *Voix du Dahomey* in Dahomey. Although he had a reputation for socialist-leaning views, the then governor, de Coppet, conducted a judicial investigation into its activities in 1933–34: '[The newspapers] are displaying their sympathy for certain extreme forms of communism. . . . Their influence is deplorable. I have resolved to fight them'.[26]

The tough stand of Governor de Coppet, who was later to become the open-minded, Socialist Governor-General of AOF, was no doubt linked to the visceral loathing of French socialists and communists for each other. The newspaper nonetheless defended itself: '[We are] not rebels, or revolutionaries, or communists, but servants of France'.[27] Following the arrest of the newspaper's directors and long and difficult legal proceedings, the trial finally came to an end in June 1936 during the Popular Front's period of office. The verdict, which took into account a wide range of mitigating circumstances, finally imposed a symbolic fine on the defendants of just one franc, and thus effectively represented a victory for the élite.[28]

The élite had in fact for the most part rallied to the Popular Front. African political radicalism was very much a minority phenomenon, confined to a small number of African immigrants in France. Thus, Tiémoko Garan Kouyaté, who had been expelled from the French Communist Party in 1933 for refusing to accept its change of direction, launched the Union des Travailleurs Nègres during this period, and also introduced a clandestine pamphlet into Africa under the title 'Histoire d'un merle blanc' (Story of a White Blackbird), which was effectively the manifesto of the 'Ligue de Lutte pour la Liberté des Peuples du Sénégal et du Soudan'. This appears to be the first time that a black African organisation called for national independence: 'We are struggling for the right of the peoples of Senegal to govern themselves . . . by forming an independent nation-state. . . . The League's groups are preparing the workers and peasant farmers for the decisive battles of the Senegalese peoples'.[29]

It was not long before the Union des Travailleurs Nègres, which had been infiltrated by the police and emasculated by the Communist Party, disintegrated. At the end of 1936 its newspaper, *Le Cri des Nègres*, ceased publication. Kouyaté had just founded a new paper, *Africa*, under the subtitle 'the most African independent voice for the defence of the interests of African peoples'. Well aware of the paralysed state of the independence movement, he changed direction at the time of the Popular Front. First of all, he created the Fédération Française des Jeunesses Africaines in Dakar, but failed, despite all his efforts, to have it recognised by the local administration. Again through his newspaper, he proposed to the Governor-General of AOF, de Coppet, a series of 'Guiding Principles for the Transformation of the Overseas Territories'. With immediate political independence no longer in prospect, there remained the federal alternative that had been put to the French government in the 'White Blackbird' manifesto: 'Either resolutely assimilate native *évolués en masse*, or adopt the federal system of dominions within a French framework.'[30]

Kouyaté was a lone voice. It seems that even Lamine Gueye was not aware of his activities. Shortly before the outbreak of war, he tried to launch the first Association des Etudiants de l'Ouest Africain before falling back on an assistance committee for native soldiers at the end of 1939. He was shot by the Germans in 1942.

CONCLUSION

Its inner coherence notwithstanding, the Popular Front's social programme still lacked one essential element: the time that would have been necessary to leave more than traces in its wake. Many of its decisions were barely followed through, if only because of the bureaucratic sclerosis and parochial conservatism of colonial officials on the ground who were in general not especially sympathetic to socialist ideas. While it is true that there were changes at the top – the new Governors-General of AOF and AEF were both convinced socialists – officials at the lower levels of the administration often dragged their feet.

The most enduring result of the Popular Front, apart from certain specific measures such as the abolition of forced labour for public works and the establishment of trade union freedoms, came less from its political initiatives in the strict sense than from the mind-set that inspired them. The conviction spread that human development would guarantee economic take-off, rather than the other way round. Nevertheless, the means proposed remained cautious: it was not a question of abolishing or restraining the colonial economy, but rather of making it more efficient and establishing it on healthier foundations, even if these foundations were not themselves fundamentally questioned.

However, despite its limited achievements and economic timidity, the Popular Front did hasten the development of the embryonic African nationalist movements, even if only by opening the door to trade union activities. The trade unions became the mouthpiece of a certain acculturated élite, in both the tertiary sector and the working class (the teachers' and railwaymen's unions), that allied itself with popular urban movements. Those Africans who had unanimously welcomed the coming to power of the Socialists with an outburst of joy followed by an unprecedented intensity of political activity had not been completely misguided. Indeed, it is for this reason that contemporary historians see the decolonisation process as beginning in 1936. It is no accident that the Popular Front initiated a highly symbolic change: the Musée de l'Ethnographie, which had been given this name at the beginning of the scramble for Africa in 1880, was renamed in 1938 the Musée de l'Homme.

Notes and References

1. 'Pour reprendre en l'adaptant aux réalités d'outre-mer la formule même du président Léon Blum, [d']extraire du fait colonial le maximum de justice sociale et de possibilité humaine'. Marius Moutet to the Ministry of Colonies, undated note, AOM, PA 28 (1).
2. F. Challaye, *Souvenirs sur la colonisation* (Picart, 1935).

3. D. Guérin, *Au Service des colonisés* (Editions de Minuit, 1954).
4. 'C'est un fait... dont la brusque disparition à l'heure actuelle engendrerait plus d'inconvénients et de dangers que d'avantages. C'est un fait que nous avons pris en charge certains pays que nous appelons des colonies.... Il s'agit de les incorporer dans l'ensemble de notre vie nationale'. Marius Moutet papers, ANSOM, PA 28.
5. '... l'activité de son travail et la productivité de celui-ci [étaient liés] au gain accru des cultivateurs sénégalais'. D. Hémery, 'Aux origines des guerres d'indépendance vietnamiennes: pouvoir colonial et phénomène communiste en Indochine avant la Seconde guerre mondiale', *Mouvement social*, 101 (1977) pp. 3–36.
6. '... la grande attente qui s'attachait à notre oeuvre'. This is a quotation from Léon Blum's investiture speech in May 1936.
7. For a discussion of the Blum–Viollette project, see Chapter 11 by France Tostain.
8. '[Elle reçut pout tâche de] préparer la rénovation du système colonial français [en recherchant] quels sont les besoins et les aspirations légitimes des populations habitant les colonies, les pays de protectorat et sous mandat.... La commission d'enquête proposera toutes réformes qui paraîtront opportunes'. Constituent Law of 30 January 1937.
9. See G. Lydon, 'The Unravelling of a Neglected Source: A Report on Women in Francophone Africa in the 1930s', *Cahiers d'Etudes Africaines*, 147 (1997) pp. 555–84.
10. '... privilégier les "centres de gravité économique" – ce qu'on appellera plus tard des pôles de développement – c'est-à-dire de mettre l'accent sur l'Afrique "utile" (celle des grands ports et de la côte) et d'abandonner les zones pauvres de l'arrière-pays à elles-même', E. Giscard d'Estaing, *Rapport au Ministre sur sa mission en Afrique occidentale*, Dec. 1931–Mar. 1932, ANSOM, Affaires Politiques, p. 539.
11. '... le silo en dur contre l'incendie et les insectes, le puits cimenté, le chemin vicinal et le pont définitif destiné à supprimer l'odieux travail de prestation, l'école artisanale et l'école rurale, nouveau cadre de vie économique et culturel du pays', Marius Moutet to the Ministry of Colonies, undated note, AOM, PA 28 (1).
12. '... par peur de voir trop petit, on a vu trop grand', Marius Moutet circular, August 1936, AOM, PA 28 (1).
13. Author's note.
14. 'C'est une grande entreprise, mais le sacrifice est lourd pour l'Africain des autres régions qui, la plupart du temps, manque l'essentiel', Conference of Governors-General, *Rapport sur le fonds d'équipement colonial*, ANSOM, Affaires Politiques, 2529.
15. '[en remplaçant] en maints cas l'ingénieur par le contremaître', Foreword to the resolutions of the Conference of Governors-General, in ibid.
16. '[afin] de ne pas fatiguer la population par des exigences inutiles', *Rapport sur le fonds d'équipement colonial*, op. cit.
17. 'Une colonie, pour être sociale, doit être fiscale', Note on the ac-

tions undertaken by the Colonial Ministry since 4 June 1936, ANSOM, Affaires Politiques, 2529.

18. '. . . [il recommandait de] garder la mesure [et de] tenir la balance égale entre les besoins de la collectivité et les besoins des individus', Marius Moutet circular, op. cit.
19. '. . . moyen essentiel de notre politique coloniale', Foreword to the resolutions of the Conference of Governors-General, op. cit. Subsequent quotations in this section also come from this conference.
20. . . . sans aucune restriction, en visant la réalisation à plus ou moins brève échéance, *d'économies complexes* nécessaires d'ailleurs à leur propre défense', L. Mérat, 'Note sur l'économie aux colonies', ANSOM, Affaires Politiques, 2529. Mérat subsequently wrote a book entitled *L'Heure de l'économie dirigée d'intérêt général aux colonies* (Sirey, 1936).
21. P. Bernard, *Les Nouveaux aspects du problème économique indochinois* (Nouvelles Editions Latines, 1937), p. 96.
22. G. Lacam, *L'Inventaire économique de l'Empire* (Sarlot, 1937).
23. A decision of 9 July 1936, applied in the decree of 11 March 1937, legalised trade unions and professional associations. A second decree of 20 March 1937 extended the metropolitan law on conciliation and arbitration to AOF, *J.O. du Sénégal*, 19 April 1937, pp. 326ff..
24. N. Bernard-Duquenet, *Le Sénégal et le Front Populaire* (L'Harmattan, 1985) pp. 131–8.
25. Iba der Thiam, *La Grève des cheminots du Sénégal de 1938*, Masters dissertation, Université de Dakar, 1972.
26. '[Les journaux] manifestent des sympathies pour certaines formes outrancières de communisme. . . . Leur influence est détestable. J'ai résolu de les combattre', Archives Nationales du Bénin, confidential circular 788A/AP, 18 Nov. 1933.
27. 'Ni révoltés, ni révolutionnaires, ni communistes, mais serviteurs de la France', *La Voix du Dahomey*, Nov. 1933.
28. C. B. Codo, *La Voix du Dahomey*, Doctoral thesis, Université de Paris VII, 1978.
29. 'Nous luttons pour le droit des peuples du Sénégal à disposer d'eux-mêmes . . . en formant un Etat national indépendant. . . . Les groupes de la Ligue préparent les ouvriers et les paysans aux grandes batailles décisives des Peuples sénégalais', AOM, Fonds SLOTFOM, III, 53. See also P. Dewitte, *Les Mouvements nègres en France, 1919–39* (L'Harmattan, 1985).
30. 'Ou bien assimiler résolument les indigènes évolués en masse, ou bien adopter le système fédératif des dominions dans le cadre français', *Africa*, 8, Apr.–May 1936.

8 Women, Children and Popular Front's Missions of Inquiry in French West Africa*

Ghislaine Lydon

On 4 July 1938, the French Minister of the Colonies wired the Government of West Africa requesting information on the 'administrative action [taken] in favour of the civil liberties of indigenous women in AOF'.[1] In response to this inquiry, the interim Governor-General submitted a lengthy account which concluded that the predicament of African women was little different from that of slaves. He ended by stating which policies had been implemented in AOF to redress the situation. It is in any case significant that the status of African women was a concern at a time when the Popular Front government was about to step down.

Although this period in French history is well known to historians, few have recognised its significance in African history. Many contributions in this volume evaluate whether Popular Front rhetoric actually translated into concrete action, whether fleeting ideals left a long-term mark in any colonial context. Whatever the verdict, it is clear that several regions of AOF witnessed a significant shift in the respective attitudes of both colonisers and colonised during the mid- to late 1930s. Colonial policy in this period opened a window of opportunity for Africans to contest the status quo. This was true for working men, but it also applied to women and children who became the focus of legal reform.

The Popular Front government led by Léon Blum naturally was inclined to address the needs of the working class. As France's first Socialist Minister of the Colonies, Marius Moutet launched an ambitious parliamentary commission

170

to investigate thoroughly the social situation in the overseas territories. Broad issues were targeted by the commission, but in the case of French West Africa, at least, this rather novel concern came to the fore: the predicament of women and children. As they represented more than half of the labour force in many parts of Africa, focusing on traditionally invisible workers was a sensible, albeit avant-garde, move. But how did this fit into the overall colonial agenda of the Popular Front government, and what impact did this concern have on the administration of the colonies? After discussing the Popular Front government's colonial mission, and its main component, the Parliamentary Commission of Inquiry, this chapter examines the reasons behind an official concern for women's prerogatives.

THE POPULAR FRONT'S COLONIAL MISSION

In the campaign leading to the Popular Front victory of May 1936, politicians appealed to humane ideals such as the equal rights of the people of all nations. On the colonial issue, Léon Blum had recommended, in 1927, 'that colonial legislation moves towards independence, towards self-government like in the Dominions . . .'.[2] The anti-colonialist factions of the Communist and the Socialist parties, although in a minority, remained committed to indigenous independence movements.[3] In the wake of the electoral victory, however, the newly formed Popular Front government did not have a coherent colonial programme. Colonial affairs remained peripheral for they scarcely raised any interest in French public opinion. The government's attention was quickly absorbed with matters of domestic urgency including the rise of fascism throughout Europe.

The Minister of the Colonies, Marius Moutet, an expert in colonial affairs, was committed to the needs and aspirations of indigenous peoples. Indochina, where he served for many years, was the colony he knew best. He also had a distant affinity with sub-Saharan Africa as his father once managed a trading post in Dahomey.[4] Before joining the Ministry, Moutet shared Blum's opinion about the future

of colonial rule. But once in office, Moutet's stance shifted
and notions of autonomy and 'self-government' were never
mentioned again by this government. Instead, the
overarching principle of France's colonial *mission civilisatrice*
was firmly upheld. In one of his first statements, Minister
Moutet assured that the Socialist government would *guarantee*
the management of France's overseas empire.[5] The assistant director of Moutet's *cabinet*, Robert Delavignette, for
his part, resolved the ideological dilemma in these terms:
'the colonial sin, we accept it with an afterthought of guilt
and a will to reform'.[6]

The turn-around was so complete that even an idealist
such as André Gide, during his visit to Senegal in the summer
of 1936, apparently said: 'I think that the natives would
be less happy without us.'[7] Like Delavignette, Gide was very
influential in the Popular Front colonial office, and a key
member of the Parliamentary Commission discussed below.
It is said that Gide, a close friend of Marcel de Coppet,
was consulted by Moutet before de Coppet's nomination
as Governor-General of AOF.[8]

As soon as he took office, the new Minister for the Colonies' first priority was the so-called 'famine file'. Moutet
was appalled at how previous colonial administrations' actions, or lack thereof, had aggravated famine situations, as
in the case of West Africa in 1914 and Indochina. He warned
that, faced with any signs of food-scarcity, colonial officers
should never be passive and that 'a *colonial system is not
viable when it is not energised from within by the natives who
should benefit from it*'.[9] Later, Moutet called a conference in
Paris in order to deliberate on colonial affairs at hand. In
his circular summoning the governors-general of the overseas territories, he itemised the essential ingredients of the
Popular Front's colonial agenda.[10] First, Moutet proposed
to reduce taxes which, since the Depression, had increased
consistently while the welfare of the masses had deteriorated. In AOF, tax reform entailed changes in the system
of *prestation*, an annual tax paid in days of obligatory labour
on public works. Secondly, Moutet ordered a down-sizing
of the colonial administration. Moutet's third point was that
colonial administrations must encourage local production
with price incentives. This would raise the general pur-

chasing power of the population and ultimately stimulate imports 'made in France'.

In addition, Moutet's aim was to curtail the power of trading companies whose unfair price fixing and usurious practices crippled local economies. Finally, Moutet proposed to abandon large public works and focus on small-scale, realistic projects in line with the 'grand programme des petits projects,' a rural plan proposed by Delavignette. He expressed his apprehension *vis-à-vis* colossal development schemes, such as the 'Office du Niger', which was expensive, inefficient and had negative repercussions in the French Soudan. He urged Governor-General de Coppet to investigate this matter further. Later, after hearing about the Office's despotic management and the use of forced labour, Moutet made a special trip to Soudan during his second ministerial visit to Africa.

The Popular Front's colonial programme, designed to address the wide-range of situations in all of France's colonies, was rather broad in scope. The colonial plan resembled more a list of ad hoc measures than a concrete plan. This was symptomatic of the Popular Front's lack of preparation for the task at hand, some authors argue.[11] Members of the Ministry of the Colonies later felt the need to implement a new plan of action.

THE PARLIAMENTARY COMMISSION OF INQUIRY IN AOF

Eight months after entering office, Minister Moutet and his cabinet chartered a Commission d'enquête parlementaire to investigate the 'political, economic and moral situation in the French overseas territories, namely in North Africa and Indochina'.[12] Oddly enough, sub-Saharan African colonies seemed a lesser priority. By determining 'the needs and legitimate aspirations of the populations' the Ministry could implement informed colonial policy.[13] In Delavignette's words, the commission was 'inspired by the preoccupations of the SFIO party and the Human Rights League, [it] served the ideal of social justice which animated the Popular Front on both the colonial and the domestic plane'.[14]

Although the Parliamentary Commission of Inquiry was founded by decree on 30 January 1937, nothing was undertaken for 6 months. It is difficult to account for the delay. Perhaps it was a question of internal co-ordination, or maybe funds were slow to clear. Colonial governments were finally instructed to advertise the creation of the commission in the official journals in August 1937.[15] Indigenous groups, associations, as well as private individuals, were encouraged to address their concerns directly to the commission headquarters in Paris.

The commission was composed of approximately 42 permanent board members.[16] It included some of France's finest experts in colonial matters of Africa, such personalities as Robert Delavignette, Hubert Deschamps, Henri Labouret, Lucien Lévy-Bruhl and André Gide. Henri Guernut, a delegate of the Human Rights League and the Minister of Education in the previous government, presided over the commission which was divided into three colonial sub-regions each headed by a secretary-general: Tunisia and Morocco (M. Hoffner), Indochina and the colonies of the Indian Ocean (M. Touzet), and the American colonies, Madagascar, Réunion and continental Africa (M. Labouret).

The organisation of the Parliamentary Commission of Inquiry was rather ad hoc. Some board members of the Commission wrote reports on topics of their choice, but most commissioners were contracted to lead research missions. Some inquiries were carried out on the basis of questionnaires dispatched from the Paris office. Commissioners enjoyed a great deal of freedom both in terms of mobility and access. As per their instructions:

> the members of mission have entry to all councils, to all local assemblies, but in no way do they have decision-making powers, nor a deliberating or consulting voice . . . [they are] delegated to collect on the spot information judged necessary, they are assimilated for the length of their trip to general inspectors on mission to the colonies with regard to transportation and baggage indemnities.[17]

With these directives in mind, commissioners set to work. Several inquiries dealt with the study of 'the aspirations of the natives'.[18] The idea was to listen to the demands of people, namely in political circles, various associations, institutions and schools. Lévy-Bruhl compiled such a report focused on 'witchcraft, ritual cannibalism and reprehensible acts committed in so-called secret societies'.[18] Lévy-Bruhl apparently never left Paris to do the inquiry. Instead, the Governor-General of AOF was invited to search in the archives in Dakar for information on this particular topic, which he did. Lévy-Bruhl consulted documentation on women killed by sorcery and cases of poisoning related to witchcraft. There is no doubt that he was most suited for such an undertaking, but one wonders what direct purpose such a study was intended to serve in guiding colonial policy.

For his part, Gide was also in charge of an inquiry on the 'aspirations of natives' and education. He, on the other hand, travelled to AOF in 1938. After a brief tour of Senegal, he proceeded to Soudan where he studied rural schools, he then headed to Haute Volta and finally Dahomey. It is not clear if he ever completed his report. Another commission investigated African customs and laws. Four commissioners focused on this subject in AOF (Niel, Quinson, Gasparin and Moutelors). Lamine Gueye, the SFIO partisan who had lost the Senegalese elections for deputy by a thin margin to Galandou Diouf in May 1936, was in charge of the same mission of inquiry for AEF.[19]

Several questionnaires were widely distributed throughout West Africa. One such questionnaire, regarding local living standards, specifically diet and dwellings, targeted African teachers. Another questionnaire sought information on 'the problem of *métis*', or the off-spring of African women and French men often abandoned in special orphanages.

In the end, this highly bureaucratic commission did not succeed in its stated goal. The initiative was slow to gain momentum, co-ordination at the ministerial level was often poor, and board members dragged their feet. Eventually, a year after its creation, the finance committee of the French Senate eliminated the credit available for operating the Commission.[20] Yet, the main reason for the failure was that the Popular Front government simply ran out of time. When the missions began turning in their reports, the Popular Front government was already being shown the door. So, in effect, this research was rarely incorporated into reform. Nevertheless, the archival record of this massive inquiry represents an exceptional source of facts and figures for historians to mine.

Although the model of 'commissions d'enquête' was a classic approach to colonial policy, the subjects chosen for investigation by the socialist administration were innovative and were usually overlooked by previous administrations. The hands-on investigatory approach was original because commissioners listened directly to the problems of the masses. Nowhere is the Popular Front's social mission more apparent than in a study of West African women and children.

OFFICIAL CONCERN FOR WOMEN AND CHILDREN

Concern for women's predicament was highly unusual in the 1930s for any administration, let alone one in French West Africa. At first glance, when considering such a report, it appears that the Popular Front's social mission was truly revolutionary. Indeed, why did the colonial administration under Governor-General de Coppet decide to organise an inquiry on women? And how did the French develop a concern for women's prerogatives?

French missionaries in Africa were the first to alert the colonial government about the plight of African women. The Fathers of the Holy Ghost were especially concerned when, in 1932, a missionary was brutally killed in Cameroun while protecting a girl. After giving refuge to the battered slave, the Father was stabbed to death by her Christian master.[21] This strange incident was to have a lasting effect on colonial policy. The Commissaire-Général of AEF responded immediately to missionary pressure by issuing legislation regulating marriages in the Equatorial colonies.[22] A clause prohibited the marriage of girls before the age of 14 and boys before the age of 16, another fixed the modalities of paying bridewealth; yet another facilitated divorce in polygamous relationships. Regional officers were encouraged to enforce this in court. The archbishop of the Holy-Ghost mission, Monseigneur Le Roy, subsequently produced a booklet entitled 'Pour le Relèvement de la

Femme en Afrique Française'. He sent a copy to Governor-General Brévié urging him to enact similar legislation to protect African women in AOF.

In response to the plea, Brévié assured Monseigneur Le Roy that the government was taking necessary measures to redress the situation in AOF.[23] Missionaries in other areas, such as the White Fathers in Ouagadougou, also communicated similar concerns about African women to the Governor-General.[24] So in effect, the missionaries successfully lobbied the AOF government to focus on women and children. Brévié, for his part, agreed to draft legislation but a milder version than what was passed in Cameroun, because: 'if we must strive to improve the fate of women, we must also not lose sight of our prime interest not to cause the dislocation of indigenous society'.[25] Brévié had touched upon a central point: how to deal with indigenous customs which offended the French, especially in the area of marriage and inheritance.

It was during the Popular Front period that women became visible in French politics.[26] This was motivated by a need to rally widespread political support rather than an ideal of social justice and equality. In fact, the French Communist Party, for instance, continued to have a very conservative image of femininity characterised by 'moral probity, a commitment to marriage and motherhood, and gender-specific activism'.[27] However, three women were appointed by Léon Blum to high political offices. Madame Léon Brunschwig was nominated Secretary of State in the national department of education, Irène Joliot-Curie was the Under-Secretary of State in scientific research, and Suzanne Lacore was in charge of the 'protection of childhood'.[28] Granted these women had minor roles with limited decision-making powers, and the jobs of two of the three related to children, their appointment was nonetheless significant.

Official publications of de Coppet's administration reveal an interest, early on, in the predicament of African women and children. In the autumn of 1936, barely one month after de Coppet assumed his position as Governor-General (after being personally installed by Moutet himself during his first visit to West Africa in August 1936), the government of AOF enacted legislation concerning women. A momentous decree 'to insure the protection of the labour of children and women' was signed in France on 18 September 1936. De Coppet promulgated this decree in AOF on 30 October 1936.[29] The decree contained 56 articles which regulated the status, working conditions, and the legal rights of working women and children, while at the same time defining 'family labour'.[30] The penalties for non-complying employers as well as the role and responsibilities of the newly created Inspection du Travail agents were also established.

In his opening speech to the Government Council in December 1936, de Coppet spoke about the need to enforce legislation on both the pawning of people, a 'barbaric practice', and 'certain backward and critical customs concerning marriage'.[31] Pawning, or the pledging of family members or slaves for securing loans was widespread in West Africa. In the years following the Depression, the prevalence of pawning was directly linked to widespread poverty. Women and children, usually girls, were the prime targets. For the creditor, the pawn's labour represented the 'interest' on the loan. But never was a pawn substituted for the actual loan unless she was converted into a wife, in which case the original loan became the bridewealth. In the first half of the 1930s, reports of multiple incidences of pawning caused alarm among some colonial administrators. In fact it was de Coppet's predecessor, Jules Brévié, Governor-General of AOF from 1930 to 1936, who originally drafted the legislation de Coppet referred to. Indeed, Brévié dispatched a number of circulars concerning the related question of pawning and indigenous marriages, namely forced marriages.[32]

Faced with these questions, which he inherited from the previous government, de Coppet became actively committed to women's issues. Besides re-enacting legislation on marriage, pawning and child labour which aimed at protecting African girls, de Coppet's government paid special attention to the education of girls. By November 1937, three new schools for girls were created in Senegal.[33] Another piece of legislation promulgated in AOF dealt with regulating police sanctions towards women.[34] Hence, it was altogether a logical step to assign a woman to examine such matters in detail.

A MISSION OF INQUIRY ON WEST AFRICAN WOMEN AND CHILDREN

Of all the missions of inquiry in AOF, the most remarkable was entitled 'La famille en AOF: condition de la femme'.[35] This lengthy report, the fruit of seven months of fieldwork throughout French West Africa, was compiled by one of the rare European women ever to serve in the colonial administration: Denise Moran Savineau. At the time the Parliamentary Commission of Inquiry was created, Moran was working for the AOF administration as a technical counsellor for education. She had lived in Africa for a number of years, namely in Chad, where she worked for the political office of the governor, who at the time, was none other than Marcel de Coppet. In March 1937, she expressed her desire to participate in the Commission in several letters addressed to de Coppet, mentioning in one of them that Delavignette was also trying to get her in.[36] Seven months later, the Governor-General appointed her to lead 'an enquiry in AOF on the condition of women in the family, in education facilities, in salaried employment, etc.'[37]

In spite of the title, Moran's research goes beyond the study of West African women and families to encompass many of the topics explored by the Commission. From October 1937 to May 1938, Moran visited most of the colonies in AOF. She investigated the colonial justice system, penitentiaries and health facilities. She inspected most schools, as this was her area of expertise. She visited agricultural businesses and local markets, examining production at all levels. She reported on the prevalence of forced labour and colonial taxation. The result of her extensive fieldwork is an outstanding investigation into the social and economic situation of women and children in AOF in the late 1930s. What makes this commissioner's study so exceptional, besides her focus on women, is her critical outlook on the colonial administration, her extensive interviews with a wide range of people, and her commitment to reporting on social injustices.

Naturally, indigenous marriage practices were an important aspect of Moran's inquiry. Moran found courtrooms an excellent source of information on marital affairs because gender boundaries were often challenged in court. Most cases brought to colonial courts dealt with domestic conflict, especially divorce. Generally, women more than men resorted to colonial courts to settle their problems, especially when local customs failed them. In a town in lower Côte d'Ivoire, only women frequented the court-house.[38] Moran closely examined how courts handled forced marriage which, like pawning, she equated to slavery. Overall, court officials tended to deny women a fair trial, opting in a majority of cases to send them back to their husbands. In Ouagadougou, court assessors laughed when Moran suggested women should have a right to choose their own husbands.[39]

To assess the status of African women, or what she referred to as 'feminine evolution', Moran gave historical depth to her ethnographic study. According to the court assessor in Bamako, 'In former times, women respected their fathers, and their mothers feared their husbands . . . they were reserved and they knew how to stay put at home. Now, they are doing the things that they love and that their father and mother and God do not allow.'[40] Similar views were held by the assessor in Porto Novo (Dahomey): 'In the days of Bchangjin, we were free to order our women around. Nowadays, they do not want to obey any more. . .'.[41] In Niger, Moran reported that both women and children were 'shaking the authority' of male heads of household.[42] In her final report, Moran concluded that 'protected by us [i.e. the French colonial administration] women are beginning to defend themselves, even to attack. We see this in the case of divorce'.[43] Judging from these observations, colonial legislation protecting and 'emancipating' women was producing positive results.

Most of the issues outlined in Moutet's colonial programme appear in Moran's report. For instance, she made a special inquiry on the Office du Niger. After assessing the situation through interviews with people whose lives had been disrupted by this agricultural development fiasco, she concluded that the project's modus operandi was reminiscent of slavery.[44] Moreover, she explained how the administration empowered African men to control the labour of their wives and children. She confirmed suspicions that the Office was ignoring labour laws protecting women and children and salaried workers, including the decree on forced labour. On another note, Moran noted that throughout AOF, colonial taxes were not commensurate with the excessively low standard of living in West Africa caused by the Depression. On the issue of *prestation*, 'yet another deplorable servitude', she reported some progress. In the Boundiali region (Niger), for example, the labour tax was successfully replaced by a fiscal one.[45]

De Coppet was extremely pleased with the outcome of Moran's research expedition and expressed this in numerous letters addressed to her and to Moutet. When he received Moran's first report, entitled 'La femme et la famille à Bamako', he immediately forwarded a copy to the Minister together with a 'personal and very confidential' letter.[46] De Coppet then wrote to the Governor of French Soudan demanding clarification on certain points raised in the report. Many issues concerned schools: the elementary school in Bamako was under-funded, both the girls and boys schools were seriously under-staffed, the *métis* orphanage was austere and depressing, the level of teaching in the Sisters' school was poor because the Sisters apparently discriminated against black students, and European teachers in charge of the school of the Office du Niger abused their authority. Other observations pertained to *métis* complaints about job opportunities, the lack of supplies in medical facilities, ill treatment of patients of the leprosy centre and the over-speculation on meat prices by trading houses.[47]

It is interesting to note that the archives contain two very distinct responses to this query formulated by two Governors of French Soudan. The first reply, by Governor F. Rougier (see below), tended to deny the validity of Moran's observations.[48] The new Governor of French Soudan, on the other hand, made confidential inquiries to confirm the information, before submitting his response. Overall he found most issues raised by Moran were indeed true.[49] This was the tactic de Coppet apparently used with all Moran's data, he confronted respective Governors of the AOF territories with the reported problems.

Clearly, not every colonial official in the field responded positively to Moran's mission. The typical reaction to the subject of her inquiry was ridicule. One notable exception was an older retired civil servant named Zounou who praised the Lord for the Governor-General's concern for women.[50] Moran had at least one brush with a French official, which caused the Governor of French Soudan, F. Rougier, to complain that 'Mrs. Savineau inconvenienced many people with her attitude of an inspector directly accredited by the Government'.[51] In another incident, Moran was invited to a *vin d'honneur* by young partisans of the SFIO in Abengourou (Côte d'Ivoire). The district officer urged Moran to change her plans for he feared that this meeting would turn into a political demonstration![52]

Moran's mission of inquiry delivered myriad data on African women's changing status in social and economic spheres, responding directly to the colonial administration's needs. While the plight of African women and families was officially recognised before the Socialist government, it became an important focus in de Coppet's colonial programme His administration chose to relieve women of practices considered 'barbaric', namely forced marriages, and pawning of girls and women because their customary treatment contradicted the aims of the *mission civilisatrice*, the motto justifying France's role in the colonies.

THE POPULAR FRONT ERA IN AOF: CONCLUDING REMARKS

Beyond his official concern for women, children and the family, it is safe to say that Governor-General de Coppet introduced a radically different approach to colonial rule in French West Africa. De Coppet, who had served in Africa for over 30 years, seemed to be motivated by a genuine commitment to social justice. One of the greatest achievements of his administration was the creation of the Inspection du Travail to survey the work conditions in both private and public establishments, and regulate labour recruitment while enforcing protective labour legislation.[53] The labour office and other institutions created at the time, such as the Institut Français d'Afrique Noire, would outlast the Popular Front era.

De Coppet is mostly remembered for being the first to

liberalise syndicalism in AOF. What followed was an impressive swell in trade unions. Strikes erupted in several towns in Senegal in 1937. The French press was quick to criticise de Coppet's soft response to strikers' demands for higher wages. But the criticism redoubled when the Thiès railway workers went on strike in September 1938. De Coppet's handling of the matter, and subsequently his entire political programme for AOF, came under fire. By this time, Moutet had been replaced as Minister of the Colonies, and one could read in *Paris-Dakar* 'AOF is no longer in vogue in the metropole, in Parliament or in the editorial rooms because of his scandalous record.'[54] Georges Mandel, the new Minister of the Colonies, soon removed de Coppet. But the seed had been planted in the consciousness of Senegalese workers. While a powerful political awakening took place only in key West African colonies, namely Senegal, Dahomey, Ivory Coast and Soudan,[55] other regions were almost unaffected by de Coppet's reforms, as Michel Brot's contribution to this volume attests for Guinée.

Although sub-Saharan Africa was not a priority for the Parliamentary Commission, it is significant that Moutet's first ministerial visit overseas was to AOF. In fact, he toured the region on two separate occasions during his short term in office. His closest advisers were 'colonial Africanists' (Gide, Delavignette), as were many of the Commission's board members. Governor-General Brévié had blazed a trail in social reform in AOF before the Popular Front era. Immediately after the Popular Front victory, even Delavignette admitted: 'Brévié behaved like a precursor in AOF; he laid the foundations of a truly social policy of economic liberation and education of the masses.'[56] Moutet appointed Brévié to a post he himself had once occupied, that of Governor of Indochina. Could it be that the Colonial Ministry of the Popular Front government believed that the situation in the AOF colonies was sufficiently researched? Or was a model of social reform to be emulated by the other overseas territories? Is this the reason why de Coppet, when addressing the Senegalese strikers in his typically paternalistic tone, said: 'You are the eldest sons of colonial France'?[57] These questions require a thorough examination of the archival record, including Moutet's papers.

It is difficult to say what prompted the new Minister of the Colonies in July 1938 to request information on the policy measures which promoted the emancipation of African women. Perhaps he was simply doing a routine examination of the previous administration's record. On the other hand, he may have been alerted by Christian women's organisations concerned with the status of women overseas, just as Brévié had been guided by the missionaries.[58] In his reply, the interim Governor-General described the 'realistic' measures taken to 'liberate' women from customs which were contrary to 'French civilisation', to 'set women free from a servitude often incompatible with our notion of individual freedom'.[59]

While the official concern for the status of African women was not a Popular Front innovation, de Coppet was fully committed to investigating women's issues, and he took the Socialist colonial mission to heart. He assigned Moran, an exceptional woman, to lead a unique inquiry in response to an official concern for the status of African women and children, and a will to reform. Moran's invaluable report was used, to some extent at least, to guide official measures. Her findings do suggest that legislation protecting African women was having a impact, and they were contesting the status quo in courts. The large-scale parliamentary commission of inquiry to determine the needs of the masses was original in scope: listening to the people; identifying problems in the administration; taking steps toward political emancipation so that the colonised could actively partake in resolving their own problems; and protecting the rights of workers, including women and children. It is in this latter sense that Popular Front reform in the West African colonies marked a radical departure.

Notes and References

* I thank Tony Chafer for persuading me to write this chapter. I also would like to thank Jason Peirce for his useful comments. Special thanks to Magida Safaoui and the Shadids.
  1. ANS 17G/160 (28). Dakar 5 September 1938, AP/2 no. 1841, Gouverneur-Général de l'AOF par intérim à Ministre des Colonies.

2. Léon Blum's 1927 address to the party, cited by D. Hémery in 'Aux origines des guerres d'indépendance vietnamiennes: pouvoir colonial et phénomène communiste en Indochine avant la deuxième guerre mondiale', *Mouvement Social*, 101 (1977) p. 11.
3. For an insider's opinion of various anti-colonial sentiments of the French Left, see R. Delavignette, 'Le Front Populaire devant l'Afrique noire' in *Bulletin du Comité d'Études Historiques et Scientifiques de l'AOF* (1936) p. 253. Copy consulted in ANS 17G/160 (28).
4. N. Bernard-Duquenet, *Le Sénégal et le Front populaire* (LHarmattan, 1985) p. 61.
5. D. Hémery, art. cit., p. 28.
6. R. Delavignette, 'Le Front Populaire', art. cit., p. 254. He was head of the ENFOM and an administrator with a long career in French West Africa.
7. R. Delavignette, 'Le Front Populaire', art. cit., p. 253.
8. N. Bernard-Duquenet, op. cit., p. 81.
9. ANS 17G/160 (28) 'Situation de la femme en AOF, 1934–38,' folder 'Dossier des famines 1936', Ministre des Colonies (Moutet) à Messieurs les Gouverneurs-Généraux, 24 June 1936. Sentence underlined in the original.
10. A copy of the circular addressed to Marcel de Coppet, Governor-General of AOF, was reproduced by Jacques Marseille in his article, 'La conférence des Gouverneurs-Généraux des colonies (novembre 1936)', *Mouvement Social*, 101 (1977) pp. 73–84.
11. W. Cohen, 'The Colonial Policy of the Popular Front', *French Historical Studies*, 7, 3 (1972) p. 371.
12. G. Lefranc, *Histoire du Front populaire (1934–1938)* (Payot, 1965) p. 441.
13. *Bulletin officiel du Ministère des Colonies*, LI, no. 2, Feb. 1937, p. 109.
14. R. Delavignette, 'La politique de Marius Moutet au Ministère des Colonies', in *Léon Blum Chef de Government 1936–1937* (Presses de la Fondation Nationale des Sciences Politiques, 1981) (1st ed. 1967) p. 392.
15. ANS 17G/101 (17), 'Commission d'enquête parlementaire dans les pays d'outre-mer', folder '1937'. Ministre des Colonies (Moutet) à Messieurs les gouverneurs des Colonies, 31 August 1937. They were meant to give wide coverage to the commission and advertise in four consecutive issues.
16. N. Bernard-Duquenet, op. cit., p. 79.
17. ANS 17G/101 (17) folder 1938, Gouverneur-Général à Messieurs les Gouverneurs, 2 Jan. 1938. Articles 4 and 6 of the instructions to the members of the parliamentary commission.
18. ANS 17G/101 (17) folder 1, Directeur de la commission d'enquête (Guernut) au Gouveneur-Général de l'AOF (De Coppet), 25 Oct. 1937.
19. ANS 17G/108 (17) folder 1938. *Journal Officiel de la République, Débats parlementaires* (8 Oct. 1938).
20. R. Delavignette, 'La politique', op. cit., p. 393.
21. G. Goyau, 'L'action missionnaire pour la protection de la femme noire', *Annales Coloniales*, 16 Aug. 1934.

22. 17G/160 (28), folder 'Pour le Relèvement de la Femme en Afrique Française', A. Le Roy, former Superior General of the Compagnie du Saint-Esprit, Archbishop of Carie.
23. 17G/160 (28), folder 'Pour le Relèvement de la Femme en Afrique Française', Gouverneur-Général Brévié à Monseigneur A. Le Roy, 19 May 1936.
24. See M. Klein and R. Roberts, 'The Resurgence of Pawning in French West Africa during the Depression of the 1930s', in T. Falola and P. E. Lovejoy (eds), *Pawnship in Africa: Debt Bondage in Historical Perspective* (Westview Press, 1994) pp. 303–20.
25. 17G /160 (28), folder 'Pour le Relèvement de la Femme en Afrique Française', folder 1935. On a scrap note (AP/2, 7 May 1936) one reads 'the draft circular gives entire satisfaction to the Fathers, while avoiding, <u>unlike what was done in Cameroun</u>, interfering with customs . . .'.
26. S. B. Whitney, 'Embracing the Status Quo: French Communists, Young Women and the Popular Front,' *Journal of Social History*, 30 (autumn 1996) p. 29.
27. Ibid.
28. A. Brimo, *Les femmes françaises face au pouvoir politique* (Editions Montchrestien, 1975).
29. *Journal Officiel du Sénégal, 1889* (3 Dec. 1936) pp. 948–51.
30. Ibid. The decree was later amended. See *Journal Officiel du Sénégal, 1918* (10 June 1937).
31. AOM, Affaires Politiques 541 'Condition de la femme indigène', Discours prononcé par le Gouverneur-Général de l'AOF à l'ouverture de la session du Conseil du Gouvernement, Dec. 1936.
32. See AOM, Affaires Politiques 541 'Condition de la femme indigène', for a list of the circulars. For Brévié's report on his 'politique indigène', see ANS 17G/160 (28) 'Situation de la femme en AOF, 1934–1938', folder 'Evolution social pour les masses et les travailleurs indigènes'. This is an excerpt from the 13 Oct. 1935 talk Governor General Brévié gave at the Academy of Colonial Sciences.
33. *Journal Officiel du Sénégal*, 1942 (11 Nov. 1937) p. 789. The schools were in Rufisque, Kaolack and Ziguinchor.
34. Decree no. 3031 AP, *Journal Officiel du Sénégal, 1946* (9 Decembre 1937) p. 848. Moran's information on prisons and the justice system could very well have prompted the enactment of this particular decree.
35. See ANS 17G/381 (126). The study, about 1,000 pages long, includes a general report, and 17 regional reports. For details, see: G. Lydon, 'The Unraveling of a Neglected Source: A Report on Women in Francophone West Africa in the 1930s', *Cahiers d'Etudes Africaines*, 147, 37, 3 (1997) pp. 555–84.
36. ANS 17G/217 (104) 'Voyages et Missions, lettres S à Z', Savineau à Gouverneur-Général de l'AOF, 1 Mar. 1937.
37. ANS 17G/217 (104) 'Voyages et Missions, lettres S à Z', Circulaire du Gouverneur-Général de l'AOF, 7 Oct. 1937.
38. ANS 17G/381 (126), Rapport no. 12 'La Basse Côte d'Ivoire'. p. 39.

39. ANS 17G/381 (126), Rapport no. 8 'Ouagadougou', p. 26.
40. ANS 17G/381 (126) Rapport no. 1 'La femme et la famille Bamako', p. 28.
41. ANS 17G/381 (126) Rapport no. 6 'Le Dahomey', p. 20.
42. ANS 17G/381 (126), Rapport no. 5 'Le Niger occidental', p. 9.
43. ANS 17G/381 (126), Rapport no. 18 'Rapport d'ensemble', p. 18.
44. ANS 17G/381 (126), Rapport no. 2 'Les villages de colonisation de l'Office du Niger'.
45. ANS 17G/381 (126), Rapport no. 9 'Bobo, Marka, Lobi, Senoufo, etc.', p. 47.
46. AOM, 17G/381 (microfilm) end of the roll contains correspondence related to Moran's inquiry. Gouverneur-Général de l'AOF à Marius Moutet, Personnel et très confidentiel, 12 January 1938.
47. Ibid. See also ANS 17G/381 (126), Rapport no. 1 'La femme et la famille à Bamako'.
48. AOM, 17G/381 (microfilm). Gouverneur du Soudan Français à Gouveneur général de l'AOF, 7 Mar. 1938.
49. AOM, 17G/381 (microfilm), Gouverneur du Soudan Français à Gouverneur général de l'AOF, 1 Apr. 1938.
50. ANS, 17G/381 (126), Rapport no. 6: 'Le Dahomey', p. 10.
51. AOM, 17G/381 (microfilm), Gouverneur du Soudan Français à Gouverneur-Général de l'AOF, 21 Feb. 1938. Doctor Cavalade of Ségou refused to give her an appointment because it was the 11 November (Armistice day). Governor of Soudan, F. Rougier, soon left office, and it is tempting to surmise that he was removed because of his negative attitude towards this particular mission of inquiry.
52. Ibid. Commandant de Cercle d'Abengourou à Gouverneur de la Côte d'Ivoire, 4 Mar. 1938. Moran ended up attending a very se-date meeting at the home of the political representative of the SFIO.
53. For an impressive comparative study of African labour history which discusses the Inspection du Travail and forced labour in AOF see F. Cooper, *Decolonisation and African Society: a Labor Question in French and British Africa* (Cambridge University Press, 1996) esp. pp. 78–81.
54. N. Bernard-Duquenet, 'Les débuts du syndicalisme au Sénégal au temps du Front populaire', *Mouvement Social*, 101 (1977) p. 51.
55. See, for instance, C. H. Cutter, 'The Genesis of a Nationalist Élite: the Role of the Popular Front in the French Sudan (1936–1939)', in G. Wesley Johnson (ed.), *Double Impact: France and Africa in the Age of Imperialism* (Greenwood Press, 1985) pp. 107–128.
56. R. Delavignette, 'Le Front populaire', op. cit., p. 255.
57. 'Vous êtes les fils aînés de la France coloniale', N. Bernard-Duquenet, 'Les débuts du syndicalisme au Sénégal', art. cit., p. 52.
58. See M. Klein and R. Roberts, op. cit., p. 37.
59. ANS 17G160 (28). Dakar 5 Sept. 1938, AP/2 no. 1841, Gouverneur-General de l'AOF par intérim à Ministre des Colonies.

9 Did the Popular Front Have Any Significant Impact in Guinée?

Michel Brot

It may seem something of a paradox to make a study of the Popular Front in Guinée, because, whereas the impact of the Popular Front was modest in much of French West Africa, in Guinée it was especially weak. An intensive search was often needed in order to find even the most scanty evidence, hence the microscopic and occasionally anecdotal nature of this chapter. Furthermore, as we shall see, it is not even clear that most of the changes introduced between 1936 and 1942 can be attributed with certainty to the Popular Front.

The population of the colony was about 2,100,000, almost entirely rural,[1] with a capital, Conakry, which was only a small town of 15,000 inhabitants. Guinée was characterised by the small number of European colonists (a few hundred officials, traders and planters) and by the economic importance of Lebanese traders and entrepreneurs: all that was often left to the Africans by way of employment was gold-washing, petty trade, farming or cattle-rearing. The few wage earners were concentrated in Conakry (labourers, domestic servants, office workers) and also in the banana plantations of Lower Guinée, the only modern productive sector. These plantations, which were expanding rapidly at this time, were principally run by Europeans as, before the war, in contrast to the situation in the Ivory Coast, there were very few African planters in Guinée. They employed underpaid agricultural labourers, often requisitioned by the government from the forest part of Guinée at the other end of the country: flight was their only means of protest.[2]

From the political point of view, Guinée was far removed from Senegal: it did not possess its Four Communes and practically all Guinéens were French subjects and not citizens. There were no elected assemblies, no trade union rights before 1937 and a system of special legislation for natives, called the *indigénat*, prevailed. From the social point of view, it was also not like Dahomey, the reputed 'Latin Quarter of Africa', nor Togo, where a dynamic African bourgeoisie flourished. The French-educated elite was tiny: there were between 3,000 and 8,000 pupils in the primary sector throughout the inter-war years and only a few individuals were sent each year to be trained in the higher schools in Dakar. There were no African newspapers. Therefore there was no agrarian or commercial bourgeoisie in Guinée to speak of and no significant educated élite. Hence the colony possessed the least favourable conditions for the emergence of any political life of a modern kind.

URBAN WAGE-EARNERS AND *EVOLUES*

An embryonic political and trade union life did however start under the Popular Front, but it was confined to a very limited milieu, the *évolués* of Conakry.[3] A group of the Socialist Party (SFIO) was set up at Conakry in 1938 (after two years of the Popular Front government) on the initiative of a European, Sialelli, an accountant on the railways, but with a majority of African members, comprising 20 Europeans and 71 Africans.[4] It was affiliated to the Senegal SFIO Federation which was larger and also included blacks and whites.[5] At about the same time trade unions for native officials and business employees were set up in Guinée, but again, later than in Dahomey, the Ivory Coast or Senegal.[6] But local legislation compelled each member of a native trade union to possess a certificate of elementary studies or its equivalent, which limited recruitment to *évolués*.[7] As a result of this, it was not possible to establish trade unions among the workers in banana plantations who represented the largest number of wage earners in the colony. These short-lived trade unions, like the SFIO group, disappeared after 1939. It still remains the fact that the first unions were formed in Guinée in 1937 or 1938 and not in 1945 (the date that Sekou Touré established the trade union for native postal workers) as is often asserted.

During the period of the Popular Front some strikes broke out in Guinée: one in 1936, eight in 1937 and two in 1938.[8] According to Pierre Tap, the Inspecteur du Travail for AOF, there were six in Conakry between September 1936 and March 1937. The strikers demanded wage increases, which Tap himself considered to be justified by the rise in prices. But these strikes were not all successful: only two firms in 1936–37 granted the increases requested, the others simply sacked their striking workers.[9] These were not the first strikes in Guinée: there had been some before, especially in the – period immediately after the First World War,[10] but the 1936–37 ones were probably inspired by the general climate of the period and by the influence of social movements in Senegal and France.

In order to apply the new worker-friendly policy, Pierre Tap went on a fact-finding mission to Guinée in April 1937. However, fact-finding missions do not necessarily produce much in the way of actual outcomes and the results of the Tap mission were limited to an increase in the minimum wage, which went up from 1.50 to 3.50 francs a day plus a 500 gram rice ration (outside Conakry), by a local ordinance of 26 October 1937,[11] and to some fine words, which tell us much about the previous mind-set of the colonial administration: 'In the minds of employers, the outdated but persistent conviction that the French administration is at their entire disposal and should support their claims with all its energy must disappear. . . . In trade disputes the administration must remain the arbiter.'[12] It was up to the staff in the colonial administration to apply these new principles.

However, in order to estimate the full impact of the Popular Front government in Guinée, one has to examine the actual situation of the vast majority of the population in Guinée, not only during the two years 1936–38 but also before and after, from the beginning of the 1930s economic crisis up to the Vichy regime of 1940–43, and even the Gaullist regime of 1943–45. By extending the period under scrutiny, we shall see if there was an appreciable improvement in the lot of the rural population between 1936 and 1938 as a consequence of the supposedly more liberal colonial policy of the Popular Front. In order to assess its impact, three of the most significant indicators of the burden of colonial rule will give a good measure of the effects of reform: direct taxation, forced labour and special legislation for natives.

THE RURAL MAJORITY UNDER COLONIAL RULE

As far as taxation is concerned, it is obvious that the population of Guinée had less difficulty in paying the *capitation*[13] in 1937, 1938 and 1939 than between 1930 and 1936. All contemporary accounts emphasise this. In a famous report, the administrative officer Gilbert Vieillard, while denouncing the terrible pauperisation (famine, forced sales, pawning children) suffered by the peasants of Fouta-Djalon because of the economic crisis and the maintenance of tax at a high level, stressed that '1936 was the last of a series of sombre years'.[14] The reports by the administration paint the same picture, and the economic data compiled by two historians also support these impressions: Trentadue's macroeconomic study shows that from 1931 to 1936 the burden of direct taxation on the population of Guinée exceeded its ability to pay, that is to say the price paid for the colony's exportable produce, which was the peasants' only means of monetary income, but that this relationship was reversed in 1937–8, when African monetary income again rose above the tax burden.[15] A more local study by Beavogui in the Macenta district (in the forest part of Guinée) also shows that, in francs adjusted for inflation, the poll tax rate increased a great deal from 1930 to 1935, then decreased just as much up to 1941 (the trough of the curve being in 1940–41), before climbing gently again thereafter (Figure 9.1).[16] But this relief from the burden of tax was largely due to the increase in prices for raw materials (palm kernels, wax, rubber) after 1936 and to the devaluations of the franc making these prices competitive, and very little due to any administrative measures. Certainly in 1936 there was some mitigation of the tax burden, owing to two political initiatives: the abolition of the tax on livestock and the raising of the age at which children became liable for tax from eight to 14.[17] But these two measures, applied in

Figure 9.1   Graph showing poll tax rates in Macenta *cercle*, 1930–45, in francs adjusted for inflation (1938=100)

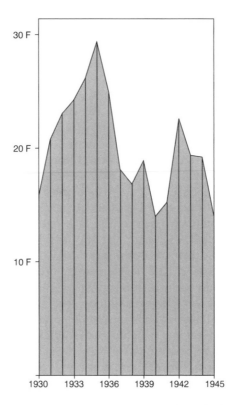

Source: Graph adapted from F. Béavogui, 'Contribution à l'histoire des Loma de la Guinée forestière de la fin du XIXe siècle à 1945', Thèse de doctorat, Université de Paris VII, 1991, p. 469.

1936, had in fact been decided in 1935 by Jules Brévié, the Governor-General, and Louis Rollin, the Minister for the Colonies.[18] The latter was a 'republican of the left', which under the Third Republic meant a man of the right, serving in the cabinets of Pierre-Etienne Flandin, Fernand Bouisson and Pierre Laval. So these measures should not be credited to the Popular Front. Besides, these tax reductions were offset by two new taxes: compulsory contributions to native savings groups, set up administratively in each district from 1932 onwards, and the additional tax replacing the *prestation* from 1938.

The reform of the forced labour system was in fact inspired by the ideas of the Popular Front: it replaced the regime of *prestations* by an additional tax which enabled those subject to the *prestation* to buy out their labour dues in cash and also enabled volunteer labourers on road construction and building sites to be paid. This very popular reform was progressively introduced between 1938 and 1942 in all the various *cercles* (administrative areas) in Guinée: four *cercles* were involved in 1938, eight more in 1939, none in 1940, eight more in 1941 and the last two in 1942. This reform, initiated by the socialist Governor-General of AOF, Marcel de Coppet in 1937, was therefore in fact carried out under the right-wing Minister Mandel, then the Vichy Governor-General Boisson. So the last years of the Third Republic and the Vichy regime in fact prolonged the 'liberal' policy of the Popular Front.[19]

The *indigénat* system was one that allowed colonial officials to punish any native with a prison sentence or a fine, as a matter of discipline and without trial. It was principally used to punish the offence of obstruction or ill-will when taxes were being levied or *prestations* carried out, but was also used to punish opposition to the colonial regime by means of a list of offences that was deliberately left vague. The statistics concerning the numbers of days served in prison between 1930 and 1943 certainly show a decrease in the number of prison convictions after 1935, with a trough between 1937 and 1940 (Figure 9.2),[20] but the decrease appears to be due mainly to the Africans' higher tax-paying ability, which was itself due to improved earnings from the sale of produce. There were therefore fewer convictions for refusal to pay. There is no evidence that it was due to a hypothetical policy of leniency carried out at a high level under the stimulus of the Popular Front.

This may not be the most significant aspect: the reality of colonial pressure and repression cannot be encompassed in legal texts and statistics. For example, in order to collect taxes, the administration could rely on its *chefs de canton* and their henchmen, the infamous *batoulabé*, who, completely out of control, ill-treated and robbed recalcitrant peasants.[21]

Figure 9.2   Annual number of days in prison to which Africans were sentenced under the *indigénat* in Guinée, 1930–43

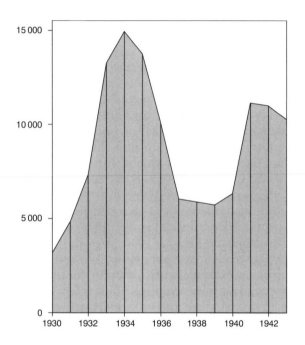

Source: Data derived from ANSOM, Aff. Pol. 978, *Rapports politiques de la Guinée, 1930–39*, and ANS, 2G40/9, 2G41/21, 2G42/22, 2G43/19, *Rapports politiques de la Guinée, 1940–43*.

It is doubtful if their exactions diminished during the periods of the Blum and Chautemps governments. Later on, during the grim years of the war effort (1943–45), when Guinéens were compelled to provide an enormous quantity of products necessary for the Allied war machine by means of compulsory cultivation and harvesting, particularly severe in the case of rubber, it was demonstrated that the abolition of *prestations* did not prevent a return to the system of forced labour when the colonial authority deemed it necessary.[22] This means that the reforms of the 1930s were precarious because they could be reversed.

Whether they were genuine or illusory, these reforms were of no value without the will of the administrative personnel to apply them. Here was the problem: indications of the reservations of certain officials can be seen in the words they use. On the other hand, the freedom of action of colonial liberals (*'indigénophiles'* as they were called then) can be assessed through the example of two men, Louis Blacher and Gilbert Vieillard.

THE ROLE OF INDIVIDUAL OFFICIALS

The words used are of some importance. One of the key words in the official discourse of the Popular Front in metropolitan France was 'worker': 'the interests of the workers', 'to improve the lot of the workers' were popular phrases. Two reactions from colonial officials can be noted. In 1937, according to Pierre Tap, the Inspecteur du Travail for AOF, the administrator of a *cercle* in Lower Guinée replied to an enquiry about the morale of the workers by 'sneering at the term "workers" applied to natives and proposing to stop all wages because too much money can lead the native into temptation'.[23] In the same year an Inspecteur des Colonies criticised Governor Blacher's decision to put a ceiling on the sale price of rice at Kindia, which penalised the colonial trading companies. He wrote that 'this measure . . . has the appearance of a weapon aimed at one category of workers'.[24] By this he meant, surprisingly, the European or Lebanese traders who were prevented from speculating. It is obvious that these two officials, by mocking the vocabulary of the Popular Front or by deliberately misusing it, revealed a clear hostility to its colonial policy.

Some officials did support the colonial policy of the Popular Front, yet it is questionable whether they had the means to steer the administration towards the 'colonial humanism' that was the official ideology of the Popular Front. Louis Blacher was a 'liberal' governor of Guinée from 1936 to 1939, at the same time as Marcel de Coppet was Governor-General at Dakar. Blacher was born in Martinique in 1883, of mixed race and illegitimate (two categories which are not unimportant in a colonial society). He had been Governor of Niger during the 1931 famine and was thereafter much preoccupied by the problem of malnutrition amongst rural populations. That is why he issued orders in 1936 and 1937 setting a ceiling on the sale price of rice, in order to encourage the peasants to build up reserves, thus penalising the European and Lebanese traders who usually bought rice from the peasants at a low price at the time of the harvest and sold it back to them at a high price during the hungry season before the next harvest. For this he attracted serious criticism from the Inspecteur des colonies, Huet, who accused him of obstructing trade. The arguments of the two sides reveal two divergent ideas concerning the role of the colonial administration in mediating between the traders and the African peasants. For his part, Huet argued that:

> Speculation is the name given to trade when you want to obstruct it in one way or another. . . . Traders are not philanthropists. It is quite normal for them to wait as long as possible before selling their stocks, otherwise these sales will not bring them any profit. . . . No one will deny that the administration has the responsibility for protecting the interests of the native population, but it would not seem fair to make part of the European population pay for this protection.[25]

Governor Blacher replied firmly:

> By protecting the native population against trading activities which would have been disastrous for its food supply, has the local administration hindered trading, has it acted arbitrarily in depriving traders of the profits which they might have made from the rise in rice prices? The Inspector General maintains that this is the case. And if it is so, the person responsible for this action has no regrets, since he considers that his primary role in the colony is to ensure the normal feeding of the population at affordable prices, especially when the food is produced by the natives themselves and when the spirit of free trade tends to snatch it from their hands in order to make them buy it back again at a much higher price. . . . If the local administration had facilitated the selling and reselling operations of the country's rice, it would not have acted in collaboration [with business interests] but acted as an accomplice to the detriment of the natives.[26]

No doubt there were other similar events during the governorship of Louis Blacher, for his biographer concluded that he left behind him: 'the memory of an honest and upright high official who knew how to defend the interests of the Guinéen population against the greed of certain colonists and certain European and Syro-Lebanese traders'.[27] However, it should also be noted that an historian, making a rapid typology of 'black colonisers' (West Indian and Guyanese officials) classifies him among the 'zealous colonisers'.[28]

It is possible, after all, that Governor Blacher succeeded in pushing the Guinée administration in the direction of a better appreciation of the interests of the peasants. But there is no evidence to suggest that he was a genuine Popular Front man. We do not know what his party ties were (de Coppet, for example, belonged to the SFIO) and he had been posted to Conakry by the centrist Sarraut government on 7 March 1936, hence before the coming to power of the Popular Front government. In any case, it was Georges Mandel, the right-wing Colonial Minister in the Daladier cabinet after the Popular Front, who recalled him at the end of 1939.

At a more junior level, Gilbert Vieillard, Administrateur-adjoint of Mamou *cercle* from 1935 to 1937, also tried to introduce reforms. He too was not a Popular Front man. According to his biographer he was apolitical: 'he was not a colonial who subscribed to *Le Temps*'.[29] He had reservations about some aspects of colonisation whilst accepting its overall principle. He was also an unusual colonialist who had a passionate interest in one African people, the Peuls.[30] He spoke their language and was entirely familiar with their culture, to the extent that the first Guinéen ethnic association, founded in 1944 by Peul intellectuals, was called 'The Gilbert Vieillard Association'. In a report of 5 July 1936 on Peul emigration to Sierra Leone he recommended some relaxation of administrative practice in respect of Peul cattle herdsmen in the districts of Kindia and Mamou, primarily by exempting them from the *prestation*, by separating them from the authority of the Susu *chefs de canton*,[31] by lifting the ban on bush fires, and by respecting their feelings better by giving them 'a polite welcome in our offices'.[32] These were reasonable proposals, formulated with moderation. However, his immediate superiors, the Commandants de cercle of Kindia and Mamou, received these proposals very badly and protested loudly to the Governor, blackening Vieillard. The Mamou Commandant de cercle was particularly virulent:

> I find it somewhat paradoxical that an official, who has shown himself incapable of running a sub-division and who has himself recognised his incompetence by asking to be relieved of his duties, should make unwarranted criticism of two Commandants de cercle. . . . No inspector of administrative affairs would ever make such criticisms . . . M. Vieillard exaggerates the advantage he has in knowing the Peul language. When I question a native, with the help of an interpreter, I am sure the interpreter only translates what I say or what the native replies. . . . In any case, I cannot accept that M. Vieillard advises 'giving the natives a polite welcome in our offices'. I like natives as much as he does, perhaps more so, and in any case better than him, and I will not tolerate any official, European or native, treating any native other than politely.[33]

It is rare for the theme of the human relations between colonisers and colonised to appear in colonial documents. The last sentence makes one suspect that Vieillard has touched on a sore point, which explains the outraged reaction of his superior. Such jealousies and personal hostility were commonplace in colonial bureaucracy. But in this case Vieillard had the support of Governors Blacher at Conakry and de Coppet at Dakar. They considered his reports admirably precise and ethnographically sound.[34] In the first instance they thought of giving him a new district to be set up in Fouta-Djalon but in the face of the hostility of the *commandants de cercle* they preferred to take advantage of his abilities as an ethnologist by posting him to the Institut Français d'Afrique Noire (IFAN) which had just been set up in Dakar in 1938.[35] His job was to travel in the Sahel to study the Peuls in the French Sudan and Mauritania. So Vieillard was promoted and the science of ethnography benefited, to the detriment of reforms that he would like to have seen carried out in Guinée.[36]

The case of Gilbert Vieillard proves that a junior official, even when supported by a governor and a governor-
general, could not initiate even modest reforms in favour
of the colonised, nor modify administrative practices into
a more humane direction if he came up against the hostility
of the *commandants de cercle*, all powerful in their area. In
such conditions the status quo had every chance of being
maintained.

CONCLUSION

In sum, the impact of the Popular Front in Guinée was
very limited. The few reforms effected at this time form
part of a sequence running from 1935 to 1942 and for the
most part cannot be especially attributed to the Popular
Front. Those individuals within the colonial administration
with ideas for reform were neutralised by the routine of
the system, the hostility of the various administrative offices
and of private interests. Folk memory is rarely mistaken:
older Guinéens still remember, and speak about, Haidara
Kontofili's Islamic revolt of 1931 and the hard times of
the war effort in 1943–45, but for them the Popular Front
means nothing.

Notes and References

1. The first reliable census, carried out in 1955, showed a rural population of 92 per cent: the proportion was certainly even higher in
1936.
2. J. Richard-Molard, 'La banane de Guinée Française', *Revue de
géographie alpine*, 3 (1943) pp. 345–91.
3. It was among the Conakry *évolués* that the Gaullist resistance networks, who were to be active in Guinée between 1940 and 1942,
also concentrated their recruitment.
4. ANSOM, Aff. Pol. 978, Rapport politique de la Guinée pour 1938.
5. N. Bernard-Duquenet, *Le Sénégal et le Front Populaire* (L'Harmattan,
1985) p. 109.
6. Ibid., p. 139. The author gives no date.
7. Ibid., pp. 141–42. A decision of 9 July 1936, applied in the decree
of 11 March 1937, legalised trade unions and professional associations.
A second decree of 20 March 1937 extended the metropolitan law

on conciliation and arbitration to AOF. *J.O. du Sénégal*, 19 April 1937, pp. 326ff.

8. Ibid., p. 139. The author gives as her source ANS, K181-26.
9. ANSOM, Aff. Eco. 103, 'Mission d'avril 1937 en Guinée de M. le Gouverneur Tap, Inspecteur du Travail', 15 May 1937.
10. O. Goerg, 'La Guinée', in C. Coquery-Vidrovitch (ed.), *L'Afrique occidentale au temps des Français* (La Découverte, 1992) p. 363.
11. N. Bernard-Duquenet, op. cit., p. 149. But this minimum had not changed since 1926 and Tap himself recognised that the rise was insufficient to compensate for the rise in the cost of living, given the successive devaluations of the franc.
12. 'Il faut aussi que disparaisse de l'esprit des chefs d'exploitations cette conviction périmée, mais tenace, que l'Administration française est à leur service exclusif et doit appuyer de toutes ses forces toutes leurs prétentions. . . . Dans les conflits professionnels, l'Administration doit rester l'arbitre'. ANSOM, Aff. Eco. 103, Mission Tap, op. cit.
13. In AOF, the tax was a flat rate for all native tax-payers and was payable per head, hence the name '*capitation*' (poll tax).
14. '. . . l'année 1936 a été la dernière d'une série d'années noires', G. Vieillard, 'Notes sur les Peuls du Fouta-Djallon', *Bulletin de l'IFAN*, II, 1–2 (1940) p. 171.
15. ANSOM, Aff. Pol. 978, Rapports politiques de la Guinée, 1937, 1938; M. Trentadue, 'La société guinéenne dans la crise de 1930: fiscalité et pouvoir d'achat', *Revue française d'histoire d'outre-mer*, LXIII, 232–3 (1976) pp. 628–39. Trentadue's very revealing graph is reproduced in O. Goerg, 'La Guinée', op. cit., p. 349.
16. F. Béavogui, 'Contribution à l'histoire des Loma de la Guinée forestière de la fin du XIXe siècle à 1945', Thèse de doctorat, Université de Paris VII, 1991, p. 469.
17. The livestock tax, established in 1930, was levied on cattle, sheep and goats and especially penalised the Peul herdsmen. The administration scrapped it when it was realised that it led to a large number of Fouta-Djalon Peuls fleeing into Portuguese Guinée or Sierra Leone with their families and their flocks, thus running the risk of diminishing the number of cattle in Guinée. The poll tax was payable by every person over the age of eight, of either sex, before 1936 and over 14 years old after that date. The reform of the age at which children became liable to pay the poll tax therefore lightened the tax burden on large families.
18. ANS, 21G62(17), Minister for the Colonies Rollin to Governor-General Brévié of AOF, 21 Dec. 1935.
19. ANSOM, Aff. Pol. 978; ANS, 2G40/9, 2G41/21, 2G42/22, Rapports politiques de la Guinée, 1938–42; B. Fall, *Le travail forcé en Afrique Occidentale française* (Karthala, 1993) pp. 222–3; N. Bernard-Duquenet, op. cit., pp. 91–104.
20. The yearly number of prison days imposed by virtue of the special legislation for natives reached a peak in 1933–5 (13,000–15,000 days), then a trough in 1937–40 (5,000–6,000), before increasing again in 1941–3 (10,000–11,000).

21. G.Vieillard, op. cit., pp. 129, 151. The author gives a precise description of the exactions of the *batoulabé* of Fouta-Djalon in the years 1935–7.

22. M. Brot, 'Les régions frontalières Guinée/Sierra Leone du début du XXe siècle aux indépendances', Thèse de doctorat, Université de Provence, 1994, ch. 5.

23. ' . . .en ironisant sur le terme "travailleurs" appliqué à des indigènes et en proposant de supprimer tout salaire, trop d'argent ne pouvant qu'induire l'indigène en tentation'. ANSOM, Aff. Eco.103, Mission Tap, op. cit..

24. 'Cette mesure . . . prend l'apparence d'une arme dirigée contre une catégorie des travailleurs'. ANG, 2D420, Rapport de l'Inspecteur des colonies Huet sur la situation économique du cercle de Kindia, 28 June 1937.

25. 'Spéculation est le nom que l'on donne au commerce lorsqu'on veut lui apporter quelqu'entrave. . . . Les commerçants ne sont pas des philanthropes. Il est normal qu'ils attendent le plus possible pour vendre leurs stocks, si ces ventes ne doivent rien leur rapporter. . . . Que l'Administration ait le souci de protéger les intérêts de la population indigène, nul n'y contredira, mais il ne paraît pas juste de faire supporter à une fraction de la population européenne les frais de cette protection'. Ibid.

26. 'En protégeant la population indigène contre des opérations commerciales qui eussent été désastreuses pour son alimentation, l'Administration locale a-t-elle brimé le commerce, a-t-elle commis à son égard un acte arbitraire en le privant du bénéfice qu'il eût pu retirer de la hausse du riz du pays? M. l'Inspecteur Général l'affirme. S'il en est ainsi, l'auteur des mesures prises ne les regrette pas. Il considère que son premier rôle dans la colonie est d'assurer le ravitaillement normal des populations à des prix abordables, surtout lorsqu'il s'agit d'une denrée produite par les indigènes eux-mêmes, que l'esprit de négoce aurait tendance à leur arracher des mains pour les amener à le racheter plus tard beaucoup plus cher. . . . Si l'Administration locale avait facilité les opérations d'achat et de revente du riz du pays, elle aurait joué non pas un rôle de collaboration [avec le commerce], mais un rôle de complicité au préjudice des indigènes'. Reply of Governor Blacher, 23 July 1937, ibid..

27. ' . . . le souvenir d'un haut fonctionnaire intègre et droit qui avait su défendre les intérêts des populations guinéennes contre la rapacité de certains colons et de certains commerçants européens et libano-syriens'. R. Cornevin, 'Louis Blacher (1883–1960)', in *Hommes et destins. Dictionnaire biographique d'outre-mer*, Tome II, vol.1 (Académie des Sciences d'Outre-Mer, 1977) p. 94.

28. S. Le Callenec in E. M'Bokolo, *Afrique noire. Histoire et civilisations*, Tome II: *XIXe et XXe siècles* (Hatier-AUPELF, 1992), p. 358.

29. *Le Temps* was the most serious Parisian daily paper, comparable to *Le Monde* but right-wing.

30. This was the name given by the French to a mainly pastoral people

who live throughout much of West Africa, usually known as Fulani or Fula in English.

31. In this area, the Peuls were a minority in a predominantly Susu area.

32. 'Je trouve d'abord pardoxal qu'un fonctionnaire, qui s'est révélé incapable comme chef de subdivision, et qui a reconnu lui-même cette incapacité en demandant à être relevé de ses fonctions, formule à l'égard de deux commandants de cercle ... des critiques injustifiées ... comme n'en aurait pas formulées un Inspecteur des Affaires Administratives.... M. Vieillard exagère vraiment l'avantage que lui donne la connaissance de la langue peule; lorsque j'interroge un indigène, avec l'aide de l'interprète, j'ai la certitude que l'interprète ne traduit que ce que je dis ou ce que l'indigène répond.... Je ne puis en tout cas tolérer que M. Vieillard donne le conseil "de réserver aux indigènes un accueil correct dans nos bureaux". J'aime l'indigène autant que lui, mieux que lui assurément, et je ne tolérerai pas qu'un fonctionnaire quelconque, européen ou indigène, ne traite pas le dernier des indigènes avec la correction nécessaire'. ANS, 21G62(17), Administrateur-adjoint Gilbert Vieillard to the Commandant de cercle at Mamou, 5 July 1936.

33. ANS, 21G62(17), Commandant de cercle at Mamou to the Governor of Guinée, 13 July 1936.

34. P. O'Reilly, 'Gilbert Vieillard (1899–1940)', in *Hommes et destins. Dictionnaire biographique d'Outre-Mer*, Tome I (Académie des Sciences d'Outre-Mer, 1975) p. 612.

35. ANS, 21G62(17), the Governor of Guinée to the Governor-General of French West Africa, 19 August 1936; note by the Political Affairs Directorate of AOF, 23 Sept. 1936.

36. He published many excellent reports on the Peuls and left valuable manuscript material to the IFAN at Dakar. He was killed during the war in France in 1940.

10 Socialism in the Colonies: Cameroun Under the Popular Front
Jean Koufan

In the 1930s, Cameroun was a segregated and unequal society. Colonial legislation was rudimentary and the administration was totalitarian and repressive in nature but ruthlessly efficient. The economy was expanding rapidly under a militaristic conception of production closely supervised by the colonial administration, with the result that the native population was in a permanent state of contained revolt. Against this background, the victory of the Popular Front in 1936 marked an important stage in the evolution of links between Paris and Cameroun. There are two main reasons for this. First of all, at the end of the economic crisis of 1929 as the colonial 'establishment' attempted to intensify economic exploitation by means of the usual authoritarian measures, the victory of the Popular Front marked the adoption of the doctrine of 'participation' by the colonial administration. Secondly, because the Popular Front came shortly before the Second World War, its reforms largely determined the conditions in which the African colonies prepared for the war effort. The purpose of this chapter is to examine the innovations introduced by the Popular Front and their significance in Cameroun.

CAMEROUN ON THE EVE OF THE POPULAR FRONT

In 1936, Cameroun, like all colonial societies, was divided into two communities of unequal demographic and social significance: a white community of approximately 1,500 Europeans, who controlled the administration and comprised Christian missionaries, business people and colonial administrators, confronted 2 million Africans, who were divided by language, lifestyle and religious belief. These 2 million Africans were subject to the *indigénat* and were frequently either fined or imprisoned by the colonial administration:[1] thus, in 1935, 91 per cent of prisoners fell into the category of administrative internee.

On the socio-political level, Cameroun in the 1930s was a country of pent-up frustrations. The undoubted unpopularity of forced labour and forced cultivation of crops, combined with the harsh living and working conditions, could degenerate at any moment into open revolt and thus compromise the promise of excessive profits. In fact, people's resentment, although silent most of the time, had flared up many times in the form of violent revolts, like that of the Gbaya; acts of often bloody collective rebellion against representatives of colonial authority, such as tax collectors;[2] songs and dances criticising both colonial officials and *colons*;[3] protest marches;[4] petitions;[5] various, ever more ingenious, subterfuges, such as the illicit use of peddlers' licences to evade labour requisitions; and finally, people's prodigious mobility.[6] Administrative authoritarianism and the marginalisation of the indigenous population can therefore be seen as the 'crutches' on which a relatively prosperous command economy was built.

Indeed, in 1936 the Camerounian economy was expanding rapidly. The recovery had started in 1932 and gathered pace in 1935–36, as the following figures show: between 1932 and 1936, the value of imports increased from 72,598 to 126,366 billion francs, while exports increased in value from 83,115 to 168,249 billion francs.[6] This prosperity was the result of the 'forced march' development of agri-business, of which agricultural plantations and forestry were the backbone. Although the importance of the latter relative to the former declined over time, it nevertheless remained the case that these two activities accounted for 95 per cent of exports, whether measured by volume or value.

This domination of the economy by agriculture and forestry is equally striking if we look at employment patterns:

between them, these two sectors accounted for 77 per cent
of waged employment in 1935 and 78 per cent in 1936.
Both sectors paid badly and were labour-intensive because
of the rudimentary methods used. As a result of the economic recovery, the number of workers employed in the
colonial cash economy increased at the rate of 30 per cent
per year from 1933–36. This began to create labour shortages in some areas by 1936, which in turn jeopardised
economic diversification. In fact, it can be argued that
European colonisation in Cameroun had by this time reached
the limit of its capacity to expand, because the granting of
new concessions of land to Europeans had to be suspended
and the development of indigenous colonisation was now
encouraged.

The intensification of the economic struggle in order to
ward off recession necessitated the extension of the colonial infrastructure into new regions of production, which
in turn involved the mobilisation of a huge number of
workers (260,000 in 1934 and 254,000 in 1935, without
counting the veritable armies of porters, who numbered
55,000 in 1934 and 109,000 in 1935). Thus, some 67 per
cent of the total able-bodied male population (estimated
at 621,000 in 1934),[8] was employed in the colonial cash
economy in 1935, a figure which gives a clear indication
of the scale of labour mobilisation on the eve of the Popular
Front. Furthermore, most of these plantation workers, porters
and labourers recruited by the colonial administration were
not volunteers. Many were conscripted by local African chiefs
working for the administration and many more were the
product of police raids.[9] Once they arrived on site, they
were subject to military-style organisation: indeed, the construction site would often be called a 'work camp' and workers
were organised into 'brigades' under the command of a
sub-officer or a civil licensee.

Until 1937, the criteria used to decide upon wage levels
were whimsical, to say the least, and some, such as the
'humanism' of the employer, were completely subjective.
In 1935, the average daily wage of the African worker was
1.5 francs per day (39 francs per month), whereas that of
a commercial clerk (whose pay scale was the same as that
of a skilled worker on a plantation) was 6 francs per day

(156 francs per month). However, as Manga Mado has pointed out, workers were lucky to receive 5 francs at the end of the month. Frequently, 2.50 or 3 francs were all that an African worker managed to earn in a month.[10] This was because of the more or less arbitrary system of deductions that were applied.

Female and child labour were also in everyday use. L. Buell has commented on the use of child labour on road construction sites,[11] while enquiries by the administration showed that the Compagnie Française des Tabacs recruited children for work on the tobacco plantations.[12] Other reports confirmed the use of adolescents for jobs normally undertaken by adults.[13]

With regard to health, although the administration had successfully extended health cover and had also had some success in reducing the number of epidemics, notably of sleeping sickness, the health system nonetheless remained inadequate. It was based on the principle of curative, rather than preventive, medicine and this, together with the lack of health education and the inadequacy of basic public hygiene in the villages, exposed them to a high risk of infection. Death rates remained high. As for the health of workers on construction sites, certain regulations had been introduced in 1922 that provided for the ill worker to be cared for and the healthy worker to be protected against the risk of sickness or accident. But in the absence of any competent authority to enforce them, no *colon* felt obliged to observe them.[14]

Labour legislation was no better observed than health legislation. An effort had nevertheless been made in this field. Apart from the 1922 decree which required the employer to look after his ill employees, there was another decree of the same year which put an end to the 'free' recruitment of labour and subjected it to 'the agreement and control of the administration'. There was also a 1925 decree that limited the working week to 60 hours, with a maximum of 10 hours in any one day. However, despite this, the working day for the African worker often started at 4.00 a.m. and lasted for 12 to 16 hours.[15]

It is therefore no exaggeration to say that, on the eve of the Popular Front, Cameroun was, for many of the indigenous population who worked for the coloniser, a kind of 'tropical gulag'. The work camps were characterised by poverty, terrible working conditions, the unrestrained use of the whip, inadequate food, and the general physical and moral degradation of the workers. This was the price paid by African workers for their integration into the capitalist economy.

POPULAR FRONT REFORMS

Given the difficult reputation of the territory, where reactionary *colons* wielded a hidden power and were hostile to the slightest suggestion of 'pro-native' policy, the choice of governor to guide it through the changes was crucial. This delicate post required someone with a strong character, convinced of the necessity of reform. Marius Moutet's choice fell on Governor Pierre Boisson. Boisson was a former primary school teacher who had studied at the *Colo* (Ecole Coloniale) after the First World War. Straight-forward, calm with a hint of Breton determination, his appointment marked a break with the problems of the past, which he tackled with imagination and humanity. No sooner had he landed at Douala than he set the tone for his future term: 'The legislation on native labour has caught my attention', he wrote on 3 March 1937. 'The current regulations seem to me to need completion and amendment on certain points.'[16]

The outcome of this will to reform the legislation was a new set of regulations governing native labour promulgated on 17 November 1937. We shall return to this below. However, first it is worth looking at some of the more cosmetic changes introduced by the Popular Front.

As the main aim of the Popular Front was to humanise the colonial system, some of the first reforms served to calm the situation by reducing the more visible symbols of oppression. Measures such as banning the carrying of canes by Europeans, the amnesty of 12 July 1937 and the reduction of the maximum sentence possible under the *indigénat* to five days (from 15) made little difference except as evidence of a new attitude. Nonetheless, these half-measures did bring a touch of humanity to a colonial system morally deformed by the operation of the *indigénat*.

More substantial reforms followed with the decree of 17 November 1937 mentioned above. This law, revolutionary in principle, extended the benefits of social legislation in the metropole to Camerounian workers, while adapting it to local conditions. A detailed analysis of the text would be inappropriate here but it is worth noting the main improvements in relation to the 1925 decree. These improvements concerned the liberalisation of labour;[17] the revaluation of the minimum wage; the establishment of savings schemes; the extension of medical care and free medicines to the families of workers; health and safety protection for workers; the possibility of creating *économats*;[18] a more precise definition of the rights and duties of the Inspecteur du Travail and most notably, the establishment of a central labour bureau, backed by a network of 20 regional offices. As a result, the number of inspections carried out by the Inspecteurs du Travail rose by over 150 per cent between 1936 and 1937.[19]

In addition to these measures which tended to make waged labour more attractive, two other reforms were significant: the increase in wages, along with moves to improve the spending power of Camerounian workers and reforms to the system of labour dues.

The crusade for justice established by the Popular Front led the administration to declare that the plethora of wage rates was unacceptable. Why run expensive campaigns against pandemics if the colonial state could not even guarantee workers the minimum wage necessary for survival of the family? There was a need to replace the existing anarchy with a standard rate and so a minimum wage was established.

The Popular Front government intended that employers should abide by the wage rates thus fixed and that workers should receive the full amount due to them without any deductions whatsoever. This concern lay at the heart of a circular from Marius Moutet in January 1938. The text was tinged with compassion for the natives and the tone was one of moralising aimed at both officials and *colons* in Cameroun. In a burst of indignation Moutet refused to accept ' . . . that anywhere on our territory it should not be possible for the families of manual workers to live on their wages. This is a basic human right and we have a moral duty to ensure that it is respected'.[20]

Setting a good example, the local administration announced measures intended to improve the lot of its own employees. Thus the pay of personnel in the 'cadres locaux indigènes' was improved and the index of salaries was raised three months later.[21] In addition, a series of decrees and decisions by the Commissaire de la République granting various allowances and bonuses further improved the financial situation of these employees.[22] All these measures would have served no purpose, given the confusion in market prices, if the complete anarchy in price-fixing for the local market had not been effectively tackled. Indeed, this problem appeared to be so important to the Commissaire de la République that he set up a Central Committee on prices. However, a more successful approach to this problem was the creation of *économats*, which had the effect of improving the purchasing power of workers.

Another major grievance for the local population was the system of *prestations* (labour dues). These were also reformed to make them less of a burden. Thus unpaid obligatory labour was abolished by the decree of 12 August 1936; age limits for those performing the labour dues were introduced; a formal obligation to feed the workers decently so that they did not need to draw on their own food reserves was recognised and the facility to buy out labour dues in goods or cash was extended to all. Buying out labour dues had existed during the period before 1936 but it was only ever granted as a 'special favour'. In addition, the rate had been set too high to be affordable for the majority of Africans. In 1937 a new rate was fixed by the Commissaire de la République at 10 francs per day for Europeans and 2 francs on average for natives.[23] This reform produced immediate results, since the number of days' work carried out under the *prestation* system went down from 1936 to 1937. Other changes were later added to the new regulations. Labourers working more than 10 kilometres from their usual homes gained the right to rations in kind throughout the time they were required to be at the work site. The quantity varied according to region and in theory was to be calculated according to wage rates in the district concerned.[24]

The results of these reforms were felt immediately. The number of days worked per person fell in comparison with 1936. In 1939 the fall was as much as 46 per cent compared to 1936.[24] The evidence suggests that Africans who were in a position to avoid their labour service in person increasingly tended to fulfil their obligations in cash. With the Popular Front, labour dues were no longer considered as forced labour, which had been the case until then. Instead they became 'a veritable tax in every way comparable to the communal dues payable in the metropole'.[25]

Thus, in Cameroun the fight against capitalism and the bourgeoisie which controlled the metropolitan economy was transmuted into a fight against the abuses of the *colons*. Administrators and politicians were moved by the material sufferings of the colony's inhabitants. By an understandable doctrinal distortion, they equated the *colons* with exploiters and the natives with victims of injustice. The role of a government of workers was thus to denounce the social organisation in force in the colonies and to reform colonial rule so as to restore their dignity to those who had been exploited. And so the Popular Front turned the glorification of the native peasant into a doctrine. They declared the development of a European settler community based on large grants of land to be against government philosophy, thus curbing settlement in the territory.

Governor Boisson made himself theoretician of this undertaking during a conference at the Académie des Sciences Coloniales. Speaking on the theme 'European colonisation or native colonialism: we have to choose', he set out Popular Front thinking on this issue with courage and determination, which provoked great hostility.[26] According to Boisson, European colonisation and 'native development' were contradictory; thus it was no longer possible to encourage both simultaneously. Equally, it was impossible to allow the number of European settlers in Cameroun to rise without instituting a system of forced labour. 'Faced with these impossibilities, we have chosen a policy of instructing the native peasantry.'[27]

Boisson's choice in favour of the Camerounian peasantry sanctioned what had already become an incontrovertible reality: support for an indigenous 'settler' population, that is, small-scale farmers owning their cash-crop plantations and, like their European counterparts, employing waged labour. This shift corresponded to the ideas of Léon Blum, according to whom no colonial administration would succeed unless animated from within by the natives who would benefit from it. As with the metropolitan proletariat, Popular Front policy aimed to inspire the participation of the masses in the creation of their own future, which implied the emergence of small-scale, land-owning farmers open to modern production techniques.

In order that this policy should bear fruit, in other words in order that Camerounian planters should play the role assigned to them after the renewal of the pillage economy which had been in force, it was essential to give priority to the training of African supervisory staff, the creation of decent living and working conditions for African workers, and the education of producers and, especially, of the producers of the future, the peasant farmers' children. Thus the administration established a pragmatic policy of peasant education based on a tripartite emphasis on health, agricultural production and the development of manual skills for young people. Native Savings Societies (SIPs: Sociétés Indigènes de Prévoyance) were another instrument of this approach.

Created by an order of 9 July 1937 the SIPs were seen as a framework for peasant training in co-operative and civic skills. Each SIP was the responsibility of the local administrative chief; membership was obligatory. They functioned on the subscriptions of their members, subsidies from the administration and income from sales of produce. Unlike previous co-operatives the SIP were assigned the role of modernising traditional agriculture, raising production levels and of transmitting technological advances. It was hoped that the SIPs would stimulate a growth in crop yields and an improvement in labour productivity for peasants.

In 1938 13 SIPs with 1,000 local divisions were set to work training co-operative members, buying agricultural inputs and equipping small factories to undertake preliminary processing of primary products. One pilot project at Mungo bought itself a diesel-operated coffee processor and produced 170 tons of coffee in 1938.[28] However, the rise in productivity anticipated by reactivating the SIPs brought benefits, first and foremost, to European commerce, which could now count on a solvent local clientèle. Thus from the end of 1938 rigorous application of business principles by the SIPs generated substantial incomes for the local peasantry, which generated an atmosphere of euphoria:

> There was great joy both in the forest and in the savannah region. The 'big men' bought cars, rich peasants were content with record-players and European-style clothes.... Pious converts made generous donations to the missions. No-one doubted that the Golden Age had returned.[29]

Encouraged by his experience in AOF, where SIPs had rescued the indigenous economy, Governor Boisson reorganised Camerounian peasant cooperatives so that the contribution of each member was more equitably rewarded.

The emphasis on training was not limited to the popularisation of African co-operatives; other forms of social and sanitary education were also combined with this agricultural guidance. In particular, the Popular Front made medical care a priority for the first time in Cameroun. Health was now seen as the most profitable of undertakings, because it guaranteed the 'human capital' of Cameroun. A major focus of the fight for improved health care and social well-being concerned the eradication of disease. The underlying causes of disease are multiple and often overlap. They include poverty, individual ignorance, malnutrition and inadequate hygiene. So the strengthening of the agricultural service dovetailed well with an active policy on public health. The main innovation in this policy concerned the strategy planned and the means made available for carrying out the new strategy. The government set up mass medical campaigns carried out in the countryside by mobile health teams, thus taking into account for the first time the rural nature of Cameroun.[30] What is more, greater resources were also allocated to the health service. Credits granted increased by 54 per cent between 1936 and 1939.

Endowed with more adequate means the public services concentrated on three fields: the reinforcement of mobile public health services outlined above, the fight against endemic and epidemic disease and the establishment of a workplace inspectorate in each region. To crown the whole edifice, particular attention was paid to training auxiliary health workers at the newly established Ecole des Aides de Santé in Ayos. However, officials in charge of this strategy were well aware that the success of the new public health system depended on more or less favourable harvests, given that food security is an indispensible precursor of good health. Thus it was necessary to institute a policy of establishing reserves of both food crops and seed.[31]

Equally it was because of this interrelationship that school reforms were also instituted. The new policy ruled out an academic curriculum in favour of a generalised technical education. The utilitarian nature of this shift is clear. It was in this spirit that the decree of 17 March 1937 broadened the content of school teaching. The Schools Inspector was charged with ensuring adequate communications between the appropriate technical services such as Finance, Agriculture, Public Works and Health, on matters relating to their functions which might have implications for public education.[32] The same concern lay behind the circular of 27 May 1937 which directed the regional schools towards a more practical, manual education. Officials therefore expressed a desire less to educate the young than to 'train good peasants, rural artisans and foremen rather than highly qualified Africans'.[33]

This was also the aim of two new institutions created in this period: the Ecole Professionelle in Douala and the Ecole Supérieure d'Agriculture in Yaoundé. The former was responsible for training monitors for the Public Works department, overseers for the maintenance of roads and buildings and African employees for the railways and Public Works department,[34] while the Ecole d'Agriculture in Yaoundé was set up to provide trained indigenous staff for the agricultural, forestry and animal husbandry services, auxiliaries in private firms with these same interests, instructors for practical subjects in the rural and regional schools and overseers for works for the SIPs.[35]

In the light of these reforms the founding of mutual societies in all the regional schools stands out as being particularly important.[36] Acting as both producer and consumer co-operatives at the same time, the mutual societies combined the dual functions of encouraging solidarity and self-help among the pupils and of equipping them with skills for their future after leaving. By the end of 1937 there were 30 such societies. It could perhaps be said that in altering the nature of education in the colonies the French assimilationist ideal had been abandoned in favour of a pragmatism tinged with paternalism.

CONCLUSION

Boisson arrived in Cameroun in 1937. By this time the *colons* were already experiencing difficulties recruiting local labour. Workers deserted because of the disastrous labour policy pursued in the colony: abusive practices, such as low levels of pay, an excessively long working day, poor housing conditions and food rations, made work on the plantations and construction sites profoundly unappealing to African workers. Thanks to the persuasive nature of Governor Boisson's personality and the timely and important measures enacted by his administration, the Popular Front achieved a considerable improvement in the conditions of life and work of the Camerounian people. In a short time it succeeded in humanising the operation of colonial rule to a significant extent. This was all the more urgent since the European plantations in the territory, which formed the main centre of white settlement along the whole of the Atlantic coast of West Africa, showed worrying signs of collapse as a result of the labour policy that had been pursued hitherto.

Boisson's talent was to have had a clear vision of the need to subordinate (in a real rather than a merely cosmetic way) the organisation of labour to the requirements of capital. For Boisson, as for the metropolitan strategists of the Popular Front, it was less a case of changing the system of exploitation than of adapting it to the imperative of increased production. Economic necessity and political conviction thus combined to oppose keeping the African population in a state of semi-slavery. The common denominator of the reforms discussed here was their almost exclusive attack on the more shocking abuses created by the *indigénat*. Although timid, clearly insufficient and full of ambiguity, these reforms served as a facelift for the destructive militarism then in force. However, even as a cosmetic exercise, they were a distinct improvement on the inactivity of the previous 20 years.

Notes and References

1. Cf. ANSOM, Fonds Cameroun, T. P. C. Box 20 D5, Rapport du Gouverneur des colonies, May 1918, p. 103: according to this report, relations between the administration and Africans were generally expressed by the words 'fine' and 'prison'.
2. See, for example, decrees no. 270, 20 Nov. 1933; no. 219, 1 Aug. 1934; no. 28, 7 Feb. 1937; no. 144, 10 May 1937.
3. There are many examples of songs of protest against the repressive nature of the production regime. One such song was 'Les chagrins de la captivité et les espoirs des compagnons des Allemands' sung by the KFDGV, a group of Germanophile Camerounians.
4. A good example of one of these protest marches was the Douala women's protest march in July 1931 against the head tax; see J. Derrick, 'Elitisme colonial au Cameroun: Le cas des Douala dans les années 30', in M. Z. Njeuma, *Histoire du Cameroun (XIXe siècle – début XXe siècle* (L'Harmattan, 1989) pp. 163–201.
5. Two examples are the 'Pétition des Douala' (1929) and the 'Pétition des Yevols' (1931). See D. Abwa, '"Commandement européen" et "commandement indigène" au Cameroun sous administration française de 1916 à 1960', Doctoral thesis, Université de Yaounde, 1994.
6. See J. Koufan, 'Travail forcé et migrations au Cameroun: le cas des Yambassa dans l'entre-deux-guerres (1918–1946)', Masters dissertation, Université de Paris VII, 1979, p. 196.
7. RASDN, 1936, p. 84.
8. RASDN, 1934, p. 127.
9. L. Kaptué, *Travail et main d'oeuvre au Cameroun sous le régime français, 1916–52* (L'Harmattan, 1986) pp. 225–6.
10. R. H. Manga Mado, *Complaintes d'un forçat* (Editions Clé, 1970) p. 23.
11. R. L. Buell, *The Native Problem in Africa* (Frank Cass, 1965) p. 326.
12. ANSOM Aff. Pol. C2689 D5 MOI, Rapport du Commissaire de la République au Ministère des Colonies, 19 Feb. 1927.
13. L. Kaptué, op. cit., pp. 124–5.
14. Even when they did consent to do so, the task of caring for hundreds of workers would often fall to one ill-equipped nurse. More commonly though, as various exchanges of correspondence show, plantation owners had no qualified nurse and no medicines avail-

able, even for the most basic of treatments. Cf. correspondence between the chief of the Bamileke region and the Governor concerning conditions on M. Bove's plantation in ANY Archives Politiques et Administratives 11119, 15 Mar. 1945.

15. H. R. Manga Mado, op. cit., p. 67.
16. 'La législation du travail indigène a... retenu mon attention. La réglementation actuelle m'a semblé d'ores et déjà devoir être complétée et amendée sur certains points'. Note of 3 Mar. 1937 on the subject of the application to Cameroun of the social laws voted by the French parliament on 20, 21, 24 June 1936, ANY Nouveau Fonds 872/1.
17. ANY Affaires Politiques et Administratives 11381, 'Services', 1938.
18. These were a sort of shop or depot established within each enterprise to sell to workers imported articles of primary importance at official prices. Their aim was to strengthen the purchasing power of wage-labourers.
19. J. Bassanguena, 'Le Cameroun sous le Front Populaire, réformes sociales et réactions du colonat 1936–1938', Masters dissertation, Université de Yaoundé, 1991, p. 67.
20. '... que quelque part dans notre domaine, il ne soit pas possible à une famille de manoeuvres de vivre en travaillant, c'est un droit essentiel de l'individu: nous avons l'obligation morale d'en assumer le respect'. Circular by M. Moutet quoted in *L'Eveil du Cameroun*, 300 (23 Jan. 1938) p. 3.
21. *JOTC* 435 (1938) pp. 384–88; see also *JOTC* 434 (1938) p. 339. The 'cadre local indigène' was the corps into which African workers were recruited, the pay scales of which were far lower than those that applied to French employees in the 'cadre supérieur'.
22. *JOTC* 433 (1938) p. 296 and *JOTC* 435 (1938) p. 393.
23. This figure is an average calculated from the various values given in the table in *JOTC*, 401 (1937) p. 20.
24. *JOTC*, 428 (1938) p. 25.
24. L. Kaptué, op. cit., p. 165.
25. '...un véritable impôt, à tous égards comparable à l'impôt communal des prestations en métropole'. RASDN.(1938) p. 129.
26. J. Bassanguena, op. cit., pp. 60–77.
27. 'Devant ces impossibilités, nous avons choisi la politique qui consiste à éduquer le paysannat indigène'. ANSOM. Cameroun, Affaires Politiques C30 D278. Note confidentielle du Gouverneur Boisson, June 1938.
28. M. Homet, *Afrique Noire, terre inquiète. Garderons-nous nos colonies d'Afrique? AOF – Cameroun-AEF* (1938) p. 138.
29. 'Ce fut une grande joie dans la forêt et dans la savane. Les notables achetèrent des autos, les paysans riches se contentèrent de phonographes, de vêtements à la mode d'Europe.... Les personnes pieuses firent de grands cadeaux aux missions.... Personne ne doutait que l'âge d'or ne fût revenu', G. Manue, *Cameroun, création française* (1938) p. 95.
30. *JOTC*, 450 (1938) pp. 1009–44. Decree of 7 February 1938 on the

organisation and workings of the health service in Cameroun.
31. *JOTC*, 421 (1937) p. 88. Decree of 4 June 1937 and circular relating to the establishment of reserves of foodstuffs and seeds.
32. *JOTC*, 410 (1937) p. 299.
33. '. . . former de bons paysans, des artisans ruraux et des contremaîtres plutôt que des bacheliers noirs'. Quoted in J. Bassanguena, op. cit., p. 77.
34. *JOTC*, 412 (1937) p. 299. Decree of 29 May 1937 establishing the technical school in Douala.
35. *JOTC*, 413 (1937) p. 524. Decree of 17 June 1937 setting up an Ecole d'Agriculture in Yaoundé.
36. *JOTC*, 439 (1938) p. 586. Decree of 5 June 1938 regulating the school mutual societies in the territory's schools.

11 The Popular Front and the Blum–Viollette Plan

France Tostain

When the Popular Front government brought Léon Blum to power in 1936, he was bound by the coalition programme of the different parties. However, as Charles-Robert Ageron has observed, 'the common programme of that popular alliance had virtually forgotten the colonies, apart from thinking of sending an official fact-finding mission to them'.[1] The fact was that, as Charles-André Julien remarked, 'Algerian matters, at that turbulent time, were not uppermost in Blum's mind and he had an incomplete grasp of the essential elements of the colonial problem in Algeria'.[2] His personal position regarding colonisation was that of the Section Française de l'Internationale Ouvrière (SFIO) in the 1920s, that is to say an anti-assimilationist position, 'colonisation being justified only insofar as it prepared the peoples for self-government'.[3] However, despite the anti-assimilationist position of the SFIO colonial commission, at its 33rd National Congress in 1936, the SFIO changed its position markedly[4] by proposing an assimilative programme of reforms through the *cahier des doléances* of Frenchified Algerians submitted by Jules Moch. The programme which was passed without debate and without prior consideration by either the colonial commission or Georges Nouelle who headed it, committed the party in its attitude towards the Frenchified Algerians who thought they had the full support of the socialists. For his part, at the Congress of the Ligue des Droits de l'Homme in February 1931, Maurice Viollette, who had been Governor-General of Algeria from 1925 to 1927, condemned any doctrine other than that of assimilation. 'The assertion', he said, 'that the indigenous population should develop in the context of its own civilisation is one that I refuse to accept: indigenous civilisations that have undergone colonisation are precisely

218

those which are almost invariably closed to development of any kind'.[5]

There being no clear-cut colonial programme, Léon Blum surrounded himself with trustworthy people who had a thorough knowledge of Algerian matters, and appointed as Minister of State the French socialist, Maurice Viollette who had a detailed knowledge of the situation there. He had even been nicknamed 'Viollette l'Arbi (the Arab)' by the French Algerians because of his strongly pro-native stance. But his remit as Minister of State was ill-defined and his 'scope for action over the administrators limited', as was stressed by Charles-André Julien.[6] As it happened Algeria, unlike the other colonies because of its particular status as a territory formally divided into *départements*, came under the control not of Marius Moutet, whom Léon Blum had appointed as Minister for the Colonies, nor of Pierre Viénot, whom he had appointed as Undersecretary of State responsible for the Protectorates and the Mandated Levant Territories at the Ministry for Overseas Affairs, nor of the Président du Conseil, but of the Minister for the Interior and his Undersecretary of State for Algerian Affairs, Raoul Aubaud, who was also the Président du Bureau of the Radical Party. The Governor-General of Algeria, Lebeau, was himself a former *préfet*. The radical elected representatives for Algeria, notably Paul Cuttoli, whose constituency was Constantine, and Senator Duroux of Algiers, who was the proprietor of the newspaper *L'Echo d'Alger*, were men of influence at the Ministry for the Interior. Furthermore, Raoul Aubaud made Maurice Cuttoli (son of Paul) *chef-adjoint* of his *cabinet* so as to remain in contact with the Algerian Radicals.[7] In Parliament and on parliamentary commissions this Radical group had the support of the Comité de l'Afrique Française under the chairmanship of Léon Baréty, and of the Groupe Colonial de la Chambre whose chairman, Léon Archimbaud, was also the rapporteur for the colonial budget. It was in the interest of this pressure group to maintain the status quo in Algeria and to thwart reform of any kind.

In 1936 and 1937 Algeria underwent a period of political turmoil similar to that of metropolitan France, but for three reasons which were not necessarily connected with

the national and international preoccupations of the Popular
Front: the resumption of the Blum–Viollette plan supported
by the Europeanised Muslim bourgeoisie; the activities of
the Congrès Musulman which was trying to bring together
all the political tendencies in a common front; and the
establishment of the nationalist Etoile Nord Africaine of
Messali Hadj in Algeria ten years after its formation in
France.

BACKGROUND TO THE BLUM–VIOLLETTE PLAN

The much talked-of Blum–Viollette Plan was in reality merely
the re-adoption of a bill introduced in July 1931 by Maurice
Viollette. Its aim was to grant French citizenship to well-
educated and influential Algerians without their having
to abandon their *statut personnel* as Muslims. It also set out
to take measures which would be of financial advantage to
Muslims, so as to establish, among other things, parity at
the institutional level between the Muslim and European
communities. For an understanding of the matter of *statut
personnel* in those territories which were French *départements*
incorporated into the French administrative system one must
go back to the time of Napoleon III and the founding of
the Third Republic.

In his famous letter of 3 February 1863 prompted by
Ismail Urbain who had been Chef de Bureau at the new
Ministry for Algeria in 1858 and then Conseiller-rapporteur
of the Conseil du Gouvernement in 1860, Napoleon III
described his Algerian colonial policy as being anti-
assimilationist. 'Algeria', he said, 'is not strictly speaking a
colony but rather an Arab Kingdom; the native people and
the colonists have an equal right to my protection'.[8] The
Senatus Consultum [senate decree] of 22 April 1863 granted
the Algerian tribes ownership of the lands they had occupied for generations. Thus Algeria was divided into military territory and civil territory: in the first of these the
Arabs were under the protection of the military who took
no active part in the day-to-day running of their affairs,
but guarded them against the territorial greed of the new
colonists who were granted possession of the civil territo-

ries. It was Ismail Urbain again who stated that 'the Senatus Consultum regarding the naturalisation of Algerians must not, on the pretext of liberalism, seek to undermine their Arab-Muslim personality'.[9] They were French in order to establish civil equality between Arabs and Europeans while at the same time preserving their *statut personnel*. Also, Muslim courts were recognised as having the right to have jurisdiction over any litigation on the subject. This system was not unlike that of the Milal (communities) of the Ottoman Empire. The Muslim community was regarded, from a political point of view, as comprising French subjects who could seek French citizenship if they chose to do so and thus surrender their *statut personnel* as Muslims. The Senatus Consultum of 1865 also enabled non-French Europeans living in Algeria to acquire French nationality.

The Third Republic brought with it the destruction of the status quo established by the Empire. In accordance with the colonial doctrine of assimilation, the French authorities introduced a law in 1889 to make compulsory the naturalisation of the European population, something which they did not particularly want and which resulted in them outnumbering the official French *colons*. Those who were at that time called the Jewish Algerians were also naturalised under the Crémieux decree, which swelled the French colonist numbers in the closing years of the nineteenth century to half a million. Thus it was more a political decision than a question of linguistic assimilation.

In the decades that followed, all the ambiguity of the colonial doctrine of assimilation hinged upon what exactly was meant by the term 'Algerian'. In the main, people in France took relatively little interest in colonisation and were unaware of the complexity of the Algerian situation during the Third Republic; as they saw it, all the measures adopted in the name of the assimilation of Algeria to France were liberal and applicable to the Algerians as a whole no matter what their origins might be, whereas for the public lawyers of the period the term 'Algerian' still implied 'Algerian European'. All in all the assimilation issue concerned the non-French Europeans, that is to say those who at the time were known as the 'Néo-Français'.[10] It was because of this that the abolition of the Bureaux Arabes and the military territories, plus the extension of the *régime civil*, in accordance with that of metropolitan France, enabled the colonists to buy back the common land belonging to the Arab tribes, and that the establishment in 1900 of a colonial assembly, which, in the name of assimilation, entrusted the management of the budget – '*les délégations financières*' – to Algerian Europeans, prevented the Paris government from implementing its decisions. Every measure taken in the name of assimilation was, in fact, meant to ensure the autonomy of Algerian Europeans in relation to Paris and yet they remained under the protection of France should there be a Muslim uprising. Thus to an increasing extent Paris acted as an arbiter between the two communities; in 1936 the French government maintained its colonial interests but for strategic, rather than economic, reasons.

The Muslim *statut personnel* had been taken into account by Ismail Urbain who, himself a convert to Islam, wished to respect the cultural and religious identity of the Muslims while at the same time associating them with France. However, he turned against the French under the Third Republic since adopting French citizenship involved the total rejection of Islam; to cross this legal Rubicon was regarded by the rest of the Muslim community as a betrayal, hence the taunting nickname 'M'tourni' [from the French '*tourner*'] which was applied to Muslim Algerians who embraced the values as well as the patterns of behaviour and dress code of French culture at the expense of their original, Arab culture.

In this sense the Blum–Viollette Plan set a precedent, for it granted French citizenship while at the same time allowing Muslims to retain their *statut personnel*. The plan was in line with assimilationist position of the Radicals of the Third Republic in that its aim was to incorporate Muslims into the French electoral body. However, in terms of assimilation the plan was so modest as to be little more than symbolic, since at a time when there were some 5 million Algerian Muslims, it made provision for only 21,000 of them to be granted citizenship in 1936. Those concerned were in a similar socio-economic bracket to those who at the beginning of the century in France had benefited under the Radicals from the social mobility towards lower middle-class status, which means that they were in the main

Muslims working in the teaching profession, the civil service, the army and social administration. The likelihood, then, would seem to be that, in the guise of an assimiliationist doctrine, the logic of the plan was, over a number of years, to enlarge the electoral body of Muslims in those categories so as to give them parity with the 200,000 Europeans who were eligible to vote. This would open the door to the progressive development of Algeria into a Franco-Muslim Dominion. In support of this view it should be noted that, at the beginning of the 1930s, Viollette drew attention to the fact 'that in Algeria there were 100,000 Muslims who had urgently to be taken into account, and that if they were not to be allowed to regard France as their homeland, then they would seek one elsewhere'.[11] In fact, as Jean-Claude Vatin has rightly remarked, 'assimilation was simply a way of achieving socio-political parity between Europeans and Muslims; it was never an end in itself'.[12]

OPPOSITION TO THE PLAN AND OBSTACLES TO IMPLEMENTATION

Viollette's plan in Algeria had the support of the Frenchified members of the Fédération des Elus, Dr Bendjelloul and Ferhat Abbas, and also of all those then commonly known as the *évolués*. Initially, however, it was opposed by the Ulema, the best-known representative of whom, Ben Badis, stated that it 'had the grave disadvantage of distancing the élite from the mass of the people from which they sprang and with whom they were to remain in permanent contact'.[13] It was also opposed by the communists and l'Etoile Nord Africaine of Messali Hadj who, as early as 1926, was campaigning for independence. Viollette also had to reach a compromise with the radical opposition. Régnier, the former Radical minister, made it known that he had said in 1935 that there could not be two categories of French citizen, and Daladier, who was Vice-Président du Conseil in 1936, announced that he would oppose the satisfying of Algerian demands for parliamentary representation for as long as the Algerian Muslims kept their *statut musulman*. All this did not augur well for Viollette's task.

The political situation in 1936, however, gave rise to U-turns in the policies of the parties in France and Algeria alike. It must be stressed, though, that the ultimate motives of the parties in France and Algeria were not precisely the same since in France their tactics tended to be prompted by opposition to fascism, whereas in Algeria they were prompted by nationalism.

The Algerian Communist Party was founded in January 1936 at the Congrès de Villeurbanne on the initiative of André Ferrat who had responsibility for the colonies. He had little influence on the mass of the people, however, owing to his atheistic stance which was rejected by both the Fédération des Elus and the Ulema. At the same time, the Communist Party which, like Messali Hadj, was in favour of the election of an Algerian parliament by universal suffrage and of the total independence of Algeria before 1936, abandoned its stance in order to support the government coalition and campaign against fascism.[14] The communists thus gave the Blum–Viollette Plan their support and moved closer to the Fédération des Elus and the Ulema.

For its part, the Etoile Nord Africaine of Messali Hadj, founded in France in 1926 among immigrant manual workers, found it difficult to escape from the dominance of the French Communist Party whose workers' struggle did not always correspond to the nationalist struggle of Messali. It was in December 1935, when Messali Hadj was forced into exile in Switzerland to avoid arrest, that the Etoile Nord Africaine, deprived of his leadership, took on a new role, led by Amar Khider,[15] under the overall control of the Communist Party, and temporarily abandoned the call for independence.

The Ulema, which included Muslim reformists such as Ben Badis, Al Uqbi and Al Ibrahimi, realised that the Blum–Viollette Plan was not directly in their interest; the purpose of their activities was in essence to restore, through language and religion, the Arab–Muslim personality of the Algerians. Their primary objective was to reform the nineteenth-century Islam of the marabouts so as to adapt it to the urban conditions of the twentieth century, in much the same way as had happened in Egypt under Mohammed Abdu and Rashid Rida. They relaunched Arabisation, set up Muslim Boy Scout groups and boosted the self-esteem of Algerian Muslims. It was above all in that spirit and wishing to make their voices heard that they joined forces at the Congrès Musulman.

The overriding objective of the Congrès Musulman held in Algiers on 7 June 1936 was to set up a common Muslim front which could rally the bulk of the Muslim electorate to support the Blum–Viollette Plan, counter the influence of Algerian radicals in Paris, and enable the Muslims to resist offers of membership from French political parties of both left and right. There was a good reason for this: the Parti Populaire Français, for example, under the leadership of Doriot and his Algerian representative, Victor Arrighi, had gained a great deal of ground in the region around Oran where their federation had a membership amounting to over 10,000 and was recruiting among Muslims and *Néo-Français* in opposition to the Blum-Viollette Plan, playing on both anti-Semitism and anti-Marxism.

However, it was inevitable that, despite all the talk of unity of purpose, the ultimate aims of those involved, which, for the time being, were overshadowed by short-term tactics, should once again come to the surface: from the outset the assimilationist and Frenchified Fédération des Elus clashed with the Ulema whose claim to an Arab and Muslim personality was a constant, albeit latent, concern.[16] The split between the two groups prompted the Ulema to reach a compromise with the Algerian Communist Party, whereas Dr Bendjelloul sought the backing of the traditional marabouts and official muftis to question the right of the reformist Ulema to represent Muslims. On 2 August the mufti Mahmud Kahhul was assassinated, and Bendjelloul severed relations with the Ulema, who in turn strongly criticised him for the arrest of one of their number, Al-Uqbi. As for Messali Hadj who returned to Paris on 10 June having been officially pardoned, he did not attend the Congress and remained opposed to the Blum–Viollette Plan, demanding the setting-up of an Algerian parliament. He strengthened the nationalist line of the Etoile Nord-Africaine and abandoned the idea of sending international troops to Spain; this marked the beginning of the break between the Etoile Nord-Africaine and the Communist Party.[17]

On 23 July 1936 Léon Blum, Maurice Viollette and Jules Moch received the delegates to the Congrès musulman who submitted their demands, calling not only for naturalisation in the *statut*, but also for the abolition of the *délégations financières* and of the Government-General.

On 2 August, in the football stadium in Algiers, Messali Hadj, who was then a delegate to the Congrès musulman, raised the question of independence. He was carried shoulder-high by the jubilant crowd, and established the Etoile Nord-Africaine on Algerian soil but, in so doing, demonstrated his opposition to the other parties in the Congrès. This led to the expulsion, on 24 January 1937, of the Etoile militants by the Algerian Communist Party which had infiltrated all the structures within the Congrès. On 27 January 1937, Governor Lebeau obtained the dissolution of the Etoile despite the protests of certain members of the SFIO, including the revolutionary Left of Marceau Pivert. Later, on 11 March 1937, it re-formed in Nanterre under the new name of the Parti du Peuple Algérien.

Meanwhile, European Algerians were also organising themselves: in the football stadium in Algiers on 9 August 1936, in response to the Congrès Musulman, the parties of the Right held a big political rally which was attended by 25,000 people. Following the tabling in the National Assembly of the Blum–Viollette Plan on 23 December 1936, all but two members of the Congrès des Maires d'Algérie voted for the rejection of the Plan.[18] The Radicals sent delegations to the Ministers, to the *groupes parlementaires* and to the commissions, and obtained formal declarations condemning the Plan from prominent figures such as Paul Reynaud. Whereas in the lower chamber the Popular Front representatives accounted for 380 votes – 270 of which came from the Socialist-Communist coalition – as against 220 votes for the opposition, the situation in the upper chamber was different. The most recent intake of new senators – one-third of the total membership – had been elected in 1935, and although the groups of the Left were in the majority, the internal balance was completely different: the Communists and the Socialists held only 15 seats and were heavily outnumbered by the Radicals under Cailleux, with the result that the Senate succeeded in having the Blum–

Viollette Plan struck off the agenda, and Blum refused to re-introduce it by decree later. On 21 June 1937 Blum fell from power; his place was taken by the Radical, Camille Chautemps who, favouring the colonists, made no attempt to resurrect the Plan. In the end, then, the Blum–Viollette Plan was never put to the vote, and it was not until eight years later that General de Gaulle eventually readopted its measures in the government ruling of 7 March 1944.

CONCLUSION

1936 and 1937 in Algeria were years of great expectations and shattered illusions. The 1944 ruling came far too late to win over the Frenchified Algerians and bring about their cooperation; they gradually set their sights on independence. In fact it was the nationalist Parti du Peuple Algérien of Messali Hadj which emerged the winner at that period. As Charles André Julien remarked, 'to bring about any kind of change in the deadlocked situation, there would have had to be a senior civil servant from France keeping a constant eye on every European civil servant in Algeria, which was financially out of the question'.[19] During the Second World War the question of independence arose once more, owing to American influence in North Africa. The San Francisco Conference proved to be yet another disappointment for Algerian Muslims.[20] When fighting broke out in Algeria, the first encounter involving the nationalists, who had done too little to ensure the support of the population at large, led to massacres in the Constantine area of eastern Algeria, extremist behaviour on the part of the political parties and the ruthless campaign of repression by the army in Sétif, some 120 kilometres west of Constantine. It was be another 17 years before the Algerian Revolution and the war of independence came to an end.

228   *Blum–Viollette Bill*

Notes and References

1. 'Le programme commun de ce Rassemblement populaire avait pratiquement oublié les colonies, sauf à penser y envoyer une commission d'enquête officielle'. C.-R. Ageron, 'L'Algérie entre le Front Populaire et le Congrès Musulman', in *"L'Algérie algérienne" de Napoléon III à De Gaulle* (Editions Sindbad, 1980), p. ?.
2. 'Les affaires algériennes n'étaient pas, en cette période troublée, la préoccupation majeure du Président du Conseil et les données essentielles du problème colonial algérien lui échappaient'. C.-A. Julien, 'Léon Blum et les pays d'outre-mer', in P. Renouvin and R. Rémond (eds), *Léon Blum, Chef de Gouvernement, 1936–37* (Presses de la Fondation Nationale des Sciences Politiques, 1981) p. 377.
3. '... ne trouvant de justification à la colonisation que dans la mesure où elle préparait les peuples à se gouverner eux-mêmes'. Ibid.
4. C.-R. Ageron, '*L'Algérie*', op. cit., p. ?.
5. 'Soutenir que l'indigène doit évoluer dans sa propre civilisation est une affirmation que je me refuse à comprendre car, précisément le plus souvent, les civilisations indigènes qui ont subi la colonisation sont des civilisations qui sont fermées à toute évolution'. *Cahiers des Droits de l'homme* (1931) p. 125.
6. '... ses possibilités d'action sur les administrateurs limitées'. C.-A. Julien, in *Léon Blum*, op. cit., p. 379.
7. B. Droz and E. Lever, *Histoire de la guerre d'Algérie, 1954–62* (Seuil, 1982) p. 43.
8. 'L'Algérie n'est pas à proprement parler une colonie mais un Royaume arabe; les indigènes et les colons ont un droit égal à ma protection'. C-R. Ageron, '*L'Algérie*', op. cit., p. 24?.
9. '... le Senatus Consulte sur la naturalisation des Algériens ne doit pas, sous prétexte de libéralisme, attenter à leur personnalité arabo-musulmane'. Ibid.
10. C.-R. Ageron, *France coloniale ou parti colonial?* (Presses Universitaires de France, 1978) p. 67.
11. '... il y avait en Algérie 100,000 musulmans avec qui il fallait absolument compter et que si on ne leur donnait pas la Patrie Française, ils iraient en chercher une autre ailleurs'. C-R. Ageron, *Histoire de l'Algérie contemporaine*, vol. 2 (Presses Universitaires de France, 1979) p. 388.
12. 'L'assimilation n'est qu'un moyen pour parvenir à la parité socio-politique entre européens et musulmans, jamais une fin en soi'. J.-C. Vatin, *L'Algérie politique. Histoire et société* (Presses de la Fondation des Sciences Politiques, 1983), p. 23.
13. '[Il] présentait le grave inconvénient d'éloigner l'élite de la masse dont elle est issue et avec laquelle elle devait rester en contact permanent'. A. Merad, *Le Réformisme musulman en Algérie de 1925 à 1940* (Mouton & Cie., 1967) p. 398. The Ulema were a group of reformist, modernising Muslim scholars, such as Ben Badis and Al Uqbi, who hoped to create an 'Islam of the towns' to counter French cultural and social influences.

14. B. Stora, *Nationalistes algériens et révolutionnaires français au temps du Front Populaire* (L'Harmattan, 1987) p. 36.
15. Amar Khider was an official of the Etoile Nord-Africaine, in charge of the newspaper *Ikhdam* until 1936. He was later to become a member of the pro-German wing of Parti du Peuple Algérien led by Messali Hadj, still in charge of their paper, *Al Oumma*. This group was expelled from the party shortly before the outbreak of the Second World War.
16. B. Stora, op. cit., p. 39.
17. Ibid., p. 40.
18. C.-A. Julien, in *Léon Blum*, op. cit., p. 381.
19. '. . . pour changer quelque chose à la situation bloquée de l'Algérie, il aurait fallu mettre un fonctionnaire de la métropole derrière chaque fonctionnaire européen, ce qui était financièrement impossible'. Ibid.
20. Algerian nationalists had hoped that American anti-imperialist rhetoric would be put into effect and that the Americans would free them from French colonialism. However, at the end of the War, the US backed the French in Indochina and dropped their opposition to colonial rule in North Africa as well.

12 The Popular Front's Colonial Policies in Indochina: Reassessing the Popular Front's 'Colonisation Altruiste'

Panivong Norindr

This study builds on the compelling work of Daniel Hémery, Jacques Marseille, Manuela Semidei, and other scholars who have examined the colonial policies of the Popular Front and their impact on the metropolitan and colonial economy. Although their analyses consider the importance of the colonies for French capitalism – thus placing political economy at the centre of the imperial enterprise – their work also fails to call into question the very notion of 'colonisation altruiste', a concept put forward by Marius Moutet, the Ministre des Colonies, during the Popular Front government. For Marseille and others, the 'politique altruiste' outlined in Moutet's speech opening the Conference of Governors-General, merely describes an old economic precept, 'the old theme of complementary economies'.[1] Economic determinism can blind as well as illuminate. I contend that such a problematic and overdetermined expression as 'colonisation altruiste' precludes us from so conveniently separating the economic from the political, and I would add, the 'humanitarian', taking as my model, Jules Ferry. I evoke Jules Ferry not gratuitously but because I consider his address in front of la Chambre des Députés, on 21 July 1884, to be an important critical intertext that enables us better to situate and understand the Popular Front's colonial policies and its so-called 'colonisation altruiste'. More than 50 years before the Popular Front's coming to power, Jules Ferry had declared:

The policy of colonial expansionism is both a political *and* an economic system; I said that we can link this system to three realms: the economic, the civilising mission of great importance, and the political and partriotic realm. On the economic terrain, the need for markets . . . there is a second point, a second order of ideas . . . that is to say, the humanitarian and civilising aspect of the question . . . one must speak openly of the fact that the superior races have a right, because they have a duty. They have the duty to civilise the inferior races.[2]

Ferry's unapologetic ideas about French colonisation resonate, in strange and complicated ways, with many of the Socialists' prononcements. His speech may also provide an appropriate entry point for our discussion of the Popular Front's colonial policies.

I must confess that as a literary and cultural critic, I am particularly responsive to the use of rhetorical language in political and critical discourse. I was struck by the expression 'colonisation altruiste' because it sought to reconcile, by juxtaposing, unproblematically, two incompatible notions, 'colonisation' and 'altruism'. The word colonisation inhabits a rather turbulent field and attests to the existence of unequal power relations between a dominant culture and a dominated nation, the former intent in transforming the later into a colony. Altruism belongs, on the other hand, to a completely different realm. It is a philosophical term that describes devotion to others as an ideal rule for moral conduct.'[3] The context in which these two terms are conjoined may shed some light on the Socialists' imperial logic. Let us therefore examine more closely an excerpt of Marius Moutet's speech to determine the main arguments he offered to support the notion of 'colonisation altruiste':

First, we must see that we support and improve the life of all of the colonised populations. The question is not to consider the colonies in terms of the mother country's selfish interests; it means to organise them so that they form with the metropole a complex whole acceptable to all. We would not achieve this if our only intent were to make certain European and indigenous oligarchies rich. As with war, such a selfish colonisation would not pay for itself. On the contrary, it would impoverish the national economy. Altruistic colonisation, based on the need to increase the buying power of the people, favours the overseas establishment of assets, stocks and credit balance, an indispensible condition for trade with the mother country.[4]

Moutet declared, from the outset, that the primary goal of the colonial enterprise was to improve the well-being of the colonised. If we are to believe Moutet, a new era was dawning. The colonies would no longer be considered for the sole benefit of the metropole. What he appeared to be proposing was nothing less than the complete reorganisation of the colonies, by transforming them into 'a complex whole acceptable to all.' However, no concrete measures that would allow such radical changes to take place, were presented. Nothing was said of the criteria or mechanisms to be put in place to determine whether these conditions were acceptable for all, and more particularly, to the Indochinese. In fact, no mention was even made of the *cahiers de doléances* sollicited by members of Commission d'Enquête named by the Popular Front after they won the legislative election.[5]

Business as usual, however, would no longer be tolerated. Neither the European nor the indigenous 'oligarchies' would reap the profits from the colonies. Moutet asserted that his policy was based on increasing the buying power of the masses, a rather difficult proposition when so many Tonkinese peasants suffered from starvation and famine, and workers earned barely enough for subsistence living. To make his ideas of a 'colonisation altruiste' more acceptable, he contrasted it with what he called 'colonisation égoïste':

> Selfish colonisation [is] that of a nation which would solely be engaged in levying from the indigenous people direct or indirect taxes, in men, services in kind or in money, in one form or another, on behalf of the mother country or metropolitan citizens; selfish colonisation [is] one which would only be concerned with export trade that would drain wealth and capital, and prevent the economic expansion of the colonies.
>
> An altruistic policy [is] one that will achieve, under our guidance and without any unjustified demand on our

part, the improvement of the standard of living and of the physical, material and intellectual life of the people. We will therefore not speak solely of net cost nor of great yields; we will speak chiefly of the worker's standard of living.[6]

What are we to make of the economic basis for this policy, especially in the light of the debate opposing those who supported real economic reform – the proponents of the industrialisation of Indochina – and the likes of Moutet and Justin Godart (the Popular Front delegate sent on an official fact-finding mission to Indochina) who resisted and were even opposed to such industrialisation?

Before we turn to a later speech where Moutet spelt out his opposition to the industrialisation of Indochina, we must come back to the issue of the 'politique altruiste'. Where was Moutet to find sufficient funds to finance these radical changes, which in effect, would bring an extensive over-haul of the colonial system? It may be useful, here, to underline the fact that French government in Indochina derived its revenues from rather dubious sources. As Godart rightfully noted: 'the budget of Indochina was supplied by three well-springs: gambling, opium and alcohol'.[7] Opium, alcohol, as well as gambling, were state-controlled 'indus-tries,' under the jurisdiction of French colonial officials in Indochina. French officials there enforced the consumption, and even more damning, imposed 'a monthly alcohol quota for each village fixed by the higher authorities'.[8] If the minimum amount prescribed was not met, sanctions were meted out against the villagers and the local authorities. He also reported that in Cambodia, opium dens were closed for not having purchased their monthly quota from the Régie.[9] The Popular Front government did nothing to sup-port Godart's proposal to 'abolish the state monopoly on gambling and opium and to reconsider the current regula-tions about alcohol'.[10] How paradoxical, then are Moutet's words if we compare them to the policies enforced in Indochina! And yet, Moutet could still claim that the Socialist programme was above all about fulfilling 'a work of human solidarity' which would bring 'a full realisation of its econ-omic potential'.[11]

As I have suggested, improving the standard of living of the natives came at a price, and it was not part of an 'altruistic' plan, but rather, it was for profit. In Ferry's words, 'the need for outlets', was at the heart of 'colonisation altruiste.' Moutet argued that:

> The premise on which altruistic colonisation is based imposes the following requirement: the sucessful development of the economy of the French colonial world is achieved by privileging colonial products in the metropole, in order to guarantee the right price to the producer which will allow him to leave behind the poverty-stricken life of the naked races; in return, metropolitan industrial products will be given preferential treatment in the colonies. This is how a solidarity of interests, based on fraternal sentiment, is established between indigenous and French workers, allowing, for instance, the Vosges weaver to recognise that his work and productivity are due to the increased earning power of the Senegalese farmer.[12]

It is quite apparent here that Moutet's 'colonisation altruiste' was not, as he claimed, a humanitarian or social programme designed to improve the well-being and standard of life of the colonised peoples: it obeyed certain economic constraints and prerogatives.

The Conférence des Gouverneurs-généraux was perhaps only designed to showcase the progressive intent of the Popular Front government's colonial policies. And, to be fair to the intent or spirit of Moutet's speech, many constraints were undoubtedly placed on the speaker. The most obvious one was the lack of time which prevented him from fully developing his ideas. And yet, one cannot but be surprised by the vagueness of his proposals. In different settings (more confidential letters and internal memos), the substance of his reform plans were presented in a rather different light.

In his speech before the Conseil Supérieur des Colonies, on 19 March 1938, Marius Moutet argued against the industrialisation of the colonies in these unequivocally strong terms:

> We must not artificially hasten this industrialisation because it is dangerous to force the worker who has al-

ready achieved a certain degree of civilisation to regress, under the pretence of creating revenues and prioritising the needs of the backward workers. We must see that this competition will not engender unemployment in the metropole. . . . If we can envisge the creation of new industries, it seems to me that our attention must focus, first and foremost, on semi-finished products. . . . It would be a grave mistake to propel our colonies towards an industrialisation which has not been thought out. We must not create a proletariat that feels exploited and unhappy, a situation that whould rapidly become dangerous for French sovereignty.[13]

He feared that increased market competition would merely amplify unemployment in the metrople. Thus, the solidarity among the 'native and French workers', was in fact just an utopian, socialist ideal, conjured up to elicit support for the socialist colonial programme. Moutet discriminated between two distinct types of workers, the indigenous, 'backward workers' and the French worker 'who has already achieved a certain degree of civilisation'. Moutet may well have only wanted to make manifest the existence of differences in the training and/or skills of metropolitan and colonial workers, but one can certainly object to his description of the metropolitan worker as being of the top of the evolutionary ladder who would 'regress' if the needs of 'backward workers' took precedence over those of French workers.

Justin Godart, Senator, former Minister, and Délégué Général du Gouvernement aux Colonies, shared the same view. In his very thorough report, *Rapport de mission en Indochine*, Godart asked the following rhetorical question: 'Is it desirable to see industrial development in Indochina?', to which he answered:

Indochina is a country of agriculture and craftsmen. An agrarian policy will protect it from the danger that industrial development brings. The world crisis caused by over-production demonstrates that the means and method that put the world in great social and economic difficulties should only be introduced in still unscarred countries only after very careful consideration.[14]

In a speech to the Institut Colonial upon his return from Indochina he reiterated the same view:

> Is it desirable . . . to wish for the industrial development of Indochina? I do not think so. The stable and definitive foundation on which Indochina lies is small ownership ['la petite propriété']. We must defend the one that already exists and create it wherever it is possible. If, in addition to this agrarian policy, we adopt 'une politique artisanale', we will bring a new and effective palliative to the current situation.[15]

Moutet favoured agrarian reforms insofar as they would appease the Indochinese population, that is to say, to restore a sense of security to Indochina.

He also added: 'Anyway, Indochinese workers are unfit for the mandatory discipline of modern production techniques', which echoes Moutet's thesis of the 'backward workers'.[16] Godart wrote of the incompetent and unreliable Indochinese worker whose 'irregularity in working, numerous absences and frequent breaks' were a problem.[17]

But the primary reason for his being against industrialisation was not even the quality of the workers. Paul Bernard, the ardent proponent of the industrialisation of Indochina, reported that Moutet confessed to him the following:

> As far as the industrialisation of Indochina is concerned, it is true that I believe it to be sufficiently advanced. It is even a source of embarrassment because many industrial manufacturers found there very profitable work conditions, a cheap labour force that could be paid a fixed salary. These concentrations of indigenous proletarian agglomerations cause difficulties.[18]

The creation of proletarian 'aglomerations' was what the French feared most in Indochina because they felt that it posed a threat to France's control there. In fact, the right of assembly, a right we take for granted today, was not permitted in Indochina. Guérin reported that the law was still in effect in 1936 and banned meetings of more than 20 people.[19] Moutet also feared the creation of 'a proletariat which, exploited and discontented, would rapidly become a danger for French sovereignty'.[20] Revolutionary movements, it was believed, recruited their members from the proletariat and, with the help of the Communists, would undermine and attack French interests in Indochina.

We can better assess the distance between the Socialists' claims as members of the opposition, and their actual colonial practice in government, if we contrast their position in government, with that taken at the debate on the 'Indochinese question', at the Chambre des Députés in June 1930. The Socialists, supported by the Radicals, endorsed a plan that would institute a gradual decolonisation of Indochina, advancing at the same time a policy of collaboration between the French and the Annamite advocated by the 'nationalistes réformistes'.[21] In effect, they demanded a type of self-government for Indochina.

Moutet questioned the actions taken by François Piétri, then Ministre des Colonies: 'Does your policy tend to enrich certain individuals or companies or, on the contrary, to liberate a whole people from both material poverty and intellectual servitude . . .?'[22] Yet when Moutet became a member of the cabinet, in charge of French colonial policies, his discourse changed dramatically:

> A Socialist colonial policy will have all the more the chance to be constructive and solidly productive if it is less engaged in disseminating, in a direct fashion, the Socialist ideology to the indigenous people. . . . One must be cautious of the unfurling of unchecked forces onto a confused and unstable situation, unpropitious to positive construction, the result of converging forces that would provoke complex and unexpected fusions among poorly assimilated notions of class struggle, certain religious fanaticisms, the emotional nature of the Africans, the Muslim and Oriental duplicity, and other subterranean influences. . . . It is in amid a modernised indigenous peasantry that our army will find healthy recruits who will not bring social turmoil. I do not have to belabour this point. It is obvious that everything is interrelated as far as colonial policy is concerned and we will be unable to recruit reliable troops if they are drawn from a feeble, anarchical and proletarianised peasantry.[23]

Moutet no longer supported 'class stuggle.' His own sense

of superiority is transparent and merits no commentary.

Alexandre Varenne, on the other hand, was much more circumspect and prudent. During the debate, he stated:

> I intend to ask for the independence of Indochina. My position is well-known: I regard the independence of Indochina, at this particular historical juncture, to be a disaster for Indochina ... I have said it before: to surrender these nations to themselves today, even those of Annam, is to lay them open very rapidly to foreign invasion; it also means to lay them open to a rapid resurgence of domestic anarchy. The solution I advocate is well-known: I have presented it on numerous occasions. I believe that the future of Indochina, and in particular of the Annamite nations, resides in a great Indochinese federation linked to and energised by France. It is in this federation that the Annamites will rediscover the nation that they believed to have been lost. We will help them to achieve the greatest autonomy. Complete independence? I do not know if it will be given one day. I do not think that it is ever going to be a possibility, at least in the terms envisaged by certain individuals. But it is not forbidden to dream of a new Indochina where France would not have all of the administrative responsibilities as it has today, and would allow the Annamites to govern themselves to a large measure.[24]

Varenne recommended the creation of a new type of federation (in the form of Etats-Associés or limited self-government) which would allow the Vietnamese to play a larger role in the affairs of their nation. Although he did not see independence as being an immediate option because of the Communist threat, he still strikes us as being the most forward looking, perhaps because he even asked for the constitution of a 'commission parlementaire extraordinaire', in charge of examining the possibility of political reforms to prepare a new political status for Indochina, a proposal supported by the nine Communist representatives. However, as Daniel Hémery notes, this was rejected.[25]

We have to wait until the victory of the Popular Front for such a commission to be named. But as Marc Lagana and Charles-Robert Ageron show, its impact on colonial policies was marginal.[26] In 1930 and even earlier, Varenne made several proposals that had been rejected, but they became part of the Popular Front's reform plans. As a former Governor-General to Indochina, he was seen as a particularly influential interlocutor. He later wrote:

> What I would have liked to achieve, had I not encountered so much resistance both here and there, was to let true political parties constitute themselves in Annam, under our surveillance and in broad day light. By stifling normal political life in this nation, we ourselves have led distinguished and sincere Annamites join secret societies where the worst activities are planned. We were only informed of these activities by agents who sometimes play a double game. What I have said for political parties in Annam, I will also say for workers' parties. As far as I am concerned, I would prefer to have full-fledged trade unions to the secret ones that abound in Indochina and against which there can be no serious or efficient apparatus of surveillance.[27]

Varenne supported political and trade-union activities not for altruistic reasons or in the name of Republican idealism, but because banning them had merely succeeded in radicalising even the most moderate among the nationalists. The ability to monitor and control political activity, then, became the primary motivation for allowing a few freedoms.

Varenne also noted the deleterious effects of industrialisation on the Indochinese population. He was concerned that workers would exchange ideas more easily and discontent with conditions would turn into revolt.[28] In the countryside, famine, was, without a doubt, one of the main causes of peasant unrest. By adopting a series of fairly extensive agrarian reforms, the Popular Front government felt that it could 'palliate the current dangerous political situation'.[29] More concretely, a number of measures were taken as early as 1936. The anti-famine plan included regulations concerning credit and usury, fiscal reform, increased aid to rice farmers, 'migration dirigée' and agrarian reform. The promulgation of the Code du Travail and measures to raise wages also aimed at relaxing social tension.[30]

Hémery interprets these measures as being part of 'an undeniable shift in priorities from the political to the economic', which he argues can be explained by 'strategic necessities of a socio-political nature as well as the will to develop the colonial economy to accommodate the important metropolitan interests'.[31] Political measures had nevertheless been taken. But, still according to Hémery, they were 'subordinated to the logic of neo-colonial policy'.[32] No one in the Socialist party spoke any longer of granting self-rule to the Indochinese. In official statements, the question of whether the French colonial presence on the Indochinese peninsula was a temporary measure was no longer on the official agenda, as if the issue of decolonisation had been postponed forever. Confidential documents are much more explicit.[33] In one speech, Marius Moutet declared rather forcefully:

> We must, above all, face colonial reality. Be reassured, we will not lose our way with lengthy and doctrinaire discussions on this issue. It is a fact that we have taken custody of certain nations that we call colonies. It means to live with these nations while making them live better. Our first duty is to excite in them all the vital energies, and to incorporate them in all of our national life. It also means to link the different types of political and economic life with ours in a harmonious fashion.[34]

The political measures taken by the Popular Front were very few and limited in scope. No one questioned the current status of the colony. So to create a progressive climate, the Popular Front found it necessary to replace 'the senior officials most associated with the policy of repression ... to prove to the natives that they are no longer enemies or suspects'.[35] With that resolve in mind, the Résident-Supérieur, Robin, who was known for the bloody repression of the political unrest in Indochina in 1930, was recalled and replaced by Brévié, a high official known for his integrity and for his opposition to colonial abuses, who took the title of governor. But as Guérin rightfully notes, all other colonial adminstrators were left in place, which showed a lack of foresight because many of these colonial civil servants would actively resist the reforms put forward by the Popular Front in Paris.[36]

The most dramatic measure taken by the Popular Front government was an amnesty. Hundreds of political prisoners were released from the penal colonies of Poulo-Condor and Guyane. In all more than 1,500 political prisoners were set free, among them a large number of members of the Indochinese Communist Party.[37] The young Phan Van Dong (who was Prime Minister of Vietnam in 1977) and Le Duan, for instance, who became a legendary figure of the Vietnamese liberation struggle, were among those released. Although all political prisoners should have been freed, not all were released and some of those liberated were placed under house arrest in their village of origin.[38] Guérin also suggests that:

> The measure the most impatiently awaited by the people of Indochina, the complete amnesty of the jailed and deported individuals following the 1930–1932 events, was not fully carried out: of the ten thousand victims of the repression, at most 1200 condemned were the object of pardons. What happened to the others? Every time we raised the question with Marius Moutet, he only answered in an evasive and sinister fashion: 'First, many of them died . . .' Of the 535 Indochinese deported in 1931 to Inini, Moutet only gave a full pardon to 23. The others? In a letter he addressed to me, dated February 8, 1937, he claims that most of the deported 'had been condemned for common law crimes that had nothing to do with a political action or motivation.' But, in another letter, dated the 15th of March, he acknowledged the following, and contradicted himself: 'For most of them, it is difficult to distinguish between a political crime and a common law crime.' And to explain his refusal to grant other pardons, he added in a prosecutorial style: 'It would be dangerous, and not a good example, to adopt another line of conduct.'[39]

The benevolent humanist aspirations of such Popular Front figures as Moutet may indeed have succumbed to the *Parti colonial* lobbying efforts as suggested by numerous critics. Although one does not want to 'underestimate an obvious reformism marked by a will to fight famine by giving priority to food crops over production for export', and although

Catherine Coquery-Vidrovitch argues that 'it would be un-
just merely to ascribe to the men of the Popular Front an
attempt to package a desire for colonial profitability as social
reform', I am not at all convinced that giving a critical
assessment of the Popular Front's 'colonisation altruiste' is
unfair.[40]

One could certainly end on a less critical note. We can
mention a number of measures, initiatives and political and
economic reforms, supported by the Popular Front. The
Code du Travail, for instance, was promulgated, on 30
December, 1936, but it was often ignored.[41] And, as Godart
argued, it needed at least four amendments to make it
consistent with the law protecting French workers.[42] The
desire to increase the Vietnamese electoral body in Cochin-
china was also a worthwhile project. But this project pales
in comparison with the Blum–Violette bill, especially when
we know that less than a year after the Comité de Convo-
cation was created on 13 August 1936 to prepare the
organisation of the Congrès Populaire Indochinois, the
Vietnamese leaders of that Congress were arrested in Saigon,
on 9 July 1937, and sentenced to terms in prison.[43]

Rules governing the 'freedom of the press' in Indochina
remained extremely restrictive. Guérin wrote that:

> Freedom of the press [is] a myth. At the very slightest
> criticism, newspapers see their preliminary permit with-
> drawn, are condemned to pay ruinous fines; copies are
> seized, and editors jailed. In Saigon, Ta Thu Thau and
> Toa, editors of *La Lutte*, and municipal worker's party
> council members, triumphantly reelected in April, are
> condemned in July to two years in prison. All of them,
> for a simple press offence! Their crime? To agitate (with
> the pen). The all powerful Sûreté calls it 'dangerous
> agitation,' 'anti-French activity'.[44]

The same could be said for the so-called liberal policy
of allowing union activities:

> All these restrictions! Subjected to the regime of pre-
> liminary permit, constantly threatened with suspension
> or dissolution, forced to send to the government the
> minutes of their meetings, and only being able to elect

officials in the presence of French public officials, prevented from meeting as a union or federation, these trade
unions only existed in name (as in a fascist regime).[45]

Did the Front Populaire lay the ground for a renewal of
the colonial system towards 'une politique altruiste', a more
humane type of colonisation? The documents analysed here
fail to support such a claim. Moutet ended his speech with
these words: 'Will we be able to show the world that our
colonial rule is not a futile and selfish lie, but a well-planned
act of fraternal solidarity?'[46] Indeed it was a deliberate
policy but one where 'fraternal solidarity' had no place,
and one with which Jules Ferry would have been in complete
agreement!

Although recent studies have interpreted the 'colonial
humanism of the Popular Front' in terms of continuity or
change, my aim was to show the ambivalence and limited
impact of the Popular Front's colonial policies on the political, social and economic well-being of the Indochinese.
What remains is an impression, difficult to shake, especially
when the colonial policies adopted by the Popular Front in
Indochina continue to be painted in rather warm and luminous colours.[47] This aura hides the lack of concrete
achievement by the Popular Front government.

Notes and References

1. 'Le vieux thème des économies complèmentaires', J. Marseille, *Empire colonial et capitalisme français: histoire d'un divorce* (Albin Michel, 1984) p. 335. See also D. Hémery, p. 27.
2. 'La politique d'expansion coloniale est un système politique et économique; je disais qu'on pouvait rattacher ce système à trois ordres d'idées: à des idées économiques, à des idées de civilisation de la plus haute portée, et à des idées d'ordre politique et patriotique. Sur le terrain économique ... le besoin de débouchés ... il y a un second point, un second ordre d'idées que je dois également ... c'est le côté humanitaire et civilisateur de la question ... il faut dire ouvertement qu'en effet, les races supérieures ont un droit vis-à-vis des races inférieures. ... Je répète qu'il y a pour les races supérieures un droit, parce qu'il y a un devoir pour elles. Elles ont le devoir de civiliser les races inférieures' (My emphasis). P. Robiquet (ed.), *Discours et opinions de Jules Ferry* (Armand Colin & Cie, 1967) pp. 199–212.

3. 'le dévouement à autrui comme la règle idéale de la moralité', *Petit Robert*, 1973.

4. 'Nous avons en premier lieu à nous préoccuper de faire vivre et mieux vivre l'ensemble des populations coloniales. Il ne s'agit pas de considérer les colonies en fonction de l'intérêt égoïste de la métropole; il s'agit de les organiser pourqu'elles forment avec la métropole un ensemble complexe acceptable pour tous. Nous n'y parviendrions pas si nous ne songions qu'à enrichir certaines oligarchies tant européennes qu'indigènes. Pas plus que la guerre, une telle colonisation égoïste ne paierait. Bien au contraire, elle appauvrirait l'économie nationale. La colonisation altruiste, établie sur la nécessité d'accroître le pouvoir d'achat des masses, favorise la constitution outre-mer du capital actif et vivant, condition indispensable des échanges avec la métropole. M. Moutet, Discours, Conférence des Gouverneurs-généraux, 5 Nov. 1936. ANSOM, P. A. 28 p. 98.

5. C.-R. Ageron, 'La commission d'enquête du Front Populaire sur les colonies et la question tunisienne', in *Les Mouvements politiques et sociaux dans la Tunisie des années 1930* (Presses de la Société Tunisienne des Arts Graphiques, 1987)

6. Colonisation égoïste, celle d'un pays qui ne se préoccuperait que de retirer des indigènes des tributs directs ou indirects, en hommes, en prestations, en numéraire, sous une forme ou sous une autre, au profit de la métropole et de citoyens métropolitains; colonisation égoïste, celle qui ne se soucierait que d'une exportation drainant richesse et capitaux et enrayant l'épanouissement économique des colonies.

Politique altruiste, celle qui réalisera, sous notre direction et sans exigence injustifiée de notre part, l'élévation du niveau de vie, de vie physique, de vie économique, de vie intellectuelle. Nous ne parlerons donc pas uniquement du prix de revient, des 'grands produits', nous parlerons surtout du niveau de vie des producteurs.' M. Moutet, Discours, Conférence des Gouverneurs généraux, 5 Nov. 1936. ANSOM, P. A. 28.

7. 'le budget de l'Indochine s'alimente à trois sources: le jeu, l'opium, l'alcool'. J. Godart, *Rapport de mission en Indochine 1er janvier– 14 mars 1937* (L'Harmattan, 1994) p. 133.

8. 'la fixation par les autorités supérieures d'une quantité mensuelle d'alcool imposée à chaque village'. Ibid. p. 134.

9. Ibid., p. 136.

10. '[s]upprimer la ferme des jeux, celle de l'opium et remettre en question le régime actuel de l'alcool'. Ibid., p. 179.

11. 'une oeuvre de solidarité humaine'; 'un plein rendement à son potentiel économique.' Discours, M. Moutet, op. cit.

12. 'Ce postulat de la colonisation altruiste exige un aménagement satisfaisant de l'économie franco-coloniale, par le privilège réservé aux produits coloniaux dans la métropole, pour garantir un juste prix au producteur et lui permettre de quitter la vie misérable des races nues, et en contre-partie assurer aux produits industriels

métropolitains un traitement privilégié dans les colonies. Ainsi doit s'établir entre les travailleurs indigènes et français une solidarité d'intérêts, base de leur sentiment fraternel permettant, par exemple, au tisseur des Vosges de se rendre compte qu'il doit l'activité de son travail et la productivité de celui-ci au gain accru du cultivateur sénégalais', Discours, M. Moutet, op. cit.

13. 'Il ne faut pas précipiter artificiellement cette industrialisation, car il est dangereux, sous le prétexte de créer des revenus, et partant des besoins aux travailleurs non évolués, qu'on oblige à régresser le travailleur qui est déjà arrivé au stade supérieur de l'évolution. Il faut veiller à ce que cette concurrence n'engendre pas de chômage dans la Métropole. . . . Si on peut envisager la création d'industries, il semble que l'attention devrait se porter surtout sur le produit semi-ouvré. . . . Ce serait une lourde erreur de précipiter nos colonies vers une industrialisation irréfléchie. Il ne faut pas créer un prolétariat qui, exploité et mécontent, serait rapidement dangereux pour la souveraineté française' ANSOM, Affaires Politiques, 2530, Conseil Supérieur des Colonies, Procès verbal de la séance du 19 mars 1938, quoted by J. Marseille, *Empire colonial et capitalism français.* op. cit., pp. 335–6.

14. 'Est-il désirable de voir se développer l'industrialisation de l'Indochine?'; 'L'Indochine est un pays agricole et artisanal. Une politique agraire doit le préserver du péril que serait pour lui le développement de l'industrie. La crise mondiale due à l'excès de la production, montre qu'il faut avec la plus grande prudence apporter à un pays encore indemne les moyens et les méthodes qui ont mis le monde dans les plus grandes difficultés économiques et sociales.' Godart, op. cit., pp. 89–90.

15. 'Est-il désirable . . . de souhaiter le développement de l'industrie en Indochine? Je ne le pense pas. Voilà la base stable et définitive de l'Indochine: la petite propriété. Il faut défendre celle qui existe; il faut la créer là où il y a de la place. Si, en plus de cette politique agrarienne, on fait une politique artisanale, on apportera un nouveau et efficace palliatif à la situation actuelle . . .'. Godart, speech to on 12 May 1937, quoted by Hémery, op. cit., p. 25.

16. 'Puis la main d'oeuvre indochinoise est inapte aux disciplines obligatoires de la production moderne' Godart, op. cit., p. 90.

17. 'irrégularité dans le travail, absences nombreuses, sorties fréquentes'. Ibid., p. 90.

18. 'Quant à l'industrialisation de l'Indochine, il est exact que je l'estime suffisamment avancée. Elle constitue même une source d'embarras, en ce sens que trop d'industriels sont allés chercher là-bas des conditions de travail particulières, une main d'oeuvre aux salaires fixes et à trop bon marché. Toutes ces constitutions d'agglomérations indigènes prolétariennes causent des difficultés' quoted by Hémery, p. 25.

19. Guérin, op. cit., p. 432.

20. 'un prolétariat qui, exploité et mécontent, serait rapidement dangereux pour la souveraineté française'. Discours, M. Moutet, op. cit.

21. Hémery, op. cit., p. 8.
22. 'Votre politique tend-elle à enrichir quelques personnalités ou compagnies ou, au contraire à libérer tout un peuple à la fois de la misère matérielle et de la servitude intellectuelle...?' (Séance du 6 juin 1930), p. 2434.
23. 'Une politique coloniale socialiste aura d'autant plus de chance d'être constructive et durablement féconde qu'elle se préoccupera moins de communiquer d'une manière directe l'idéologie socialiste aux indigènes.... Il faut prendre garde au déchaînement de forces incontrôlables, à la situation confuse et instable, impropre à toute construction positive, qui pourraient sortir d'une action où des notions mal digérées de lutte de classes, certains fanatismes religieux, la nature émotive des Africains, la dissimulation islamique et asiatique et toutes sortes d'influences souterraines se rencontreraient en des réactions complexes et imprévisibles.... C'est dans un paysannat indigène rénové que notre armée pourra vraiment trouver un recrutement sain, qui n'apportera pas de trouble social. Je n'ai pas besoin d'insister sur ce côté du problème. Il est évident que tout se tient en matière de politique coloniale et que nous ne pourrons pas avoir de troupes sûres si celles-ci sont tirées d'un paysannant débile, anarchique et prolétarisé.' ANSOM, PA 28/4; quoted by Marseille, *Empire colonial et capitalisme français*. op. cit., p. 336.
24. 'J'entends demander l'indépendance de l'Indochine. Mon opinion est connue: je considère l'indépendance de l'Indochine, à l'époque et dans la situation présentes, serait un désastre pour l'Indochine.... Je l'ai dit: livrer actuellement ces pays, même ceux d'Annam, à eux-mêmes, c'est les exposer à l'invasion étrangère, qui ne tarderait pas, c'est aussi les exposer à un rapide renouveau d'anarchie intérieure.... Ma solution, on la connaît: je l'ai formulée à maintes reprises. Je vois l'avenir de l'Indochine, en particulier des pays annamites, dans une grande fédération indochinoise, dont la France resterait l'associée et l'animatrice. C'est là seulement que les Annamites pourront retrouver la patrie qu'ils croient avoir perdue. Nous les aiderons jusqu'à la plus large autonomie. L'indépendance totale? Je ne sais si elle viendra un jour. Je ne crois pas que, dans les termes où certains l'envisagent, elle soit jamais possible. Mais il n'est pas défendu de rêver d'une Indochine nouvelle où la France n'aurait pas toutes les responsabilités administratives comme elle les a aujourd'hui, où elle laisserait dans la plus large mesure, les Annamites se gouverner eux-mêmes.
25. Hémery, op. cit., p. 9.
26. M. Lagana, 'L'échec de la commission d'enquête coloniale du Front populaire', *Historical Reflections*, 16: 1 (1989); C.-R. Ageron, op. cit.
27. 'Ce que j'aurais voulu faire si je n'avais rencontré ici et là-bas tant de résistance, c'eût été de laisser se constituer dans les pays annamites, sous notre regard et en pleine lumière, de véritables partis politiques. En étouffant toute vie politique normale dans ce pays, nous avons nous-mêmes précipité des Annamites distingués et sincères dans ces sociétés secrètes où peuvent se préparer les pires besognes sans

que nous en soyons informés autrement que par des agents qui,
parfois, joue un double jeu. Ce que je dis des partis politiques que
nous aurions dû laisser se constituer dans les pays annamites, je le
dirai encore pour les groupements ouvriers. Je préférerais quant à
moi des syndicats ouverts à ces syndicats secrets qui foisonnent en
Indochine et sur lesquels vous n'avez aucun moyen sérieux et efficace
de surveillance.'

28. Varenne, séance du 20 juin 1930, p. 2601.
29. Ibid.
30. ANSOM, PA28, c4, d128; quoted by Hémery op. cit., pp. 27–28.
31. 'un indéniable transfert de priorités du politique à l'économie, . . .
    [explained by] des nécessités stratégiques de type socio-politique
    que par la volonté de réaménager l'économie coloniale en fonction
    des grands intérêts métropolitains' Hémery, op. cit., pp. 27–8.
32. Ibid.
33. Kept at ANSOM and cited in ibid.
34. 'Avant tout, nous devons regarder en face le fait colonial. Rassurez-
    vous, nous ne nous égarerons pas dans de grandes discussions doc-
    trinaires à ce sujet. C'est un fait que nous avons pris en charge
    certains pays que nous appelons les colonies. Il s'agit de vivre avec
    ces pays-là tout en les faisant vivre mieux. Nous avons pour pre-
    mier devoir d'exciter en eux toutes les forces vitales et de les
    incorporer dans l'ensemble de notre vie nationale. Il s'agit de com-
    biner harmonieusement leurs différents genres de vie politique et
    économique avec le nôtre . . .', undated speech, ANSOM, PA28, c4,
    d128; quoted by Hémery, op. cit., pp. 27–8.
35. 'les hauts fonctionnaires les plus représentatifs de la politique de
    répression . . . en prouvant aux indigènes qu'ils ne sont plus des
    ennemis ou des suspects [. .]' Charles-André Julien, chargé de mis-
    sion pour les questions coloniales; quoted by J. Delperrié de Bayac,
    Histoire du Front Populaire. (Fayard, 1972) p. 267.
36. Guérin, op. cit., p. 433.
37. The Vietnamese Communist Party was formed on 3 Feb. 1930. In
    Oct. 1930 it changed its name to the Indochinese Communist Party.
38. Guérin, op. cit., p. 442. See also Hémery p. 310 fn. 90.; *Les Secrets
    des Iles Poulo-Condore. Le grand bagne indochinois* (Paris: J. Peyronnet
    et Cie, 1956).
39. 'La mesure la plus impatiemment attendue par le peuple d'Indochine,
    l'amnistie intégrale des emprisonnés et déportés à la suite des
    événements de 1930–1932, ne fut que très incomplètement réalisée:
    sur dix mille victimes de la répression, tout au plus 1200 condamnés
    firent l'objet de grâces amnistiantes. Que sont devenus les autres?
    Chaque fois que nous avons posé la question à Marius Moutet, nous
    n'avons pu en tirer que cette réponse évasive et sinistre à la fois:
    "D'abord, il y en a beaucoup qui sont morts . . . "Sur les 535
    Indochinois déportés en 1931 en Inini, Moutet n'en a grâcié
    totalement que 23. Les autres? Dans une lettre qu'il m'adressait, le
    8 février 1937, il prétendait que la plupart des déportés "avaient
    été condamnés pour crime de droit commun sans rapport aucun

avec un fait ou un mobile d'ordre politique". Mais, dans une autre lettre du 15 mars, se contredisant, il avouait: "Pour la plupart, le départ est difficile à faire entre le crime politique et le crime de droit commun". Et pour motiver son refus d'accorder d'autres grâces, il ajoutait, dans un style de procureur: "Il serait dangereux, et d'un mauvais exemple, d'adopter une autre ligne de conduite".' *Solidarité Internationale Antifascite*, 1er décembre 1938; Guérin, op. cit., p. 442.

40. 'mésestimer un réformisme évident marqué par la volonté de lutter contre la famine en privilégiant les cultures vivrières aux dépens des cultures d'exportation'. Marseille, op. cit., p. 337; 'il était injuste de prêter aux hommes du Front populaire la seule tentative de plaquer un habillage social sur une volonté de rentabilité impérialiste'. C. Coquery-Vidrovitch, 'Continuité ou Rupture? L'Humanisme colonial du Front Populaire' in Thobie *et al.* (eds), *Histoire de la France coloniale*, 2 vols, .

41. Guérin, op. cit., p. 439.

42. Godart, op. cit., p. 178.

43. Guérin, op. cit., pp. 431–2.

44. 'Liberté de la presse, un mythe. A la moindre critique, les journaux se voient retirer l'autorisation préalable, sont condamnés à de ruineuses amendes, leurs exemplaires saisis, leurs rédacteurs incarcérés. A Saigon, Ta Thu Thau et Tao, rédacteurs de *La Lutte*, conseillers municipaux ouvriers, réélus triomphalement en avril sont condamnés en juillet, à deux ans. Les uns et les autres, pour simple délit de presse! Leur crime? Faire (par la plume) de l'"agitation". . . . La toute puissante Sûreté générale appelle cela "agitation dangereuse", "activité antifrançaise"' Guérin, op. cit., p. 439.

45. 'Quelles restrictions! Soumis au régime de l'autorisation préalable, constamment menacés de suspension ou de dissolution, contraints d'envoyer dans les huit jours à l'administration les procès-verbaux [minutes] de leurs assemblées, ne pouvant élire leurs responsables qu'en présence d'un représentant des pouvoirs publics, empêchés de se grouper en unions et fédérations, les syndicats n'auraient (comme une régime fascite) de syndicats que le nom.' Guérin, op. cit., p 440.

46. 'Puissions-nous montrer à tous que notre colonisation n'est pas un vain et égoïste mensonge, mais un acte réfléchi de fraternelle solidarité?" M. Moutet, Discours, Conférence des Gouverneurs généraux 5 Nov. 1936. ANSOM, P. A. 28.

47. See, for example, Régis Wargier's 1993 film *Indochine*.

Select Bibliography

Abdessalam, A., *Sadiki et les sadikiens* (Tunis: Cérès Productions, 1974).

Abwa, D., '"Commandement européen" et "commandement indigène" au Cameroun sous administration française de 1916 à 1960', Thèse de Doctorat, Université de Yaoundé, 1994.

Adamthwaite, A., *Grandeur and Misery* (London: Edward Arnold, 1995).

Ageron, C.-R., 'Le Mouvement "Jeune-Algérien" de 1900 à 1923', in C.-A. Julien (ed.), *Etudes Maghrébines: Mélanges Charles-André Julien* (Paris: Presses Universitaires de France, 1964).

Ageron, C.-R., *L'anticolonialisme en France de 1871 à 1914* (Paris: Presses Universitaires de France, 1973).

Ageron, C.-R., *France coloniale ou Parti colonial?* (Paris: Presses Universitaires de France, 1978).

Ageron, C.-R., *L'Algérie algérienne de Napoléon III à de Gaulle* (Paris: Bibliothèque Arabe, Editions Sindbad, 1980).

Ageron, C.-R., 'La Commission d'enquête du Front Populaire sur les colonies et la question Tunisienne', in *Actes du 3e Séminaire sur l'histoire du Mouvement National: Les mouvements politiques et sociaux dans la Tunisie des années 1930* (Tunis: Ministère de l'Education, de l'Enseignement et de la Recherche Scientifique, 1985).

Ageron, C.-R., 'La commission d'enquête du Front Populaire sur les colonies et la question tunisienne', in *Les Mouvements politiques et sociaux dans la Tunisie des années 1930* (Tunis: Presses de la Société Tunisienne des Arts Graphiques, 1987).

Ahmad, E. and Schaar, S., 'M'hammed Ali and the Tunisian Labour Movement', *Race and Class*, XIX (1978) pp. 253–76.

Aldrich, R., *The French Presence in the South Pacific, 1842–1940* (Honolulu: University of Hawaii Press, 1990).

Alexandre, F., 'Le PCA de 1919 à 1939 – données en vue d'éclaircir son action et son rôle', *Revue Algérienne des sciences juridiques, économiques et politiques*, XI:4 (1974) pp. 175–214.

Almeïda-Topor, H. d', 'Recherches sur l'évolution du travail salarié en AOF (1930–1936)', *Cahiers d'Etudes Africaines*, 61–2 (1976) pp. 103–18.

Almeïda-Topor, H. d', 'La Question du travail forcé', in Institut Charles-de-Gaulle and Institut d'Histoire du Temps Present, *Brazzaville, aux sources de la décolonisation* (Paris: Plon, 1988).

Bassanguena, J., 'Le Cameroun sous le Front Populaire, réformes sociales et réactions du colonat, 1936–1938', Mémoire de Maîtrise, Université de Yaoundé, 1991.

Bernard, P., *Les Nouveaux aspects du problème économique indochinois* (Paris: Nouvelles Editions Latine, 1937).

Bernard-Duquenet, N., 'Les débuts du syndicalisme au Sénégal au temps du Front Populaire', *Le Mouvement Social*, 101 (1977) pp. 37–60.

250 *Select Bibliography*

Bernard-Duquenet, N., *Le Sénégal et le Front Populaire* (Paris: L'Harmattan, 1985).

Bessis, J., 'Le mouvement ouvrier tunisien: de ses origines à l'indépendance', *Mouvement social*, IMIX (1974) pp. 85–108.

Betts, R. F., *Assimilation and Association in French Colonial Theory 1890–1914* (New York and London: Columbia University Press, 1961).

Betts, R. F., *France and Decolonisation, 1900–1960* (London: Macmillan, 1991).

Bonneuil, C., *Des Savants pour l'empire: la structuration des recherches scientifiques coloniales au temps de la 'mise en valeur des colonies françaises', 1917–1945* (Paris: Seghers, 1991).

Bouche, D., 'La Réception des principes de Brazzaville par l'administration en A.O.F.', in Institut Charles-de-Gaulle and Institut d'Histoire du Temps Present, *Brazzaville, aux sources de la décolonisation* (Paris: Plon, 1988).

Bourguiba, H., *La Tunisie et la France* (Paris: René Juillard, 1964).

Brimo, A., *Les femmes françaises face au pouvoir politique* (Paris: Editions Montchrestien, 1975).

Buell, R. L., *The Native Problem in Africa* (London: Frank Cass, 1965).

Burchell, G., Gordon, C. and Miller, P. (eds), *The Foucault Effect: Studies in Governmentality* (Chicago: University of Chicago Press, 1991).

Chaibi, M. L., 'La Politique coloniale du Front Populaire en Tunisie (1936–1938): Essai d'évaluation', in *Les Mouvements politiques et sociaux dans la Tunisie des années 1930* (Tunis: Presses de la Société Tunisienne des Arts Graphiques, 1987).

Challaye, F., *Souvenirs sur la colonisation* (Paris: Picart, 1935).

Codo, C. B., '*La Voix du Dahomey*', Thèse de 3e cycle, Université Paris-VII, 1978.

Cohen, W. B., *Rulers of Empire: The French Colonial Service in Africa* (Stanford: Hoover Institute Press, 1971).

Cohen, W. B., 'The Colonial Policy of the Popular Front', *French Historical Studies*, VII: 3 (1972) pp. 368–93.

Cohen, W. B. (ed.), *Robert Delavignette on the French Empire* (Chicago: Chicago University Press, 1977).

Colás, A., 'Internationalism in the Mediterranean, 1918–1942', *Journal of North African Studies*, I: 3 (Winter 1996) pp. 211–233.

Comité, Exposition internationale de New York, *France: New York World's Fair, 1939* (Paris: Higher Council of the French Section of the New York World's Fair, 1939).

Conklin, A., 'A Mission to Civilize: Ideology and Imperialism in French and British Africa, 1895–1930', unpublished PhD thesis, Princeton Universty, 1989.

Cooper, F., *Decolonization and African Society: The Labor Question in British and French Africa* (Cambridge: Cambridge University Press, 1996).

Coquery-Vidrovitch, C., 'Colonisation ou impérialisme: la politique africaine de la France entre les deux guerres', *Mouvement social*, 107 (1979) pp. 51–76.

Coquery-Vidrovitch, C., 'The Colonial Economy of the Former French, Belgian and Portuguese Zones, 1914–35', in A. Boahen (ed.), *Africa*

Under Colonial Domination 1880–1935, UNESCO History of Africa, vol. VII (Berkeley: University of California Press, 1985).

Delafosse, L., *Maurice Delafosse: le Berrichon conquis par l'Afrique* (Paris: Société française d'histoire d'outre-mer, 1976).

Delavignette, R., *Service Africain* (Paris: Gallimard, 1946).

Delavignette, R., *Freedom and Authority in French West Africa* (London: International African Institute, 1950).

Delavignette, R., 'La Politique de Marius Moutet', *Actes du Colloque Léon Blum chef de gouvernement 1936–1937* (Paris: Armand Colin, 1967).

Delinotte, H., 'The Fight Against Leprosy in the French Overseas Territories: Rôle of the *Commission consultative de la lèpre* of the Ministry of Colonies in the Organization of Antileprosy Prophylaxis', *International Journal of Leprosy*, 7: 4 (1939) pp. 517–47.

Delperrié de Bayac, J., *Histoire du Front Populaire* (Paris: Fayard/Les Grandes Etudes contemporaines, 1972).

Demaison, A., 'Nouvelle-Calédonie et dépendances', in A. Demaison, *Exposition coloniale de Paris: Guide officiel* (Paris: Editions Mayeux, 1931).

Derrick, J., 'Elitisme colonial au Cameroun: Le cas des Douala dans les années 30', in M. Z. Njeuma (ed.), *Histoire du Cameroun* (Paris: L'Harmattan, 1989).

Deschamps, D., 'Les sources scientifiques et la politique indochinoise de Jean-Marie de Lanessan', in P. Le Failler and J.-M. Mancini (eds), *Viêt Nam. Sources et approches, Actes du Colloque internationale Euroviet* (Aix-en-Provence, Université d'Aix-en-Provence, 1996).

Deschamps, H., *Méthodes et doctrines coloniales de la France* (Paris: Presses Universitaires de France, 1947).

Deschamps, H., 'Et maintenant, Lord Lugard?', *Africa, 33* (1963) pp. 293–306.

Deschamps, H., 'France in Black Africa and Madagascar between 1920 and 1945', in L. H. Gann and P. Duignan (eds), *Colonialism in Africa 1870–1960*, 2 vols, vol. II (Cambridge: Cambridge University Press, 1970).

Deschamps, H., *Roi de la brousse: Mémoires d'autres mondes* (Nancy: Berger-Levrault, 1975).

Dewitte, P., *Les Mouvements nègres en France, 1919–39* (Paris: L'Harmattan, 1985).

Dubief, H., *Le Déclin de la IIIe République, 1929–1938* (Paris: Seuil, 1976).

Elwitt, S., *The Third Republic Defended: Bourgeois Reform in France, 1880–1914* (Baton Rouge: Louisiana State University Press, 1986).

Ennis, T. E., *French Policy and Development in Indochina* (Chicago: University of Chicago Press, 1936).

Evans, M., *The Memory of Resistance* (Oxford: Berg, 1997).

Ewald, F., 'Insurance and Risk', in G. Burchell, C. Gordon and P. Miller (eds), *The Foucault Effect: Studies in Governmentality* (Chicago: University of Chicago Press, 1991).

Exposition coloniale internationale, *Congrès national d'action et de propagande coloniales: compte rendu des séances* (Paris: Editions de l'Institut colonial français, 1931).

Faberon, J. Y., *La Nouvelle-Calédonie laboratoire de statuts de territoire d'outre-mer* (Nouméa: Société d'études historiques de Nouvelle-Calédonie, 1992).

Fage, J. D., 'When the African Society Was Founded, Who Were the Africanists?', *African Affairs*, 94: 376 (1995) pp. 369–81.

Flandin, C. and Ragu, J., 'Origine, mode de contagion, durée d'incubation de la lèpre dans 95 cas dont 6 contractés dans la région parisienne . . .', *Bulletin de l'Académie de médecine*, 11: 117 (16 Mar. 1937) pp. 337–44.

Foucault, M., 'Omnes and Singulatim: Towards a Criticism of "Political Reason"' in M. Foucault, *The Tanner Lectures on Human Values*. Vol. II (Salt Lake City: University of Utah Press, 1981).

Foucault, M., 'The Political Technologies of Individuals', in L. H. Martin, H. Gutman and P. H. Hutton (eds), *Technologies of the Self* (Amherst: University of Massachusetts Press, 1988).

Foucault, M., 'Faire vivre et laisser mourir. La naissance du racisme', *Les Temps Modernes*, 535 (February 1991).

Gaulle, C. de, *Mémoires de guerre*, 3 vols (Paris: Plon, 1954–59, repr. 1970).

Gifford, P. and W. R. Louis (eds), *The Transfer of Power, Decolonization 1940–1960* (New Haven, CT and London: Yale University Press, 1982).

Girardet, R., *L'Idée coloniale en France* (Paris: Table Ronde, 1972).

Godart, J., *Rapport de mission en Indochine 1er janvier–14 mars 1937* (Paris: L'Harmattan, 1994).

Greenhalgh, P., 'Education, Entertainment and Politics: Lessons from the Great International Exhibitions' in P. Vergo, (ed.), *The New Museology* (London: Reaktion, 1989).

Guérin, D., *Au Service des colonisés* (Paris: Editions de Minuit, 1954).

Guérin, D., *Front Populaire: Révolution manquée* (Paris: Librairie François Maspéro, 1970).

Guérin, D., *Ci-Gît le colonialisme* (Paris: Mouton & Co., 1973).

Guezmir, K., *Les Jeunes Tunisiens* (Tunis: Editions Alif, 1986).

Gussow, Z., *Leprosy, Racism, and Public Health: Social Policy in Chronic Disease Control* (Boulder, Colorado: Westview Press, 1989).

Hamed, M., 'L'Union Intercoloniale: première école d'activité politique des immigrés coloniaux en France au lendemain de la première grande guerre', *Les Cahiers de Tunisie*, 162–3 (4ième semestre 1991/1er semestre 1992) pp. 159–165.

Hargreaves, J. D., 'The Comintern and Anti-Colonialism: New Research Opportunities', *African Affairs*, 92: 367 (1993) pp. 255–61.

Hargreaves, J. D., *Decolonization in Africa*, 2nd edn (London: Longman, 1996).

Harrison, C., *France, Islam and West Africa. 1860–1960* (Cambridge: Cambridge University Press, 1988).

Haslam, J., 'The Comintern and the Origins of the Popular Front, 1934–1935' *The Historical Journal*, 22: 3 (1979) pp. 673–691.

Haslam, J., *The Soviet Union and the Struggle for Collective Security in Europe, 1933–39* (Basingstoke: Macmillan, 1984).

Hémery, D., 'Aux origines des guerres d'indépendance vietnamiennes: pouvoir colonial et phénomène communiste en Indochine avant la Seconde Guerre mondiale', *Mouvement social*, 101 (1977) pp. 3–36.

Hémery, D., *Révolutionnaires vietnamiens et pouvoir colonial en Indochine:*

communistes, trotskystes, nationalistes à Saigon de 1932 à 1937 (Paris: François Maspero, 1975).

Henningham, S., '"The Best Specimens in All Our Colonial Domain": New Caledonian Melanesians in Europe, 1931–2', *Journal of Pacific History*, 29: 2 (1994) pp. 172–87.

Holland, R. F. and G. Rizvi (eds), *Perspectives on Imperialism and Decolonization* (London: Cass, 1984).

Institut Charles de Gaulle and Institut d'Histoire du Temps Present, *Brazzaville, aux sources de la décolonisation* (Paris: Plon, 1988).

International Leprosy Association's Subcommittee on Classification, 'The Classification of Leprosy', *International Journal of Leprosy*, 6: 3 (1938) pp. 389–409.

Jackson, J., *The Popular Front in France: Defending Democracy, 1934–38* (Cambridge: Cambridge University Press, 1988).

Joly, D., *The French Communist Party and the Algerian War* (Basingstoke: Macmillan, 1991).

Julien, C.-A., *L'Afrique du Nord en Marche: nationalismes musulmans et souveraineté française* (Paris: René Juillard, 1952).

Julien, C.-A. (ed.), *Etudes Maghrébines: Mélanges Charles-André Julien* (Paris: Presses Universitaires de France, 1964).

Julien, C. A., *Une pensée anti-coloniale* (Paris: Editions Sindbad, 1979).

Kaptué, L., *Travail et main d'ouevre au Cameroun sous le régime français, 1916–52* (Paris: L'Harmattan, 1986).

Kedward, R. and Wood, N. (eds), *Liberation: Image and Event* (Oxford: Berg, 1995).

Kent, J., *The Internationalization of Colonialism* (Oxford: Oxford University Press, 1992).

Kervingant, M. and J. Baré, 'La Lèpre en Nouvelle-Calédonie en 1936', *International Journal of Leprosy*, 7: 2 (1939) pp. 175–200.

Klein, M. and Roberts, R., 'The Resurgence of Pawning in French West Africa During the Depression of the 1930s', in Falola T. and Lovejoy P. (eds), *Pawnship in Africa: Debt Bondage in Historical Perspective* (Boulder: Westview Press, 1994).

Koufan, J., 'Travail forcé et migrations au Cameroun: le cas des Yambassa dans l'entre-deux-guerres (1918–1946)', Mémoire de Maîtrise, Université de Paris VII, 1979.

Kraiem, M., *Le Mouvement social en Tunisie dans les années trente* (Tunis: Cahiers du CERES, 1984).

Kraiem, M., 'Le Néo-Destour: cadres, militants et implantation pendant les années trente', in *Actes du 3e Séminaire sur l'histoire du Mouvement National: Les mouvements politiques et sociaux dans la Tunisie des années 1930* (Tunis: Ministère de l'Education, de l'Enseignement et de la Recherche Scientifique, 1985).

Kuisel, R., *Capitalism and the State in Modern France* (Cambridge University Press, 1981).

Labouret, H., *Colonisation, Colonialisme, Décolonisation* (Paris: Larose 1952).

Lacam, G., *L'Inventaire économique de l'Empire* (Paris: Sarlot, 1938).

Lagana, Marc., 'L'échec de la commission d'enquête coloniale du Front Populaire', *Historical Reflections*, 16: 1 (1989) pp. 79–97.

Larcher, A., 'L'ordre par la concorde: essai sur les réformismes coloniaux en Indochine, 1902–1945', Thèse de D.E.A., Université de Paris VII, 1994.

Larcher, A., 'D'un réformisme à l'autre: la redécouverte de l'identité culturelle vietnamienne, 1900–1930', *Etudes indochinoises*, 4: (1995).

Larkin, M., *France Since the Popular Front*, 2nd edn (Oxford: Clarendon Press, 1997).

Lebovics, H., *True France: The Wars Over Cultural Identity 1900–1945* (Ithaca and London: Cornell University Press, 1992).

Lefranc, G., *Le Mouvement socialiste sous la troisième République (1875–1940)* (Paris: Payot, 1963).

Lefranc, G., *Le Front Populaire (1934–1938)* (Paris: Presses Universitaires de France, 1965).

Lefranc, G., *Histoire du Front populaire (1934–1938)* (Paris: Payot, 1965).

Lewis, J. I., 'The French Colonial Service and the Issues of Reform, 1944–8', *Contemporary European History*, 4:2 (1995) pp. 153–88.

Liauzu, C., *Aux origines des Tiers-mondismes. Colonisés et anti-colonialisme en France entre 1919 et 1939* (Paris: L'Harmattan, 1986).

Liauzu, R., *Salariat et mouvement ouvrier en Tunisie: crises et mutations (1931–1939)* (Paris: Editions du CNRS, 1978).

Lugard, F. D., 'The International Institute of African Languages and Cultures', *Africa*, I (1928) pp. 1–12.

Lydon, G., 'The Unravelling of a Neglected Source: a Report on Women in Francophone West Africa in the 1930s', *Cahiers d'Etudes Africaines*, XXXVI: 3 (1996) pp. 555–86.

Lyons, M., *The Colonial Disease: A Social History of Sleeping Sickness in Northern Zaire, 1900–1940* (New York: Cambridge University Press, 1992).

Mahjoubi, A., *Les origines du mouvement national en Tunisie 1904–1934* (Tunis: Publications de l'Université de Tunis, 1982).

Mann, M., *The Sources of Social Power*, 2 vols (Cambridge: Cambridge University Press, 1993).

Marchoux, E., 'La lutte contre la lèpre dans les colonies françaises', *International Journal of Leprosy*, 2: 3 (Aug.–Oct. 1934) pp. 311–14.

Marcovich, A., 'French Colonial Medicine and Colonial Rule: Algeria and Indochina', in R. Macleod and M. Lewis (eds.), *Disease, Medicine, and Empire: Perspectives on Western Medicine and the Experience of European Expansion* (New York: Routledge, 1988).

Marseille, J., 'La Conférence des Gouverneurs-Généraux des colonies (novembre 1936)', *Mouvement social*, 101 (1977) pp. 61–84.

Marseille, J., *Empire colonial et capitalisme français: Histoire d'un divorce* (Paris: Editions Albin Michel, 1984).

McConnell, S., *Leftward Journey: The Education of Vietnamese Students in France 1919–1939* (New Brunswick: Transaction Publishers, 1989).

Mérat, L., *Fictions . . . et réalités coloniales* (Paris: Sirey, 1946).

Mérat, L., *L'Heure de l'économie dirigée d'intérêt général aux colonies* (Paris: Sirey, 1936).

Ministère des Colonies, *La Conférence Africaine Française* (Paris: Ministère des Colonies, 1945).

Michel, M., 'La co-opération inter-coloniale en Afrique Noire, 1942–

1950: un néo-colonialisme éclairé?', *Rélations Internationales*, 34 (1983) pp. 155–71.

Moneta, J., *La Politique du Parti communiste français dans la question coloniale, 1920–1963* (Paris: François Maspero, 1971).

Mumford, W. B. and Orde-Brown, G. St J., *Africans Learn To Be French* (London: Evans, 1935).

Néré, J., *The Foreign Policy of France from 1914 to 1945* (London & Boston, Mass.: Routledge & Kegan Paul, 1975).

Neton, A., *Delcassé (1852–1923)* (Paris: Académie diplomatique internationale, 1952).

Nouschi, A., 'La politique coloniale du Front Populaire: le Maghreb', *Les Cahiers de Tunisie*, XXVII: 109–110 (1979) pp. 143–60.

Osborne, M. A., *Nature, the Exotic, and the Science of French Colonialism* (Bloomington: Indiana University Press, 1994).

Oved, G., *La gauche française face au nationalisme marocain*, 2 vols (Paris: l'Harmattan, 1983).

Person, Y., 'Le Front Populaire au Sénégal (mai 1936–octobre 1938)', *Le Mouvement social*, 107 (1979) pp. 77–102.

Piétri, F., *Veillons au salut de l'empire . . .* (Paris: Les Editions de France, 1937).

Renouvin P., Rémond, R. and Labrousse E. (eds), *Léon Blum, Chef de Gouvernement, 1936/1937* (Paris: Presses de la Fondation Nationale des Sciences Politiques, 1981).

Roberts, S. H., *History of French Colonial Policy (1870–1925)*, 2 vols (London: P. S. King & Son, 1929).

Robinson, K., *The Dilemmas of Trusteeship* (London: Oxford University Press, 1965).

Robinson, K., 'Experts, Colonialists, and Africanists, 1895–1960', in J. C. Stone, (ed.), *Experts in Africa: Proceedings of a Colloquium at the University of Aberdeen, March 1980*.

Roche, J. de la and Gottman, J., *La Fédération française* (Montréal: Editions de l'arbre, 1945).

Rodinson, M., *Marxism and the Muslim World* (London: Macmillan Press, 1978).

Sarraut, A., *La Mise en valeur des colonies françaises* (Paris: Payot, 1923).

Sarraut, A., *Grandeur et servitude coloniales* (Paris: Editions du Sagittaire, 1931).

Schachter-Morganthau, R., *Political Parties in French-Speaking West Africa* (Oxford: Clarendon Press, 1964).

Semidei, M., 'Les socialistes français et le problème colonial entre les deux guerres (1919–1939)', *Revue Française de Science Politique*, XVIII: 6 (1968) pp. 1115–53.

Shipway, M., 'Madagascar on the Eve of Insurrection, 1944–1947: The Impasse of a Liberal Colonial Policy', *Journal of Imperial and Commonwealth History*, 24: 1 (1996) pp. 72–100.

Shipway, M., *The Road to War: France and Vietnam, 1944–1947* (Oxford & Providence, R.I.: Berghahn Books, 1996).

Sivan, E., *Communisme et nationalisme en Algérie 1920–1962* (Paris: Presses de la Fondation Nationale des Sciences Politiques, 1976).

Sraïeb, N., *Le Collège Sadiki de Tunis 1875–1956: Enseignement et nationalisme* (Tunis: Alif, Editions de la Méditerranée, 1995).

Stoler, A. L., *Race and the Education of Desire: Foucault's History of Sexuality and the Colonial Order of Things* (Durham: Duke University Press, 1995).

Stora, B., *Nationalistes Algériens et Révolutionnaires Français* (Paris: L'Harmattan, 1987).

Suret-Canale, J., *Afrique noire. Ere coloniale, 1900–1945* (Paris: Editions Sociales, 1962).

Tai, Hue-Tam Ho., *Radicalism and the Origins of the Vietnamese Revolution* (Cambridge: Harvard University Press, 1992).

Thiam, Iba der, 'La Grève des cheminots du Sénégal de 1938', Mémoire de Maîtrise d'histoire, Université de Dakar, 1972.

Thobie, J., Meynier, G., Coquery-Vidrovitch C. and Ageron, C.-R. (eds), *Histoire de la France coloniale 1914–1990*, 2 vols (Paris: Armand Colin, 1990/91).

Topouzis, D., 'Popular Front, War and Fourth Republic Politics in Senegal: From Galandou Diouf to L. S. Senghor, 1936–52', unpublished PhD thesis, University of London, 1989.

Vatin, J.-C., *L'Algérie politique. Histoire et société* (Presses de la Fondation des Sciences Politiques, 1983).

Vaughn, M., *Curing Their Ills: Colonial Power and African Illness* (Oxford: Polity Press, 1991).

Wall, Irwin M., 'Socialists and Bureaucrats: The Blum Government and the French Administration, 1936–1937', *International Review of Social History*, 19 (1974) pp. 325–46.

Weber, E., *The Hollow Years* (New York: Norton, 1994).

Weinstein, B., *Eboué* (New York: Oxford University Press, 1972).

Whitney, S. B., 'Embracing the Status Quo: French Communists, Young Women and the Popular Front', *Journal of Social History*, 30 (autumn 1996) pp. 29–53.

Wright, G., *The Politics of Design in French Colonial Urbanism* (Chicago: University of Chicago Press, 1991).

Index

Abd el-Krim 91
Abdu, Mohammed 224
Abengourou 182
Académie des Sciences
    Coloniales 210
administration 5, 10, 11, 19, 23,
    26, 34, 37–8, 39–41, 46, 49–50,
    60, 76, 82, 98, 131–6, 139,
    140–1, 145–6, 159, 160, 165,
    166–7, 170, 172, 175, 176, 177,
    179, 181, 182, 184, 190, 193–9,
    203, 204, 205, 207, 211, 213,
    227, 233, 240
Africa see Black Africa, French West
    Africa, French Equatorial Africa,
    Madagascar, North Africa
Africa 166
Ageron, Charles-Robert 218, 238
Ahmad Bey 92
Al Uqbi 224, 225
Al Ibrahimi 224
Algeria 2, 20, 24, 25, 26, 82, 89,
    91, 101, 103–4, 116, 155, 157,
    218–27
Algiers 225, 226
Ali, Mohammed 93
Annam see Vietnam
anti-colonialism 74–6, 90–1, 100,
    105, 144, 155, 156, 163, 164,
    171, 229
Arabs 220, 222, 225
Archimbaud, Léon 219
Arrighi, Victor 225
assimilation 7, 16, 17, 18, 19, 21,
    57, 83, 91, 104, 110, 112, 135,
    140–1, 142, 147, 161, 165, 166,
    214, 218, 220, 221, 222, 223
    (*see also évolués*)
association 7, 40, 57, 110, 111,
    112, 114–18, 121, 125, 126,
    141
Association des anciens élèves du
    collège Sadiki 93
Association professionnelle de la
    formation intellectuelle et
    morale des Annamites 122
Association Révolutionnaire de la
    Jeunesse 124

Association des Etudiants de l'Ouest
    Africain 166
Atlantic Charter 137
Aubaud, Raoul 219
Austria 78
Ayos 213

Ballard, J. G. 68
Bamako 180, 181
Bamileke 216
Baré, J. 58, 63, 64, 65, 66
Bataille, La 92
Baya see Gbaya
Bchangjin 180
Beau, Governor-General Paul 24,
    110, 114, 115, 116, 117, 121,
    125, 126
Béavogui, F. 191
Belgium 78, 80–1
Ben Badis, Sheikh 223, 224
Bendjelloul, Dr 223, 225
Berlin Conference 80
Bernard, Paul 161, 236
Bert, Paul 117
Bessis, Julliette 94, 101
Blacher, Louis 195–7, 198
Black Africa 155, 157, 158, 164,
    167, 171, 173, 174, 237
Blum, Léon 1, 34, 75, 83, 84, 96,
    97, 104–5, 132, 135, 155, 157,
    170, 171, 177, 194, 211, 218,
    219, 226, 227
Blum-Viollette Bill 24, 104, 157,
    218, 220–3, 226, 226–7, 242
Boisson, Pierre 26, 133, 193, 207,
    210, 214
Bonn, M. J. 74
Bordeaux 161
Borodin, Mikhail 124
Bouisson, Fernand 192
Boundiali 181
Bourguiba, Habib 94, 95–6, 99,
    101, 102, 105
Bourret Laboratories 64–5
Boy Scouts, Muslim 225
Brazza, Savorgnan de 156
Brazzaville Conference 2, 26, 131,
    132–47

257

DATE DUE
